THE SPIRIT AS LORD

THE SPIRIT AS LORD

The Pneumatology of Karl Barth

Philip J. Rosato, S.J.

T. & T. CLARK
36 GEORGE STREET, EDINBURGH

*TO MY EVER GRACIOUS
AND DEEPLY CHERISHED PARENTS
IRMA CILLI FERRETTI
AND
DANIEL LOREFICE ROSATO*

Copyright © T. & T. Clark Ltd., 1981

PRINTED IN THE U.S.A. BY
WM. B. EERDMANS PRINTING CO.
FOR
T. & T. CLARK LTD., EDINBURGH

0 567 09305 0

First Printed 1981

PROLOGUE

It is most intriguing that shortly before his death Karl Barth, acclaimed and accused as the christocentric theologian of the century, clearly hinted that he was willing to renounce this title for a different one. In an essay written in 1968 he states that he had already conceived much of his own theology, and that he also could have conceived the rest of it, perhaps more appropriately, as a theology of the Holy Spirit. Barth asserts that he was rightly led in his *Church Dogmatics* (IV/1-3) to place at least the Church and then faith, love and hope explicitly under the heading of the Holy Spirit. Then he adds the provocative comment that justification, sanctification and vocation could have been incorporated under this heading as well. The same could be said of his doctrine of creation and even of the dominant christology *(conceptus de Spiritu Sancto)* which had become his trademark: "Is not God—the God known to His people through His revelation in the covenant and as such the God who is proclaimed in the world—not totally and entirely Spirit *(Jn.* 4:24; 1 *Cor.* 3:17)—that is, the God who in His own freedom and power, wisdom and love makes Himself present to and bestows Himself on man?" ("Afterword" to the *Schleiermacher-Auswahl,* Siebenstern, 1968, p. 311). Karl Barth a pneumatocentric theologian? Did the renowned expositor of the Word of God view himself in all seriousness as primarily a theologian of the Holy Spirit? What did he mean? How accurate was his judgment?

Discovering the answers to these questions is the aim of this study of Barth's Spirit theology. Though other aspects of the Barthian corpus have been examined thoroughly, no work specifically on the cardinal theme of pneumatology has yet been published. Because of his own rather surprising and seemingly revisionist remarks on the possibility of interpreting his entire theology as an expatiation on the Johannine definition of God as Spirit, it is an exciting enterprise to trace the genesis, to summarize the content and to analyze the import of Barth's pneumatology. Mention of the Holy Spirit is by no means rare, but even more significant is the pervasive theological methodology of Barth which depends on his understanding of the spiritual nature of the Word, of the Scriptures and of Christian preaching. One cannot but be amazed, therefore, at the veritable miniature dogmatics of the Spirit which can be culled from Barth's writings through the years—both the shorter books and articles partially or totally on this topic and the long sections and individual passages dealing with it in the *Church Dogmatics.* This study attempts to be as comprehensive as possible, though it centers chiefly on Barth's major work into which the minor pieces gradually flow like many streams into a main artery. The leitmotif of the ensuing study is the extent to which Barth the reputed christologian is also, or even primarily, Barth the genuine pneumatologian. As the various aspects of his Spirit theology are investigated, the reader is invited to judge whether Barth's evaluation of himself as a theologian of the Spirit is a correct one. What is beyond doubt, however, is that Barth devotes much more space to the introspective task of identifying his own theological intention than is often assumed when one categorizes his work as self-assured. Pneumatology aids Barth in this effort, since it illumines for him the solution to the perennial problem of clarifying the very essence of Christian theology. It is hoped that the reader will find this entire thematic as fascinating and as haunting as Barth himself did up to the very end of his long career.

Since the main purpose here is to answer a specific question accurately, this study is designed to allow Barth to speak for himself at great length without being interrupted. To achieve this end, the study is divided into three distinct sections which are interrelated by their common goal, but different in their approach to the problematic. Part I comprises an historical investigation; it sets out to explore the background of Barth's pneumatology by centering on his lifelong reaction to Neo-Protestantism, Christian Existentialism and Roman Catholicism. Were his adversaries really covert theologians of the Holy Spirit? Barth excoriates their tendency to confuse the Holy Spirit and the holy man, and yet he must continually make a concession to the truth behind this confusion as well: Christian pneumatology necessarily contains an anthropology; it must provide a study not only of the Redeemer Spirit but also of the redeemed man. Thus the germ of Barth's pneumatology is his search for an authentic theology of the Christian. The period from 1919 to 1931, a time chiefly dominated by Barth's interior struggle with this key theme, is given particular attention in the introductory division. Part II contains an exposition of the Spirit theology in the *Church Dogmatics*. Here the trinitarian, christological, anthropological, ecclesiological and ontological dimensions of Barth's pneumatology are treated in considerable detail without any commentary whatsoever, except of course for the fact that important decisions had to be made as to what should be highlighted and what not. As much objectivity as possible is intended here; only occasionally are comments on other theologians and doctrinal variations made which seem especially worthy of discussion in the closing analysis. Part III consists of a critical evaluation which takes the form of two "improvisations" on Barth's Spirit theology. This word is used loosely here, since true improvisations are completely spontaneous, impromptu compositions, whereas the remarks which conclude this study are carefully weighed. Yet the image appears to be the one most apt to describe the character of this last section. It is constructive as well as critical, since it tries to sketch the lines of a pneumatology which is at variance with that of Barth, though clearly indebted to the thought-provoking questions which he raises.

A further word about the methodology employed in the second, expository part of this study is called for. The very numerous references to the Spirit in the *Church Dogmatics* and the substantial portions which deal almost entirely with this topic cause a dilemma. How should Barth's ideas be presented? It seems preferable to maintain his own line of reasoning, so that the gradual progression of thought throughout his main work can be directly observed. Thus Barth's own sequence of treating revelation's content will be followed rather than a fabricated division according to predominant themes which occur frequently in different volumes. At the expense of some minimal repetition, this study will also adhere to Barth's admittedly circular method of argumentation as the one which best reflects his evolution as a Spirit theologian. Thus, from a sincere effort to be faithful to his thought, Barth's pneumatology will be presented chronologically and extensively, not thematically and succinctly. Besides the nature of the exposition its length is significant. The somewhat problematic option for a sharp separation between exposition and evaluation is motivated by the desire that this study interpret Barth *in optimam partem*. Barth repeatedly complained that many who found it easy to criticize him had not really read his text carefully. Since a sound final judgment about Barth's Spirit theology can only be assured if the entire breadth of his reflections on the divine Pneuma is considered, a rather prolonged and unannotated analysis of the logic behind his positions is of utmost importance.

The critical stance which is taken at the close of this study is the result of listening to Protestant, Catholic and Orthodox critics, as well as to those who are conservative, moderate or radical in evaluating the aspects of Barth's theology which touch directly or indirectly on his pneumatology. A decidedly ecumenical and properly balanced judgment is sought after. This study locates itself somewhere on the critical spectrum between those who deplore Barth's restriction of Christian theology to the second credal article and thus point out the limited role of the man created by the Father and renewed by the Spirit, and those who lament Barth's early retrenchment from a socio-cosmological perspective and thus point out the limited role of the Spirit and of man in the penultimate attainment of the Kingdom promised at the end of history. The appraisal of Barth's pneumatology which emerges from this study will therefore oscillate between the philosophico-anthropological and the historico-eschatological poles of Barthian criticism. However, the improvisations which are offered do not merely reiterate the opinions of others. Their purpose is to generate originally formulated ideas which might incite further theological reflection on the Holy Spirit in the light of the problems which are uncovered in Barth's pneumatology. The intent of the critique is clearly not to deny the positive contributions of Barth to Spirit theology or so to modify them that they are no longer recognizable. Rather, the object is, through unfavorable observations of an admittedly serious nature, to show how man's relative autonomy and the Spirit's ontic role apart from Christ could have been granted much more attention in the *Church Dogmatics* without endangering either the sovereignty of the Spirit in the first case or the centrality of Christ in the second.

Though this study envisions a Spirit theology in a different key, admiration rather than reservation is unquestionably its prevailing mood from beginning to end. Barth's pneumatology is so extensive and so imposing that this comparatively lengthy study cannot possibly encompass it, let alone do it justice. What Barth achieves, despite all the shortcomings that will be mentioned, is an unmatched description of the Holy Spirit as God Himself being revealed in Christian experience; Barth furnishes an account of how the Spirit as Lord, as he likes to put it, actually bestows Himself on man. To probe, expose and evaluate the almost unthinkable thesis that Karl Barth is also, and perhaps first and foremost, a pneumatologist is a daring as well as a demanding and profitable undertaking. Since this study will offer a positive, even if somewhat qualified, response to the question of Barth's pneumatocentrism, it does diverge from the contemporary trend of Barthian scholarship and thus hopes to foster new avenues of research. To prove that the grounds for such a reinterpretation of Barth's central intention are actually found in his writings is the chief burden of the present study. The guarded yet confident conclusion of these pages is that a pneumatocentric interpretation of Barth's theology is not a doomed project. Instead, it provides a promising new explanation of the work of a theologian who was always underway towards a genuine theology of the Christian in the framework of a solidly grounded and majestically proportioned pneumatology. Professors and students who are searching for new insights into Barth as well as pastors and parishioners who are looking for ways to rejuvenate the Church's spiritual life can find ample material in the Spirit theology of the *Church Dogmatics*.

Only in the process of doing so does one realize that to write a book one must be trained and affirmed, recognized and aided. The initial training this author attributes to Walter J. Burghardt and Avery R. Dulles, both of the Society of Jesus. Without the years at Woodstock College in New York under their tutelage a passion for the study of God would not have been enkindled. At the University of Tübingen two professors generously provided the affirmation needed to pursue this study of Barth. Walter Kasper acted as an energetic and insightful *Doktorvater,* ever ready to challenge and to sharpen one's mind; Jürgen Moltmann, at whose seminar on pneumatology in 1975 many of the ideas here were germinated, made a foreigner feel at home while he exposed him to an original and exciting intellect. The much appreciated recognition of this study first came from Dr. Geoffrey F. Green of T. and T. Clark Limited in Edinburgh. Without his encouragement and prudence from afar this book would not have appeared in print. The aid came in various forms. Financial help was supplied by The Cardinal Bea Fund, the Maryland Province of the Society of Jesus and the Jesuit Community at St. Joseph's University in Philadelphia; Joseph P. Whelan, James F. McAndrews and Alfred J. Jolson are particularly to be thanked. Two other Jesuits, true literary descendants of Gerard Manley Hopkins, assisted with the manuscript: Francis F. Burch and Joseph J. Feeney. In Miss Donna-Marie Oberthaler, the typist, two indispensable fruits of the Holy Spirit were evident—kindness and patience.

Pentecost, 1980   Philip J. Rosato, S. J.

TABLE OF CONTENTS

ix

PART I

TOWARDS A THEOLOGY OF
THE CHRISTIAN LIFE

CHAPTER I

THE HAUNTING AMBIGUITY
OF PNEUMATOLOGY

Although Karl Barth's thought undergoes many significant changes throughout his career, one strain remains constant: he would have both to appreciate Friedrich Schleiermacher fully and yet depart from him radically if he were to change the tide of Protestant theology. This consistent attempt to understand Schleiermacher and his followers leads Barth to one haunting impasse—Spirit theology. In crucial passages of Barth's longer essays on Schleiermacher and in shorter references to him in almost all his major works through the years, pneumatology is the recurring theme. It becomes most explicit, however, in his publications dating from the year 1947. Barth invariably begins to leave his readers with one startling reflection in the form of a question: did Schleiermacher really intend to write a theology of the Holy Spirit? These crucial passages deserve careful attention since Barth's own pneumatology is clearly influenced by his tireless effort to redeem the valid insights and to excise the dangerous errors of Schleiermacher's Spirit theology. That this one aspect of Schleiermacher's thought so fascinates Barth lends credence to the daring assertion that Barth himself gradually became more properly a pneumatocentric than a christocentric theologian. In any event, these passages form the nucleus around which this investigation of Barth's Spirit theology is centered.

The first of such often repeated references appears in 1947 in the section on the Holy Spirit in *Dogmatics in Outline* where Barth is defending man himself as the object of faith within the third article of the creed. Barth states that man participates in the work of God and thus coexists in a free and active relationship with Him. Barth is intent on preserving the subjective side of God's self-revelation in the Christian which perfectly corresponds to its objective side in Jesus Christ: "It would be comfortless if all were to remain totally objective. There is also a *subjective* aspect, and one can understand the modern exaggeration of this subjective side, which had already begun in the middle of the 17th century and which was brought to systematic order by Schleiermacher, as a tortured attempt to respect the truth of the third article."[1] The same year Barth states in *The Heidelberg Catechism for Today* that Pietism and Neo-Protestantism, which found their classic expression in Schleiermacher, could both be understood as licit attempts to accentuate the truth of the third article: "Whoever understands the third article is able perhaps even to recognize Schleiermacher in it, and does not need to think of him and of the theologians of the 19th century with wrathful indignation over their 'God in us' and all that is bound up

3

with that assertion; he can recognize the true key to understanding Liberalism."[2]

Both these quotes find an echo in *Protestant Theology in the 19th Century* which was also published in 1947. There Barth searches for the underlying design of Schleiermacher's theology. At a key point in the volume's important essay on Schleiermacher Barth wrestles with the question: "whether the divinity of the Holy Spirit can be proved as the center of Schleiermacher's thought, that is, not only whether it was Schleiermacher's intention to do so, but whether it really is the *divinity* of the Holy Spirit which forms the proper center of his theology."[3] Further on in the same work, while discussing the influence of Schleiermacher on the Revivalist theology of the 19th century and especially on August Tholuck, Barth asks: "whether Revivalism had not understood better than the prevailing theology that man's concrete situation, by which the very truth-content of theological statements necessarily in conditioned, is not, as one might be inclined to think, totally in man's control, but that man's situation in this case can only be understood as the situation of faith, indeed of faith as the work of the Holy Spirit."[4]

These persistent questions understandably find their way into the *Church Dogmatics* (III/3) which was published in 1950. There Barth inquires if Schleiermacher's theology could be adapted and developed in a very different direction as a theology of the subjective reality and possibility of revelation, which is not exclusive, but inclusive of its objective reality and possibility—"a theology which, beginning with man, is intended as a theology of the Holy Spirit."[5] The intriguing recurrence of this question and its appearance exactly at those points where Barth is trying to comprehend the very nature of Protestant theology indicate that pneumatology might afford him a meeting place with Liberal Protestantism. For, in an essay which he wrote in 1957 entitled "Evangelical Theology in the 19th Century," Barth confirms his willingness to interpret the anthropocentric theology of Neo-Protestantism *in optimam partem,* as he claims that it is indeed possible and profitable to do. The question which one could legitimately pose is "whether that theology must not be understood, at least as far as its intention was concerned, as an attempt at a theology of the third article, more precisely: of the Holy Spirit."[6]

Finally, the repetition of this theme at the end of Barth's life provides a most convincing corroboration of its centrality and raises a most provocative question concerning its actual influence on Barth himself. Two publications, *Evangelical Theology: An Introduction* (1963) and an *Afterword* to a selection of Schleiermacher's writings (1968), indicate that Barth is preoccupied up to the very end of his theological career with the nagging possibility of a pneumatocentric reinterpretation not only of Evangelical theology and of Schleiermacher but of his own theology as well. Barth states that Evangelical theology as the modest, free, critical and joyous science of the God who reveals Himself through His Word, through His witnesses and through His community "can only be understood as pneumatic theology; it can only exist in the courage which springs from the Spirit as the truth who both raises and answers the question concerning the truth at the same time."[7] In light of this fact, Barth endeavors one last time to understand what binds him to Schleiermacher. Does Barth suspect that his own pneumatology accomplishes what Schleiermacher's system intended to do, but did not? Barth remarks: "everything which is to be believed, to be reflected on and to be said about God the Father and God the Son in understanding the first and second articles would be able to be exposed and illuminated in Schleiermacher's system through God the Holy Spirit, the *vinculum pacis inter Patrem et Filium*. The entire action of God for the creature, for and in and with man, could be made visible in Schleiermacher's single teleology which excludes all contingency."[8] Moreover, in a way consistent with his queries since 1947, Barth sums up his entire relationship to Schleiermacher explicitly in terms of Spirit theology: "what I have occasionally mentioned as an explanation of my relationship to Schleiermacher and what I have now and then indicated among friends, is that there might be the possibility of a theology of the third article—predominantly and decidedly, therefore, of the Holy Spirit."[9]

For the purpose of this study these statements on pneumatology are enticing. They always appear at a decisive point in Barth's evaluation of Schleiermacher and of Neo-Protestantism insofar as it was influenced by him. Despite the overwhelmingly negative critique which Barth directs at the devastating implications of 19th-century theology, the possibility of a fresh reinterpretation, precisely in terms of a theology of the Holy Spirit, stands out as a unique sign of profound appreciation for this theology. For all his condemnation of Liberal Protestant thought, Barth repeatedly locates one thread which could at least save and even justify the whole attempt to start theology with the believing Christian as the focus. Barth's stubborn clinging to this saving thread seems aptly to serve as a springboard for this study of his pneumatology. Since Spirit theology lies at the very core of Barth's interpretation of 19th-century Protestantism, it affords a logical explanation both of his initial fascination with this thought system and of his ultimate reluctance to dismiss it. Exactly at the point where a pneumatological solution becomes possible, Barth ceases to condemn because he recognizes there a deep resonance with his own theological intention.

1. Latent and Misguided Theologies of the Holy Spirit

There is no denying that Barth views the theology of Rudolf Bultmann and of Christian Existentialism in general as the culmination of Neo-Protestantism. Yet it is often overlooked that Existentialism's similar pneumatological intention induces Barth to do so. But why does Barth apply this pneumatological reinterpretation not only to Christian Existentialism, but also the spiritualist movements in 17th-century Protestantism, to certain elements in Luther's and Calvin's theology and to the central tenets of Roman Catholicism? The one preoccupation which Barth finds common to all of them is mysticism. As repelling as this subjective emphasis is to Barth, he can never disclaim that the personal apprehension of God's revelation on the part of the individual Christian belongs at the heart of Protestantism and of all genuine Christian theology. Yet neither does he ever fail to be suspicious of the danger of subjectivism. Ambiguity seems necessarily to result, since the hallmark of all individualistic tendencies in Christianity is an exaggerated enthusiasm which leads its proponents to confuse the being of Jesus Christ with their own mystical experience of God: "It is only in this enthusiasm that the actuality of Jesus Christ can be equated with what the better Christian can know and experience as his *unio mystica* with God . . . this enthusiasm tries to interpret Christ in light of the Christian rather than the Christian in the light of Christ."[10]

Barth discovers in the mystical bent of Liberal Protestants and their spiritual ancestors a blurring of the revelatory history of Jesus Christ with what the believer experiences as his personal openness to God's Spirit. As a result, the historically unique relationship of all men to Jesus Christ is sacrificed for the sake of an abstract, universal presence to the Holy Spirit. In reaction to this aberration, Barth insists that the spirituality of Christians is a consequence of the temporal work of the Holy Spirit who makes the Christ-event an historical factor in their own existence. The life of faith is not simply one particular instance of a generally valid mystical approach to God, but the result of a specific encounter with the Spirit of an historical person. Christian faith is not a "veiled cosmology, anthropology, theology or mysticism—a partial consideration of the system of that which is always and everywhere, but which has never taken place as such and never can or will take place . . . It is only in and with the outpouring of the Holy Spirit that the faith of the disciples is revealed as such and becomes an historical factor."[11] Barth therefore opposes to the vague mysticism of Liberal Protestantism and its counterparts the historical work of the Spirit of Jesus Christ. By calling on Calvin's teaching concerning the *unio mystica* between Christ and the Christian, Barth grants that mysticism has a legitimate place in a pneumatic theology, one in which all depends on the Spirit of Jesus Christ personally transforming the individual Christian. Barth repeatedly admits that Christian faith includes a subjective mystical element, which enables the Christian to pray and thus to enjoy an interpersonal relationship with God. If Barth had at first failed to yield adequate place to the individual Christian's experiences at prayer, "it was at a time when we had to deal with Neo-Protestantism and since in the investigation of its origins we rightly came on Mysticism and Pietism it was natural that we should be sharp-sighted and rather severe in this respect."[12] Later Barth concedes that interior experiences can be defined as true encounters with the Holy Spirit only if they cause a man to meet with another man, the God-Man Jesus Christ. Barth thus stresses that "the operation of the Holy Spirit is neither anonymous, amorphous nor irrational. It is an operation from man to man."[13]

Their mutual penchant to overlook this real meeting which takes place between the Christian and Jesus Christ through the Holy Spirit leads Barth to associate Protestant Liberalism and Existentialism with mysticism. Such a failure to perceive the christological as well as pneumatological character of Christian faith lures these forms of Protestantism onto the path of mystifying an unknown God and an unknown man. Barth finds such a failure concretely illustrated in Reformed Protestantism's misunderstanding of the divine election of the Christian. Instead of viewing predestination as a *de-*

cretum concretum grounded in Jesus Christ, this theology reduced it to a *decretum absolutum* to be accomplished by man's own merits: "Face to face with the absolute decree . . . there remains only the escape into mysticism or moralism, i.e., a self-chosen salvation, idolatry, the righteousness of works."[14] This inclination to move from the concrete to the general marks for Barth the birth of the spiritualism and subjectivism manifested in Neo-Protestantism as well as in Christian Existentialism. Since this subjective theology purported to stand under the aegis of the Holy Spirit, Barth discovers here a distortion of the Reformation's teaching on the Holy Spirit as none other than the Spirit of the historical figure Jesus Christ. Protestant mysticism in all of its forms was thus a misdirected theology of the Holy Spirit.[15]

For this reason, Barth finds in the hermeneutical method of Rudolf Bultmann both a variation on and a culmination of the mystical, subjective strand of Liberal Protestantism. Existential theology is essentially christianocentric, since it neglects the historical foundation of faith in the person of Jesus Christ and substitutes the believer's own experience and self-understanding as the object of theology. Barth thus connects Christian Existentialism to the dominant subjective orientation of modern Protestant theology: "Today we usually describe a theology which looks in this direction as anthropocentrism (though christianocentrism would be a more exact definition), and we rightly regard Schleiermacher as its classical exponent, though we must also point to its beginnings in the Pietism and Rationalism of the 18th century and even in the spiritual movements of the Reformation and the great mystics of the Middle Ages, and also to its unmistakable developers in the modern theological existentialism influenced by Kierkegaard."[16] This proclivity to make the Christian believer the object of theology severs faith from its christological roots and pneumatological power; that is, it separates the existential union of the Christian with God from its basis in the historical revelation of Jesus Christ and His Spirit. Thus, Christian Existentialism is in Barth's eyes a modern footnote on Schleiermacher, since both thought systems confuse anthropology and pneumatology, the pious consciousness and the power of the Holy Spirit. Everything which Barth finds distorted in Bultmann's theology is an echo of the major failure of the father of Neo-Protestantism: "Schleiermacher mentioned as the anthropologically conceived theme of theology not, as one in the present case might expect, the outpouring of the Holy Spirit—as would in itself have been possible—but precisely the pious consciousness as such. Faith was not understood as the revelation of God, but as the experience of man. And such an understanding of faith allowed, indeed, demanded, that even christology be understood *in a corresponding way*, that is, *not* under the presupposition of a strict contrast to pneumatology, not as a correlate to the concept of the Holy Spirit which was understood in a trinitarian fashion, but rather as a correlate to the experience of man."[17] By placing man at the center, theology risks replacing classical pneumatology with the prevalent anthropology of the day, and once this is done it begins refashioning classical christology along similar lines.

Put differently, Barth's nagging question with regard to Existentialism is whether it substitutes soteriology, the Christian community's experience of salvation, in place of christology. Barth is never sure that Existentialism's stress on being saved, for all its pneumatological import, does not pre-empt the place of the Savior. Is the salvific experience of the redeemed person so independent in this system that the person and work of Jesus Christ become superfluous? "Soteriology and ecclesiology, either as a doctrine of grace, justification and sanctification which comes to us or simply as a doctrine of Christian piety, can never escape the tendency to commend itself in relation to christology and ultimately to free itself from it, as that which is true and essential, as that which is of practical importance and necessity, as that which is 'existentially relevant' . . . Is not christology only so much ballast which can be jettisoned without loss?"[18] Barth cannot fully overcome his suspicion that Existential soteriology is as much an escape from the scandal of true christology as is Schleiermacher's theology of the Christian consciousness. Specifically with regard to Bultmann, Barth fears that the *extra nos* of Jesus Christ is interpreted as a "mere predicate and instrument, cipher and symbol of that which truly and properly took place *in nobis*."[19] The *in nobis*, which is the correct theme of traditional pneumatology, becomes an end in itself, excluding for all practical purposes the *extra nos* of christology. Man's self-understanding as a redeemed being occupies so prominent a place here that christology seems threatened by soteriology with extinction. In his book *Rudolf Bultmann: Ein Versuch Ihn zu Verstehen* Barth claims that the cause of Bultmann's neglect of christology for the sake of soteriology can be traced back to Luther himself: "Are there not even in the last edition of Luther's *Galaterbriefkommentar* passages in which christology seems almost to be merged with soteriology: passages on which Bultmann could rely in a strangely proper fashion to support his own existential method?"[20]

Barth's dilemma up to the end of his life concerning the degree of theological validity in Bultmann's existential approach rests ultimately both on the central pneumatological tenets which the Reformers felt compelled to incorporate in their writings and on the embarrassing consequences which too exaggerated a pneumatological emphasis produces in contemporary Protestant christology. Barth thus poses some serious questions to Bultmann. Does Bultmann's soteriology presuppose christology or exclude it? Can Bultmann's exclusive concern with Christian freedom be understood as a disguised theology of the Holy Spirit or not?[21] Would it be possible to reinterpret Bultmann's seemingly philosophical hermeneutics in the spirit of Melanchthon's *Loci*, which states: "There is one teacher, who, precisely because he is the most guileless, is also the most dependable one: the Holy Spirit, who expresses himself in the Scriptures most directly and most simply," or in the spirit of Luther's *Tischreden:* "the Scriptures seek a humble reader who simply says: teach me, teach me, teach me; Divine Spirit, you resist the proud"? Barth even confronts Bultmann directly with a pneumatic reading of hermeneutics: "is not even the modern hearer of the New Testament message (in us and in others) addressed most responsibly, when he is directed to *this* 'possibility' of understanding?"[22] Thus Barth implies that Bultmann could say everything differently if he were to allow the Holy

Spirit to be the sole hermeneutical possibility of understanding the New Testament message concerning redeemed existence. These questions reveal that what Christian Existentialism really intends to do—and Barth wants to interpret it *in optimam partem* and link it to genuine Protestantism—is to create a much needed theology of the third article of the creed, a pneumatology. Only if it is a cloaked theology of the Holy Spirit, is the thought of Bultmann and of Christian Existentialism acceptable as legitimate Christian theology. But is that what is intended? This ambivalence explains why Barth invariably links Mysticism and Existentialism to the latent pneumatological character of Neo-Protestantism.

Moreover, the same ambiguous attitude persists in Barth's mind concerning the Roman Catholic tendency to stress various aspects of ecclesiology at the expense of christology. The only sure correction is a theology of the Holy Spirit. In the preface to the *Church Dogmatics* (IV/2) Barth describes the very intent of this volume as "an Evangelical answer to the Marian dogma of Romanism"; he also makes explicit mention of "Roman Catholic readers . . . to whom I turn more and more in the *Church Dogmatics.*"[23] Barth does this at the very point in his major work where pneumatology, the study of the divine Spirit's activity on behalf of man, comes to the fore. Why does Barth so clearly associate Roman Catholic theology with pneumatology? Why does he consider theology of the Holy Spirit the most apt subject matter for ecumenical dialogue and thus for theological consensus with Roman Catholicism? The answer to these questions is found where Barth expresses willingness to accept the theology of the Rationalists, of the Anabaptists, the Spiritualists and mystics of the Middle Ages, the mariological teachings of both Western and Eastern Catholicism and even the Existential theology of the present century as latent theologies of the Holy Spirit.[24] This suspicion explains why in various passages in which Barth discusses the theology of the Holy Spirit the particular dogmas of Roman Catholic theology gain his attention. In *Zur Lehre vom Heiligen Geist*, Barth criticizes aspects of Augustines's theology in terms of their too static pneumatic character.[25] When Barth praises the work of Heribert Mühlen on the Holy Spirit, he observes that it could have "rather astounding consequences in the direction of a mariology."[26] Likewise, pneumatology provides hope for the divided Churches: "I think that we in the various confessions and churches are particularly in need of a more serious theology of the third person, or as I prefer to say, of the third way of existence of the one God, who is also the Holy Spirit. He can very briefly be defined as the inextinguishable power of the work and word of Jesus Christ and thus of the work and word of God for and in the creature."[27] These last few words are decisive; it is Roman Catholicism's concern to guard the role of the creature in theology, and Barth concedes that this must be done! As a Reformed theologian, however, Barth cannot fully agree with Catholicism's way of attaining this goal; it relies stubbornly on an independent theology of man. Whereas Barth grants the need to consider man's role in theology seriously, he feels that it is only a valid pneumatology which can rightly do so.

Why this laudatory evaluation of Catholic pneumatology on one hand and this endless suspicion of it on the other? The problem is the excessive autonomy which Catholic Spirit theology attributes to human experience and activity. An example will clarify this charge of autonomy. Although Barth's ambivalant attitude towards Protestant mysticism holds for its Catholic manifestations as well, Barth pinpoints the distortion of the pneumatological character of all Christian subjectivism in Catholicism's institutionalized form of mysticism, monasticism. Barth's evaluation of this phenomenon undergoes an evolution throughout the *Church Dogmatics*. At first Barth warns of the danger of perversion which can result from failing to heed the command of God concerning the necessary relation of man to woman and woman to man; monasticism, for all of its apparent religious motivation, can be a deceitful escape from man's need for the opposite sex.[28] Gradually, however, Barth admits that the central notion of Christian vocation, rightly understood as the Holy Spirit's call of the community to total generosity, was always preserved in Catholic monasticism: "Protestantism successfully expelled monasticism by recalling the fact that *klesis* is the presupposition of all Christian existence. But it lost sight of the grandeur and purity of this *klesis*, which were always in some sense retained even by monasticism."[29] Finally, in the *Church Dogmatics* (IV/2) Barth offers a surprisingly positive treatment of the ascetical and spiritual life of the monk, once he discovers the pneumatological character of Catholic monasticism. As dangerous as retreat from the world can be, "it might well be the law of the Spirit to which regard was had in the form of these withdrawals and the possibility of new and better Christian action which was sought and found in them." Barth's understanding of monastic obedience is likewise pneumatological: "if what is impossible with men is possible with God and the Spirit blows where He wills, it cannot be disputed that a genuine fellowship of the saints could and can take place in the form of genuine commands and genuine obeying even in the sphere of this kind of institution." In short, even monasticism, as an expression of Christian fellowship and service, has a proper place in the framework of Spirit theology.[30]

Because monasticism is concerned with the reconciled man, Barth connects it to a legitimate theology of God's action for and among His creatures; it is based on belief in the community of the saints, and is thus a logical corollary to the third article of the Christian creed, "I believe in the Holy Spirit." The same is true of mariology which Barth considers under the heading of grace—the gift of the Holy Spirit received by reconciled man. For all Barth's insistence that "mariology is an excrescence, i.e., a diseased construct of theological thought" which must be excised, he attempts to redeem mariology when in the *Church Dogmatics* (I/2) he considers the subjective reality and possibility of revelation in man as the work of the Holy Spirit. Yet constant precaution is needed lest the gifted existence of the Christian community crowd out the unique existence of Jesus Christ. Given the fact that the reality of grace and the pneumatic character of Church leadership is as exaggerated in many forms of Protestantism as it is in Catholicism, Barth wonders why a "Protestant mariology" is not thriving.[31] Despite his obvious misgivings, Barth shows himself ready to tolerate mariology as a secondary reflection, that is, as a complement to christology, if the former is securely planted in a theology of the Holy Spirit and therefore is also a theology of graced and reconciled man in the community of saints. Since Barth views his pneumatology as an Evangelical answer to Roman mariology, and since he subsumes Mary's *fiat mihi* under "the act of the majesty of the Holy Spirit,"[32] Barth intends to find a place for mankind, for Israel and for Mary precisely as the necessary consequence of the divinity of the Holy Spirit. Redeemed man, Mary, the Catholic monk and mystic, as well as the Pietist and the Schwärmer are necessarily to be included in a genuine Christian pneumatology, that is, only in a theology of the subjective aspect of God's self-revelation and self-impartation to man as Holy Spirit.

In a synthetic passage, which explains his uneasiness about the excessive pneumatic bias of Neo-Protestantism, Christian Existentialism and Roman Catholicism, Barth points out their common preference for the holy man and their common neglect of the event which procured such holiness: "Sanctification is not justification. If we do not take care not to confuse and confound, soteriology may suffer, allowing justification (as in the case of much of Roman Catholicism in its following of Augustine, but also of many varieties of Neo-Protestantism) to merge into the process of his sanctification initiated by the act of the forgiveness of sins, or by allowing faith in Jesus Christ as the Judge judged in our place (this is in my view the most serious objection to the theology of R. Bultmann) to merge into the obedience in which the Christian in his discipleship has to die to the world and himself"[33] Though Barth finds justifiable the emphasis placed by these thought systems on the existential relevance of the atonement, he is not convinced that they regard the free giver of this grace with as much earnestness as they do the gift. Is Jesus Christ in the power of His Spirit the sole cause of the Christian's new life of faith?[34] This and the many questions which Barth puts to the theologies he considers pneumatological in intention reflect the ambiguity he feels concerning their success at developing a truly Christian theology of the third article of the creed. Barth suspects that they fail, but he seems never totally sure. On the one hand, they rightly highlight the existential dimension of New Testament language about man's life in the Spirit; on the other, they tend to jeopardize the uniqueness of Jesus Christ's Spirit by relegating pneumatology to the category of an unspoken presupposition of soteriology and ecclesiology. Yet, since Barth's ambiguous relationship to these latent pneumatologies remains unquestionable, why is he continually haunted by a theology which begins with redeemed man rather than with the redeeming acts of God?

2. *The Spirit as Ellipse, Christ and Christians as Foci*

What then lies behind Barth's attempt positively to construe the ideological standpoints of his opponents as quiescent theologies of the Holy Spirit? If one examines the contexts in which references to this possibility of a pneumatological reinterpretation appear, it becomes clear that the feasibility of such a reading arises whenever Barth is grappling with the very nature of the relation between God and man in Protestant theology.[35] Since

Barth's basic intention is to return Protestantism to the insights of the Reformation, which he believes have been obscured, if not lost altogether, during the last century, he is nevertheless unwilling to bypass this era or condemn its main figures unconditionally. They too, despite their many failures, at least claim to share the same desire to be loyal to the Reformation. But how can the 19th-century Protestant theologians, especially Schleiermacher, set out in such a clearly anthropocentric direction and still place themselves with the Reformers? Have they not taken significant steps toward Romanism? Again Barth's openness: they have first to be studied and understood correctly, even admired fully for what they have accomplished, before they can be corrected or dismissed. This purposely ambivalent relation to his intellectual forebears is a recurring theme of Barth's thought which finds its first clear expression in his review, "Brunner's Schleiermacherbuch," in 1924. Emil Brunner had finished with Schleiermacher in *Die Mystik und das Wort* by assigning him to the category of distorters of the Reformation. Yet Barth's review, while it manifests sympathy for Brunner's main critique, stresses that the magnitude of Schleiermacher's theological achievement is such that, to rectify the admittedly dangerous tendencies of his thought, not an outright condemnation is required but a great counterwork precisely as impressive, but in a different direction.[36] Barth, the relentless critical redactor of 19th-century Protestant theology, is ironically also its staunchest defender. How is this possible? Where is Barth able to find Liberal Protestantism's saving character?

The intriguing passages quoted above concerning the possible pneumatological revaluation of Liberal Protestantism offer the answer. If they can be viewed as theologians of the Holy Spirit, that is, as exponents of the subjective side of Christian revelation, their theology takes up and develops an essential component of the Reformation: not christology, the main pole which the Reformers chiefly emphasize, but its counterpoise, faith in Christ through the work of the Holy Spirit, pneumatology. Barth expatiates on this theme at great length in his essay on Schleiermacher in *Protestant Theology in the 19th Century*. In the final analysis, Barth suggests that Schleiermacher attempts to write a theology of the Christian, and, in wanting to do so, remains squarely in the Protestant tradition, since the christological coinage of the Reformation always pictured on its reverse side the Christian who accepts Christ in faith through the Holy Spirit. Certainly the Reformers situate God, Christ and revelation at the center of their theology, but at the same time they realize that this center is fundamentally a split one. They thus allowed a relatively different reality from God, Christ and revelation also to stand at the center "in that they firmly placed in opposition to the Word of God the human correlate of *faith*, even though the latter was totally and entirely grounded in the Word of God and created and maintained through the Word of God."[37]

Reformation theology necessarily has two motifs: it must speak of God and man and of man and God. Whereas the Reformers themselves, well aware of the duality of their central motif, place predominant stress on the Gospel, on the Word of God and on Christ, three hundred years later Schleiermacher reverses this emphasis and puts religion or piety, the consciousness of the Christian believer, in the dominant place which Christ had occupied up to then. As Barth exposes Schleiermacher's reversal of traditional Protestantism's ordering of the two facets at the center of theological reflection, he does so very subtly and even approvingly, since the one facet without the other would reduce theology either to metaphysics, by stressing only God's action apart from its relation to man, or to mysticism, by concentrating only on man's action apart from its relation to God. "With this consideration in mind, the Reformers fashioned their teaching on the Word of God in its correlation to faith as the *work of the Holy Spirit in man.*"[38] Therefore, Barth claims that Schleiermacher's option to begin with the "faith-aspect" instead of the "Christ-aspect" should not incur a negative judgment from the start; rather his intent has to be evaluated positively since it corresponds to modern man's "Copernician" way of viewing the world with himself at the center. A theology beginning with man does not have to mean "man without God, man in his own world. It could mean: man in the face of God, man's action over against the action of God. Genuine, true theology could be constructed from the point of view of man."[39] Here Barth isolates most painstakingly what he finds to be the saving factor of Neo-Protestantism as well as of Catholicism which it patently resembles. In their aim to start theology with the man who is placed by God in His presence and touched by grace, Barth registers the deepest resonance with 19th-century theological trends. Not only does a theology beginning with the Christian have its roots in Reformational thought, but it also legitimately elucidates and deepens an aspect of this thought which, though not totally neglected, remained secondary, and only came to the fore as man became more conscious of himself and viewed his world from an almost exclusively anthropocentric standpoint. The Reformers are essentially theocentic or christocentric. Schleiermacher and his followers, having reversed the trend, are essentially anthropocentric, or better, since they fully intend to be Christian theologians, christianocentric or pneumatocentric.[40]

To be pneumatocentric certainly seems to be their goal, and Barth stands out as the theologian of this century who, in explicitating this goal, caused an astounding renewal of interest in 19th-century Protestant theologians. Barth detects their most positive contribution to be that they employ the categories of Idealistic thinkers, especially of Hegel and Schelling, without however deducing the truths of revelation from a purely speculative starting point. Schleiermacher and his successors never pretend to ground their Christian belief on science or philosophy but on the very experience of faith.[41] But once Barth makes their positive intention clear, he raises such keen and persistent questions concerning whether they actually accomplish their goal that subsequent scholars complain of Barth's cramping and debilitating influence especially on Schleiermacher studies. Richard R. Niebuhr, for example, laments the prevalent "Barthian captivity" under which modern interpreters of Schleiermacher have fallen sway.[42] What accounts for Barth's ultimately negative judgment when it is evident that he never ceases being fascinated with Schleiermacher in all that he writes about him as possibly the first expositor of a theology of the Holy Spirit? Despite Barth's continual attempt to defend Schleiermacher's genuine determination to remain faithful to Reformational insights, though from a different, pneumatological point of view, he is never really certain that his predecessor does anything more than reduce Christianity to anthropology. Instead of producing a Christian theology from an anthropocentric starting point, Schleiermacher seems to Barth to have ended up an anthropologian. The central focus certainly switches from God to man, but is the switch rooted in a pneumatocentric insight or is it mere anthropologizing?[43] Barth leans throughout the years towards a negative response, all the while harboring one glimmer of hope for a future positive judgment by holding out the possibility that Schleiermacher is the first great pneumatologian.

The root of Barth's embarrassing ambivalence toward Schleiermacher, therefore, rests not in the latter's attempt at a theology of the Holy Spirit, but in the execution of this intention. Does Schleiermacher, by reversing the Reformation's primary stress on christology and by focusing on the secondary, though equally important aspect of pneumatology, in effect abandon the first for the second?[44] The Reformers did not sacrifice the one for the other: "Their theology which began with the Word of God was at the same time a theology of the Holy Spirit, in that it could also be understood as a theology of faith and thus assure that the divine Word of God formed its proper center."[45] In Barth's eyes, however, Schleiermacher does not keep the two poles, Christ and Christians, in an equal tension like the two foci of an ellipse. By underlining the self-consciousness of the believer as the proper object of theology, Schleiermacher tends to subsume the objective reality of Christ into the subjective experience of faith. The ellipse threatens to become a circle with the subjective element forming the sole center. In short, Barth finds Schleiermacher culpable of avoiding the scandal of a genuine christology.[46] Schleiermacher never quite passes the test when his theology is measured against the balance which the Reformers achieve between the historical and the psychological poles of Christian theology. Here is the crux of the problem. For all Barth's admiration of Schleiermacher's pneumatological orientation, the result of the latter's constant stress on the Christian must undergo the test of fire: is Schleiermacher also a christocentric theologian?

Barth always leaps at the chance to affirm Schleiermacher's genius in taking a pneumatic path parallel to the christic path of the Reformers, but Barth invariably stops his praise short at the point where the divinity of Christ is apparently compromised for the sake of the divinity of the Holy Spirit. For, once the divinity of the Logos has been virtually subsumed into that of the Pneuma, Barth then doubts the validity of Schleiermacher's pneumatology as such: "It can at least be questioned whether the divinity of the Logos was as unambiguously presumed in Schleiermacher's theology as the divinity of the Spirit was for the Reformers and whether, if this was not the case, the divinity of the Spirit which apparently forms the center here, was really the divinity of the *Holy* Spirit."[47] Barth is undecided about this "Spirit's" very identity in Schleiermacher's theology when the person of Christ is so relativized that the faith of the Spirit-filled Christian becomes the sole object of theological reflection. As soon as the christocentric or historical pole of the theological ellipse is engulfed by the christianocentric or psychological pole, where the effects of Christ are applied to the believer by the *Gemeingeist* of the community, the very religious nature of the remaining pole is put in question: "The two foci of the ellipse fall irresistably back onto one another, and how can it be avoided that the objective impulse must merge and disappear into the subjective one? Here the independence of the Word over against faith is not so assured as would have to be the case if this theology of faith were a genuine theology of the Holy Spirit. In a genuine theology of the Holy Spirit a dissolution of the Word cannot come into question. In Schleiermacher's theology of the Spirit such a dissolution comes in all earnestness into question."[48] Barth therefore concludes that it is not the Holy Spirit, but man's religious consciousness which forms the actual ellipse uniting the "Christ-focus" and the "faith-focus" of Schleiermacher's system. In attempting to be pneumatocentric instead of christocentric, Schleiermacher's theology is in effect neither, since by replacing the divine Spirit with man's consciousness as the mediating factor between Christ and the believing community, this thought system is in the end exclusively anthropocentric.

The negative decision seems to take definitive shape in Barth's essay on Schleiermacher in *Protestant Theology in the 19th Century.* Furthermore, Barth applies the critique of Neo-Protestantism's unipolar theology to Christian Existentialism and Roman Catholicism as well. Whereas Schleiermacher places man's consciousness at the center, Existentialism does so with the individual's apprehension of the Word of God, and Catholicism with the creature's participation in God's own being. Thus, Barth's expressly pneumatological reinterpretation of these theologies leads him to conclude that the validity of their latent intention is irreparably compromised by their particular anthropological blurring of God's Spirit and man's spirit; such an identity causes their anthropology to absorb christology into itself. Barth employs the image of an ellipse, which has become a circle with only one center, in order to depict the tendency towards identifying the divine and the human in these theological systems. The new center which emerges is nothing else than a confusion of God and man; the real qualitative difference between the two foci is lost. In the *Church Dogmatics* (IV/3, 1) Barth locates the genesis of this confusion in a misguided concept of the Spirit. The proper function of the Holy Spirit is that of holding the two foci—Christ and the Christian—in tension, and not that of collapsing the bipolar ellipse in such a way that a fluid amalgamation of the speaking God and the hearing man results: "Why should not the fellowship between the speaking God and the hearing man in the gift and reception of the Holy Spirit be understood as this relative, fluid and on both sides provisional distinction yet interconnection of the two foci? And why should not the Holy Spirit in particular be understood as the impelling force of the process in which the two foci find their common center and therefore hasten beyond mere distinctions and particularities? This dissolution of distinction is positively the blessed union of above and below, of there and here, of God and man."[49] A legitimate pneumatology ought not to fuse the Christian and Christ; the work of the Holy Spirit is that of the ellipse proper; it preserves a tension and a balance between two points while it inseparably connects them to each other. If this coordinated tension is not maintained, then Christian fellowship in the Holy Spirit renders the historical events of the life of Jesus Christ superfluous, since the latter simply become symbols of what the Christian himself experiences, and not matchless paradigms without which his experiences would have no ground in reality. In the light of the unique presence of God in Jesus Christ, man's graced existence in the Christian community is clearly secondary; the ethico-anthropological depends on the christological pole and not *vice versa*.[50] For this reason, Barth insists on the need for perfect balance between the existential pole of Christian faith and the christological pole of the divine model of faith, Jesus Christ. In order to protect and yet to moderate the former, Barth's entire theology almost exclusively gives weight to the latter. In order to be a true pneumatologian, Barth realizes that he must first be a christologian. To counteract the unipolar character of most contemporary theology, and thus to restore the supremacy of Christ in Christianity, Barth must become decidedly bipolar, and that means concretely: also and primarily christocentric. Only a pneumatology grounded in the Christ-event would be able to reestablish the needed balance not only in Protestant, but in Catholic theology as well. This lifelong effort at a balance invariably causes Barth to be branded a christomonist. Yet, the tension which Barth constantly advocates as the hallmark of Christian theology is the tension between the christocentric and the christianocentric foci of revelation itself. It is no exaggeration, therefore, to state that Barth's christology may have a latent pneumatological intention, for the former sets out to reinstate the bipolar dimension which he finds missing not only in Schleiermacher's theology but also in the theology of Rudolf Bultmann and Hans Urs von Balthasar.[51] All these theologians, according to Barth, represent Christian existence in the Spirit as an independent experience of redemption which soon degenerates into a blurred anthropocentrism. Their initial concern to preserve the legitimate role of the reconciled man in theology invariably alleviates the tension which must exist between the Spirit-given experience of redemption and its objective historical ground in Jesus Christ. This search for a balance, for a conjunction but not a confusion between a theology of Christ and a theology of man, is undoubtedly the germ of Barth's own pneumatology.

At the end of his life, more than twenty years after his initial reluctant judgment on the matter, Barth turns to an evaluation of Schleiermacher's achievement once again. The haunting ambivalence of Barth's findings, though a negative verdict seems imminent, lends weight to the theory that, precisely in confronting the possibly revolutionary quality of Schleiermacher's pneumatology, Barth uncovers the point where the weakness of every other aspect of Schleiermacher's thought can be overlooked and his entire theology interpreted positively. For, in 1968 Barth raised five double questions about Schleiermacher's thought which echo his early attempts to grapple with Neo-Protestant theology, and which remarkably leave open the possibility of a basic misunderstanding of its major concern on Barth's part, and, therefore, also of an ultimate rapprochement with Schleiermacher. Since pneumatology dominates the total context in which these questions appear, the one dealing with the Holy Spirit reflects Barth's unending dilemma: "Pneumatology: is the Spirit who moves the believer a particular Spirit distinct from all other "spirits" and thus to be called "holy", or is the Spirit a universally effective and diffuse spiritual power?"[52]

The dilemma remains to the end! Since this new evaluation is as equally ambiguous as the first, Barth once more is forced to underline the danger of "anthropologizing" Christianity which is inherent in a man-centered theology. Lest someone should misunderstand his strongly conditioned praise of Schleiermacher's genius, Barth warns against too quick a resolve on the part of a promising theologian to embark on Schleiermacher's path and to construe a theology with man at the center: "As if pneumatology were anthropology! As if I had dreamed, instead of the possibility of a better understanding of Schleiermacher's main intention, of a continuation in a totally naive way along the path which he had chosen! I give a warning! If I am to be spared the accusation of sheer insanity, then only very spiritually and intellectually competent people, truly 'kundige Thebaner' will be of use in designing and developing a theology of the third article. Those who are not such or are not yet such should, instead of boldly wanting to actualize a possibility of the millenium, rather prefer with me to hold out a little longer in my conscious 'embarrassment'."[53] Barth thus leaves posterity both with an enticing possibility of reinterpreting Schleiermacher as a theologian of the Holy Spirit and with the warning that to do so, to continue on this path, is a task for only the most gifted of men; the possibility being that pneumatology offers the advantage of illuminating the subjective aspect of revelation as the work of the Spirit in and for man; the danger being that such an undertaking can result in a unipolar theology of man apart from and over against the revelation of the Spirit-filled Jesus Christ, that is, not in theology at all, but in anthropology.

3. The Act of the Spirit: Barth's Mediating Principle

The bipolar structure of Neo-Protestant, Existential and Catholic theology intrigues Barth not only because it is consonant with the original intent of the Reformers, but for another reason as well. Barth cannot decisively repudiate the latent pneumatic character of Liberal Protestant and Roman Catholic theology because he recognizes behind it an equally latent yet attractive pneumatic methodology. Barth is convinced that he must develop the main lines of this methodology in some new direction if his own theology is to exhibit the breadth of vision which is required of truly Christian dogmatic theology.[54] At the heart of the pneumatic methodology, which Barth admires in the thought systems of his opponents, lies the key element of a mediating principle between God's self-revelation in Jesus Christ and the Christian's response of faith. In Barth's eyes, the ultimate ambiguity of these systems is due to the adoption of either a philosophical or hermeneutical concept of mediation rather than an explicitly theological one. Barth wants to correct the error of these theological systems, but never totally to repudiate their ingenious substructure. For Barth discovers hidden in these mediating principles a theological methodology which can be interpreted pneumatologically—and is really meant to be understood as such—but which is distorted beyond recognition by what Barth calls a filtering element. Barth thus determines to remove the filter from these principles of mediation and to expose the necessarily pneumatic character of theological methodology.

It is Schleiermacher's Idealistic methodology and mediating principle which most fascinate Barth. Why is this so? Hans Urs von Balthasar conjectures that Barth himself is at heart an Idealist, and thus in the end has no other choice but to adopt Schleiermacher's Idealistic theological framework as his own. Schleiermacher is for him "the printing stamp which imprints a mark which can no longer be obliterated, the form, from which one can never free oneself despite all his efforts at a difference of content."[55] The *Zusammenschau*, or total vision, which Barth inherited from Schleiermacher is essentially a synthesis of German Idealism and Protestantism. These two systems of thought, Barth concludes, are not incompatible since the latter has already been freed by the Reformers themselves of the thought structure of Roman Scholasticism and been made receptive to new patterns of organization. Because of his own inclination and education, Barth finds himself drawn to using the conceptual vessel of Schleiermacher's thought, but to replacing its content with the genuinely different and opposite truths of revelation, as the Reformers themselves, the real initiators of "secularized" theology, had once done.[56] Thus, Barth's very search for a fitting mediating principle of Christian theology is due to his conviction that Schleiermacher along with Hegel provide orthodox Protestantism the same kind of metaphysical framework which Thomas of Aquinas offers Catholicism and Soren Kierkegaard Existentialism.[57] The elliptical or bipolar structure of Barth's own thought demonstrates a strong affinity towards and yet an abiding uneasiness concerning his Idealistic predecessor.

While Barth accepts the need for a *Vermittlungsprinzip*, or mediating principle of theological methodology, Schleiermacher's selection of man's consciousness, through which the objective becomes subjective and the historical becomes psychologically possible, strikes Barth as inadequate.[58] Through the filter of man's consciousness Schleiermacher forces the biblical understanding of Christ and the Spirit to pass; in the process both are deformed and robbed of their uniqueness. Christ is reduced to an historical figure with an ever-present impulse on man's individual consciousness, and the Holy Spirit is likewise identified with the communal consciousness of redemption on the part of members of the Church.[59] The objectivity of biblical revelation is thus lost, and the exclusive emphasis on man's subjective experience as the locus and the object of Christian faith is firmly established. The content of man's faith and his personal experience of faith are first unified and then embedded totally in the all-important mediating principle, man's consciousness. By means of this form of mediation, Schleiermacher simply merges revelation's theological content with a given anthropology's tenets. Barth's main difficulty with Schleiermacher, therefore, is that, where the Holy Spirit should stand as the one true mediator between Christ and the believer, Schleiermacher places man's consciousness, thereby reducing Christ and faith to the two theologically immunized concepts history and experience. If graphically represented, Schleiermacher's attempt to mediate between these opposed poles by means of the unifying principle of man's consciousness would appear as follows:

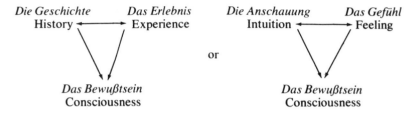

Die Geschichte   *Das Erlebnis*   *Die Anschauung*   *Das Gefühl*
History ←——→ Experience   Intuition ←——→ Feeling

or

Das Bewußtsein   *Das Bewußtsein*
Consciousness   Consciousness

Barth is dissatisfied not with the dialectical framework of this scheme in itself, but with its de-theologized content. He thus deems it imperative to transform its content by reintroducing the categories of biblical revelation which the Reformers themselves use so unambiguously. Barth substitutes for history and experience, or for intuition and feeling in the sense of receptivity and spontaneity, the much more diametrically opposed biblical categories of God's revelation in Jesus Christ and man's faith in this revelation. These poles can be brought together only by the activity of the Holy Spirit whose task is to lead and to unite men to Christ.[60] Barth's transformation of Schleiermacher's purely philosophical framework produces this schema:

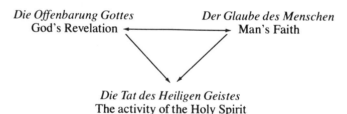

Die Offenbarung Gottes   *Der Glaube des Menschen*
God's Revelation ←——————→ Man's Faith

Die Tat des Heiligen Geistes
The activity of the Holy Spirit

The insertion of the work of the Holy Spirit in place of the key idea, indeed the most central category of Schleiermacher's thought, man's consciousness, indicates that Barth views the Holy Spirit alone as the true mediator between objective revelation and subjective faith. Barth thus introduces trinitarian categories into Schleiermacher's schema so as to preserve a clear distinction between Christ, the Spirit and the Christian.

Here is the wellspring of Barth's own pneumatology: through this replacement of man's consciousness by the act of the Holy Spirit, Barth both corrects Schleiermacher's vague christology and pneumatology, and forges his own pneumatic methodology which is original yet clearly indebted to the dialectical structure of Schleiermacher's thought. Thus, Barth's theological method is to be Idealistic in form, but Evangelical in content: "Above all at the point where the Idealists Fichte, Schelling and Hegel posited an identity between God and man at the origin of their thought, and where Schleiermacher manifested the strongest tendency towards identity, Barth posited the meeting of two opposites: God, gracious and totally different, and man, sinful and closed up within himself."[61] In so doing, Barth intends to overcome Schleiermacher's philosophical identity of God and man, Christ and faith, and the Holy Spirit and the *Gemeingeist* within man's consciousness. Confronted with Schleiermacher's philosophico-pneumatic principle of identity, Barth opts for a schema diametrically opposed to it; he stresses the biblico-pneumatic concept of mediation: the Holy Spirit. Pneumatology thus stands at the core of this correction and transition. In Barth's pneumatic methodology the Holy Spirit alone unites the nonidentical, qualitatively different beings God and man. The framework remains Schleiermacher's, the content Barth's biblical appeal to the union of God and man solely through the Spirit.

In a logical fashion, Barth follows the same line of argumentation with regard to the mediating principles of Christian Existentialism and Roman Catholicism. In each case he is convinced that the real intention of these theologies is to account for the perennial Christian belief that the Holy Spirit is God's own self-mediation between the unique event of Jesus Christ and its universal import for mankind. Barth surmises that the Holy Spirit is the latent principle of mediation which Existentialism and Catholicism imply in their own search for a methodology which will mediate Christ and the Christian. Barth concludes, however, that in each case an extraneous philosophical principle manages to veil the underlying biblico-pneumatic thought structure and thus to distort it. In Existentialism's case it is clearly an independent hermeneutic rooted in man's self-understanding which mediates between history and faith.[62] Although Barth is sympathetic to the need of modern man to interpret the meaning of the New Testament message in terms of his own experience, he would disagree that man's existential and hermeneutical self-understanding alone mediates between the kerygma and the faith of the Christian; in its place below Barth would substitute the act of the Holy Spirit:

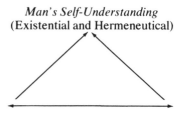

Man's Self-Understanding
(Existential and Hermeneutical)

New Testament Kerygma   *Christian Faith*

Barth discovers that a similar pattern emerges in Catholicism. Between the historical person of Christ and the individual Christian stands man's share in supernatural life either as a creature of God or as a member of the Church.[63] This mediating principle is really a disguised expression of the one pneumatic principle of mediation found in the New Testament; in the diagram below Barth would replace man's transcendental being with the act of the Holy Spirit:

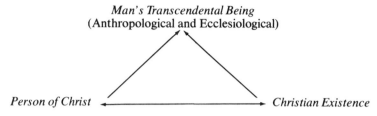

Man's Transcendental Being
(Anthropological and Ecclesiological)

Person of Christ   *Christian Existence*

In unearthing their misguided concepts of pneumatology, Barth confirms his haunting suspicion that Neo-Protestantism, Christian Existentialism and Roman Catholicism invariably reduce theology to anthropology despite their good intentions. He corroborates this theory by a close study of the mediating principles which in fact replace the traditional function of the Holy Spirit and which can thus be judged as theologically immune. Barth thus feels justified in his reinterpretation of these theologies as potential pneumatologies, since this hypothesis certainly explains the central role of a mediating principle within their several methodologies. Barth also feels justified in his continually ambiguous stance concerning the validity of their Spirit theologies, since the content of their respective dogmatic systems contains so much about man's consciousness, man's self-understanding or man's nature, that the believer himself proves to be the true subject of pneumatology and not the Holy Spirit. Theologies which begin with man and pretend to produce genuine theologies of the Holy Spirit usually end with man as the sole concern of theological investigation. This danger is certainly the reason behind the explicitly pneumatic character of Barth's own theological methodology. In order to give primacy to the mediating role of the Holy Spirit, Barth purposely downplays man's role in the process of divine-human mediation; not to do so is to sacrifice pneumatology to anthropology or to sacrifice Christ to a vague notion of the Spirit. Barth's own pneumatology is at its core a search for a theologically legitimate principle of mediation at the center of Christian dogmatics—at the point where the transition is made between Christ and the Christian. Only the Holy Spirit, the divine mediator, can validly serve this function.[64]

The import of Barth's emendations of the theological methodologies of his chief adversaries should not be overlooked, however. Though he clearly supplants their philosophical mediating principles with a decidedly pneumatic one, Barth does opt to keep their dialectical structure intact. Behind this decision is the realization that a theology based on the incarnate and written Word alone is not sufficient; there is a third aspect to revelation, namely, the living Word proclaimed in the Church and effective in Christian hearing. By tacitly approving the structure if not the wording of his opponents' methodologies, Barth concedes that Christian theology must take into account the objective basis of the subjective experience of faith. This fact explains why Barth adheres to three forms of the Word of God: incarnation, Scripture and preaching, whose efficacy he respectively attributes to the Father, the Son and the Holy Spirit.[65] In effect, Barth cautiously relativizes the centrality of the Word by permitting the work of the Spirit in the Church to serve as the ongoing revealing light by which the Word is to be interpreted. Some Protestant critics balk at this "irrational" procedure which seems to put the definitiveness and inerrancy of Scripture into question. They find Barth's pneumatic methodology ironically close to that of his rivals. By allowing the Holy Spirit to play a key role in the passage from the Word made flesh and recorded in Scripture to the Word heard and witnessed by Christians, Barth seems to unfreeze the connection between Scripture and revelation which many Protestants insist on.[66] Thus, Barth takes a great risk in his adoption and adaptation of his opponents' methodology. In separating himself from them, Barth weds himself to them at the same time.

Thus, has the whole truth been said once Barth is shown to have made a clear demarcation between his concept of the Holy Spirit and those of his adversaries? Can one also aver that Barth's pneumatology not only reacted to but also profited from the pneumatological insights of both his Protestant and Catholic predecessors and contemporaries? The answer in decidedly affirmative. For Barth is as convinced of the justifiable role of the soteriologico-pneumatological element in Christian theology as he is outraged at the failure especially of Protestant theology to highlight that role without coming dangerously close to unipolar anthropocentrism and sheer subjectivism. What is it—beyond the fact that the Reformers include a subjective as well as an objective pole in their theology—which lies behind Barth's conviction that something in Neo-Protestantism, Christian Existentialism and Roman Catholicism is eminently worth saving? Is the perpetual wavering, the perduring love-hate relationship to his opponents a disguised confession that their rejection of fundamentalism and their daring affirmation of man's part in revelation strikes Barth as offering theology a breadth and depth, a social and a spiritual relevance unmatched by more staid dogmatic systems?

And there are still other questions. Is Barth himself a "kundiger Thebaner" who is able in his own pneumatology both to retain the positive contribution of Schleiermacher and to avoid the ambiguous distortions and the anthropocentric dangers into which the latter's pneumatology falls? Is this at least Barth's intention as he develops his theology of the Spirit in the *Church Dogmatics* and in the smaller works which both precede and accompany it? Is Barth, besides being a patent defender of the objective "Christ-focus" of revelation, more essentially, though less forthrightly, a zealous advocate of the subjective "Christian-focus" of revelation as well? Or, more boldly, is Barth's theology secretly meant to be the great counterwork to Schleiermacher, a pneumatic theology "done properly" which therefore is necessarily encircled by a strong christological bulwark only to defend and to enhance all the more its real core?

CHAPTER II

REDISCOVERING THE THIRD CREDAL ARTICLE

This account of Barth's genesis as a pneumatologian has begun, as it were, in *medias res*; its starting point is the pivotal year 1947 in which Barth's reinterpretation of his opponents' positions as covert Spirit theologies starts to generate a captivating perplexity in him which lasts until his death. Now it will be helpful to go back to the beginning of Barth's development as a theologian and to trace the evolution of his Spirit theology from its inception in *Der Römerbrief* of 1919 up to its systematic expression in *Die Kirchliche Dogmatik* (I/1) of 1932. Once this is done, both the present and the previous chapter can serve as background for the central portion of this study, the pneumatology of Barth's major work. For it is not only in 1947 that Barth's thought undergoes a radical change; he admits, for example, that his extensive reading of Kierkegaard in 1919 took place "at the critical turning-point between the first and second editions of my *Romans*."[1] No doubt the very composition of the first edition of *Romans* marks a crucial transformation, as does his study of Anselm of Canterbury in 1931. Since this series of significant transitions in Barth's thought is thoroughly documented by many commentators on his life and work, the purpose of this chapter is not to repeat these details, but to dwell on their pneumatological importance. For this reason, the ensuing survey of Barth's nascent Spirit theology concentrates chiefly on three developments: the two editions of *Der Römerbrief*, the shorter works leading up to *Die Christliche Dogmatik* of 1927 and the publication of *Fides Quaerens Intellectum*.

Within the time frame which this chapter scans, Barth's thought progresses through three important methodological phases which the works mentioned above concretely symbolize. Thus, in addition to the over-all unity which the historical perspective itself affords the following survey, another theme emerges as well: the role which pneumatology plays in the main stages of Barth's intellectual growth. Is the hypothesis of Hans Urs von Balthasar correct that within this period Barth's theological methodology shifts from dialectics, then to christocentrism and finally to analogy?[2] Can this theory be corroborated by testing its applicability to the evolution of Barth's pneumatology? Though Spirit theology is not the central theme of these formative years, the relation between God and man indeed is. Barth is not interested primarily in the Church or the sacraments, in Scripture or tradition at this time, but chiefly in the nature of the union between the divine and the human.[3] Since pneumatology is later to be the subdivision of Barth's dogmatic system in which this union is explicitly treated, it seems tenable to claim that Barth is always covertly and often overtly struggling with Spirit theology from the very start of his professional career. The Spirit is essential in clarifying this God-man relationship. The two editions of *Romans* represent first a broad cosmological and then a strict christological conception of the Spirit's activity among men; the works between 1922 and 1931 witness Barth's strengthening of the link between the Spirit of the Christian and the Spirit of Christ; with his Anselm book, tones of dialectical opposition and of excessive christocentrism give way to an understanding of the Spirit's role in creating an analogy between the existence of Christ and the faith of the believer.[4] Thus, weaved throughout this chapter's central motif is the leitmotif of steadily changing methodologies. How does Barth's conceptual formulation of the Spirit's being and work reflect and perhaps even influence his entire intellectual orientation?

Yet another theme is threaded throughout this historical survey. The work of Eberhard Busch, *Karl Barth: His Life from Letters and Autobiographical Texts*, offers a new interpretation of Barth's development as a theologian. It is not purely an intellectual odyssey which Barth undergoes, but a social and pastoral one as well. What Barth says of the *Dogmatics* can certainly be applied to the period in which this major work was germinating: "It is good to think that the *Dogmatics* have emerged not only from my studies but also from a long and often difficult struggle with myself and with the problems of this world and of life. So if they are to be understood properly, they should be read not only with theoretical interest, but in an attempt to join me in the response to practical issues which has been my concern over all the past years."[5] Barth's own suggestion compels the commentator on his life's work to take into consideration the ecclesial and social milieu in which it is carried out. Though in general this study treats Barth's pneumatology theoretically, this present chapter lends itself to viewing the genesis of his thought against the backdrop of his involvement with the Social Democratic Party, his disenchantment with Liberalism, his reaction to the wedding of Church and State and his fear of the totalitarian dominance of culture over Christianity. Besides wrestling with Paul, Anselm Luther, Calvin, Schleiermacher and Kierkegaard, Barth is equally concerned with effective preaching, with the temporal well-being of Christians, with a just society and a peaceful world. In fact, Barth would tend to regard the latter as the germinal concerns which instigate his very understanding of Church dogma as the one force which can relativize the present and denude it of tyrannical power.[6]

A case in point, which indicates how historical events themselves form the bedrock of Barth's pneumatology, is his reaction as the young "comrade pastor" of Safenwil to the outbreak of World War I. On learning that his former theology professors support the Kaiser's war policy, Barth becomes disillusioned with the Liberal theology which these educators advocate; it now seems shallow and inadequate, since it confuses the Church and the State, the Spirit of God and man's spiritual faculties. Though Barth is convinced, simply through the duty of preaching to working people, that "faith in the most elevated things does not exclude but rather includes the suffering and labors within the imperfections of this world," he is not satisfied with the solution of Christof Blumhardt, Hermann Kutter and Leonhard Ragaz who all but identify the coming Kingdom of God with Social Democracy.[7]

Somehow a new theological framework has to be fashioned which relates the Gospel to world-occurrence, but does not confound Christian hope in the absolutely transcendent God with the short-term material hopes of socialism. After long talks with Edward Thurneysen, his neighboring pastor and friend, Barth initiates such an "intellectual-pastoral-social" framework with the publication of *Der Römerbrief* in 1919. This pattern of juxtaposing yet interrelating faith and society concretely illustrates the type of existential reflection which underlies Barth's entire theology. The hostile feelings towards natural theology which result from Barth's theological reading of Anselm also have a prophetic as well as an academic basis. To preserve the sovereignty of God's self-revelation against political manipulation of the Gospel for idolatrous ends, Barth assures that Christianity cannot rationally ground the being of God, but can only meditate on and act in accordance with the incomprehensibility of God's self-disclosure. The intellectual, pastoral and social stances of Christianity are thus at heart dimensions which spring from grace and can only be attained by prayer.[8] From Barth's particular reading of the needs of his world, therefore, a pneumatology is born which clearly demarcates the abyss between the power of parliaments, armies and weapons and the surpassing power of God.

1. The Letter to the Romans: The Spirit and Dialectics

Der Römerbrief of 1919 marks Barth's personal return to a biblical and eschatological perspective which firmly plants God and His promise at the center of Christian theology. Even at this early stage, however, "God" means for Barth the Father, the Son and the Holy Spirit. Thus it is no exaggeration to say that the first edition of *Der Römerbrief* is his initial attempt to unravel Spirit theology from the anthropological setting into which his own German professors insisted on embedding it. Yet this first cutting of roots does not lead Barth to sever his attachment to the mystical and universalist attitudes which his education fostered in him. There is in the first *Romans* a mixture of theological liberalism and Christian socialism; Plato, Origen, Hegel and Schleiermacher stand side by side with the Blumhardts, Kutter and Ragaz. A hopeful cosmology permeates Barth's vision of the doomed social order heading steadily towards a total restoration of all things, an apocatastasis which will take place once mankind has turned from individualism to the new corporate history of the world inaugurated by Christ and being furthered by His Spirit.[9] As the architect of the new creation, the Spirit directs the distorted being of man forward to its true being in God. Thus, Barth still maintains a continuity between the original and the second creation; though Christ's role is pivotal, the restoration of the cosmos is essentially seen as a work of the Father through His creative Spirit. The Holy Spirit performs the task of bringing disarranged creation to the "enduring objectivity of the true and the good,"[10] since He is the harbinger of the new eon of human life and freedom, the divine organizing principle of the unnatural cosmos, the crystallization-point of a new order of being, drawing matter which is still groaning under the old order of sin and death to Himself. The Spirit is already operative in the social sphere driving man's efforts towards the ultimate unity with God which he has not yet attained. He is the eschatological power of victory over evil and the pledge of the totally new being of the universe. As such the Spirit is Himself the new being of man who exists beyond man. He comes to man only as gift, is not found in human experience, and transforms all expectations: "The Spirit of God is a being, a transcendental presupposition, a divine gift and as such (not as a religious-moral possession!) He is 'the true life of Christians.' Man does not have the Spirit of God, rather He has us, whatever we might be, you in Rome as well as us in Corinth! That is the reality of life in Christ; all 'theories' can contribute nothing here and all 'experience' has nothing to add. This is what God has done for us in Christ—we have been freed through Christ from an old passing world and have been taken hold of for a new coming world. The Spirit of God is now in us, among us, with us as the principle and the power of a new free life."[11] Barth is clearly breaking away from the static, subjectivist tones of 19th-century Protestant Liberalism. The "not yet" of Christian eschatology has been rediscovered. But God and man still share the same being, though in different degrees, and the Spirit is essentially the *Spiritus Creator* yearning to bestow divine life on the lost cosmos. The support of the third article of the creed in the 1919 edition of *Der Römerbrief* is predominantly the first article; the eschatological and cosmological theology of the Blumhardts, and not the radical christocentrism of the Reformers, is the means Barth employs to distance himself from an anthropologically conceived Spirit theology.[12]

At the heart of Barth's dialectical theology there stands a dialectical pneumatology; to counteract the arrogance of self-redemption, Barth insists that God is the Subject and therefore the object of theology. The Holy Spirit is the power of God who is diametrically opposed to the powerlessness of man; the Spirit's cosmic function far surpasses man's individualism. Emil Brunner, a sympathetic reviewer of the first *Romans*, lauds Barth's efforts to fight against the tide of psychological subjectivism by reintroducing into theology the "timeless, supra-psychological, absolute nature of faith," a "metaphysical-eschatological realism;" "It is only a question of divine objectivity over against subjective feelings and activities, of the divine Spirit over against a purely human 'religious-moral consciousness.' "[13] To guarantee the Spirit's objectivity, Barth relies on the Idealists' notion that the Holy Spirit is the "objective Spirit," who leads mankind from his disrupting tendencies into the "realm of Absolute Spirit."[14] Barth's chief concern is to redirect theology back to the "what" and to the "truth" of revelation, but once he realizes that he has been misunderstood by Jülicher as a holy egoist, by von Harnack as a reincarnate Thomas Münzer, by Ragaz as an idle questioner and by Bultmann as an enthusiastic revivalist, he determines to abandon the first *Romans* and to begin the same project once again. Like Abraham sacrificing Isaac, Barth is intent on removing the pantheistic tinge and the luxuriant growths of the first edition, and thus on rescuing it from its "still very nebulous and speculative form" by assuring that the new attempt will be marked by "sharply contoured antitheses."[15] Though Plato, Kant, Overbeck, Dostoyevsky and Kierkegaard will provide Barth with dialectical insight, he is now ready to incorporate the thought of the Reformers and to concretize the inestimable distance between the objective and the subjective by introducing a Christ-centered perspective.

If the pneumatological message of the first version of *Romans* is the need for a dialectical relationship between the Spirit of God and man's spirit, the same can be said of the second edition. There are, however, considerable differences; whereas the first edition stresses a cosmological and social concept of dialectics, the second opts for a christological and transcendental standpoint. This becomes clear when one compares Barth's two treatments of Paul's eighth chapter; although in both editions Barth entitles his commentary "The Spirit", the subtitles themselves hint at his essentially different approach. In the 1919 edition they are called: "The Past," (*Romans* 8:1-11), "The Present" (12-27), and "The Future" (28-39); in the 1922 edition: "The Decision" (1-10), "The Truth" (11-27) and "The Love" (28-39). Both editions manifest Barth's effort to construct dialectical counterpoles which are mediated by the Spirit of God. In 1919 the two poles of the dialectic are man's present activity and God's future Kingdom; they are mediated by the cosmological power of the Spirit of the Father. In 1922 the two poles are man's universal sinfulness and God's unique act of redemption if Jesus Christ; they are mediated by the transcendental power of the Spirit of the Son. In the second edition, however, it is not a matter of equilibrium; the divine pole enjoys supremacy over the human: "Here we are in death, there we are in life. Both decisions—rejection and election, condemnation and justification, death and life—form the foci of an ellipse, which approximate more and more closely to one another until they unite as the center of one circle. The unity of both decisions—which is incapable of mathematical representation—is not the unity of an equilibrium, but of the infinite preeminence which the one has over the other, whereby time is swallowed up in eternity, and the flesh in the infinite victory of the Spirit."[16] The victory spoken of is not that of man's social achievements but of Jesus Christ's resurrection, God's historical decision for man which both reveals His truth and calls man to acknowledge His love.

Although both editions underline the difference between God's Spirit and man's spirit, the second links God's Spirit inseparably to the Spirit of Jesus Christ. Thus the first edition can accurately be described as a resounding plea for an essential distinction between the "already" and the "not yet" of biblical pneumatology; the second a pounding and impassioned warning against a watered-down and innocuous christology. In 1922 eschatology gives way to christology, continuity to discontinuity, the first article to the second, being *(Sein)* to meaning *(Sinn)*; in short, creation gives way to eternal election in Jesus Christ. Pneumatology is now welded to christology; the Spirit is the Spirit of Christ and thus demands a human decision in response to God's decision for man. The previous stress on the difference between "already" and "not yet", though not totally absent, is complemented by a realized eschatology; the temporal and social tone of the first *Romans* is tempered by the personal and existential decision of the "either" and the "or"; man stands not so much between the past and the future, but before the contemporary choice of two possibilities: his own world marked by the undiminished evil of the flesh, and the new world of the risen Christ, whose Spirit induces man to say "no" to the first possibility: "Spirit is the eternal decision which was made in God for man and in man for God. For Spirit means that man belongs to Christ, that he belongs to Him in his question and therefore in his answer, in his "Yes" and therefore in his "No," in his sin and therefore in his justification, in his death and therefore in his life. Spirit is therefore existential giving of meaning, determining of meaning, creating of meaning. Meaning enters into being and being becomes meaning. . . . Spirit means "either-or", but an "either" which has already been taken away from man over against an "or" which has already been accomplished for him. Spirit means being elected and therefore in no way being rejected."[17] Christian anthropology must be based on pneumatology. Man's being is the meaning granted to him by the Spirit of Jesus Christ. With the second edition of *Der Römerbrief* Barth thus arrives at both a dialectical and christological concept of pneumatology. The Spirit of Jesus Christ cannot be confused with the spirit of man, just as the latter cannot be properly viewed apart from the former.

Barth apparently lends pneumatology, even at this early stage, a key mediating role in the dialectical relationship of the Christian to Christ: the Spirit permits an individual man to belong to Christ. Therefore the pneumatic methodology which Barth later formulated in reaction to Schleiermacher, Bultmann and Roman Catholicism, is already evident from the very outset of his theological career.[18] The Spirit is the dynamic power of Christ, who challenges man, gives his life meaning and relates him to the eternal source of meaning: man's election from eternity by the Son of God. Between Christ and the Christian there is neither a vacuum nor merely a psychological effort on man's part to reach back to the distant Jesus of history; nor is there a vague consciousness emanating from Christ, by which He reaches out to the Christian community. The Holy Spirit, the spiritual power of God Himself, forms a living relationship between Christ and the believer. At the center of human weakness the sovereign Spirit of Christ is present allowing man's groanings to share the very efficacy of Christ's own prayer: "The groaning of the creation and our own groaning is naught but the impress and seal of the Spirit; our cry, *Abba Father*, is naught but the echo of the divine Word. The action of the Spirit is independent: He goes as He wills. We do not possess Him; He possesses us. He anticipates us, and forestalls our infirmities. He is the *Creator Spiritus*."[19] The Spirit alone bridges the gap between the dialectical poles of history and faith, and makes man's sinful being capable of participating in intimacy with the Father along with Jesus Christ. The Spirit is the divine *Vermittlungsprinzip* who brings man to actual contact with Christ.

Yet Barth makes it very clear that this contact with Christ is not a merging of God and man, not an exaltation of the human to the divine and not an overflowing of God's being into nature. As close as the Spirit is to man, as effective as His mediating activity is in man's weakness, there is an eschatological chasm between man and the Spirit. Man only experiences the emptiness of the cross; he only has access to hope through faith in the Crucified and in the Spirit who raised Him from the dead: "Were we to know more of God than the groans of creation and our own groaning, were we to know Jesus Christ otherwise than as crucified, were we to know the Holy Spirit otherwise than as the Spirit of Him that raised Jesus from the dead, were the incognito in which salvation has come to us, does come to us and will come to us, broken through—then there would be no salvation. . . . If Christianity were not altogether thoroughgoing eschatology, there remains in it no relation whatever to Jesus Christ. Spirit which does not at every moment point from death to the new life is not the Holy Spirit."[20] Barth thus grants the Holy Spirit the central function of crossing the eschatological barrier and of bringing the life of the new world to the believer. What Jesus Christ accomplished by intersecting the plane of creation with the plane of the transcendent Father, the Holy Spirit continues in His work as mediator, intercessor, harbinger of the Kingdom. Yet this activity of the Spirit does not supernaturalize man. The Spirit brings crisis, decision, a divine "No!" to man's subjective, psychological and religious attempts to find the new world of God. The Spirit, in casting the light of hope into man's darkness, does not make man into God, but convinces man of God's Godness and touches man only so that his "No!" can become a "Yes!" The Spirit allows the power of the resurrection to be present in man's vulnerability.

In transforming man, therefore, the Holy Spirit does not transform him. Herbert Hartwell aptly characterizes the language of *Romans* as "graphic-mathematical-paradoxical."[21] In the following passage Barth summarizes the pneumatology of his first work by employing precisely such language: "The Resurrection is the revelation; the disclosing of Jesus as the Christ, the appearing of God, and the apprehending of God in Jesus. The Resurrection is the emergence of the necessity of giving glory to God: the reckoning with what is unknown and unobservable in Jesus, the recognition of Him as Paradox, Victor, and Primal History. In the Resurrection the new world of the Holy Spirit touches the old world of the flesh, but touches it as a tangent touches a circle, that is, without touching it. And, precisely because it does not touch it, it touches it as its frontier—as the new world."[22] What Barth intends to emphasize is clear: the Holy Spirit is the eschatological power of God who exists on the far side of all human possibilities. Yet, the patently paradoxical and contradictory surface of the second *Romans* may be deceiving. Is it possible that in three years Barth manages to overcome his conviction of the underlying unity of God and man? Are the latent presuppositions beneath the second edition really not the same as those of the first? Is the insistence on the duality of Adam and Christ, of the human spirit and the Holy Spirit only a thin veneer overlaying man's direct unity with God? This is the opinion of Hans Urs von Balthasar who suspects that Barth the "nihilist" is essentially Barth the "ominist." Although man seems to be a hallow cavity and a minus sign in the second *Romans*, the supremacy of the Spirit's role in the Christian implies that "the personality of man coincides with the Holy Spirit, the new man in Christ."[23] The eschatological distance between man's spirit and the Holy Spirit may belie a much deeper identification of the two than the outer shell of negativity suggests.

Though not in terms as radical as those of von Balthasar, other commentators surmise that the "No!" cannot be understood apart from the "Yes!" of the 1922 *Römerbrief*. In fact, crisis is a dialectical idea; it implies not only a negative but a positive relation as well. God is indeed totally other than man, but God and man are also meant for community with each other. Thus, behind Barth's dialectical theology there may exist a hidden concept of analogy: "Barth often repeats that the ephemeral is a parable of the eternal. It is true that he clarifies this by stating that the former is *only* a parable. But is this not the same as affirming a certain analogy? One who uses an analogy understands it to express a resemblance and a difference without being able to define the one or the other aspect precisely . . . Analogy is a dialectical concept. It is out of place to oppose dialectics and analogy as if they were exclusive in every regard. Barth does not want to admit of unity except in difference; this position excludes certain conceptions of analogy, but not the entire idea of analogy."[24] Barth himself comes to realize this problem in time. In 1922 he begins to do so by invariably contrasting man's negation of God to God's affirmation of man. Dialectics thus form the bridge between the more cosmologically oriented theology of the first edition and the expressly christocentric theology of the second. Barth's pneumatology is affected by this transition. In order to guarantee man a real share in what God has promised and in order to ground that promise in an historical event, Barth turns to pneumatology as the link between the poles of history and experience. As diverse as the two poles are, there is a similarity between them. The Father's condemnation and exaltation of His Son is paralleled in the Spirit's conviction and pardon of man.

The Holy Spirit, the divine connection between Christ and the Christian, is no less powerful than the author of the realized promise, the Father, and the divine realization of this promise in history, Jesus Christ. Barth does indeed insist that all continuity between the divine Spirit and the human spirit must disappear; only discontinuity marks their "tangent-circle" relationship. But the Holy Spirit, although not conjoined in any way with man's spirit, does form a relationship between Christ, with whom He is identical, and man to whom He comes. In Barth's opinion the cosmological pneumatology of the first edition does not fully account either for the discontinuity of God and man or for the real relationship between the Christian and Christ. In the second edition Barth shifts to christocentrism in order to give the Spirit's eschatological creation of meaning in man a solid basis in the source of all meaning: the eternal and temporal history of Jesus Christ.[25] Though today many join Jürgen Moltmann in lamenting Barth's transition from a politically-oriented eschatology to a decidedly transcendental concept of the Kingdom of God, Barth makes this decisive turn in 1922. The ramifications of this decision for his pneumatology are significant. Although Barth continues to designate the Spirit the *Spiritus Creator* in the second *Romans*, the meaning of the term is radically altered. It is no longer meant to signify the spiritual power of the Creator operative in nature itself and in human history beyond and within the Church, but the recreative power of the risen Jesus Christ. In reacting to excessively anthropological conceptions of the Spirit, Barth concentrates from now on exclusively on the Spirit's soteriological function. Johann Blumhardt's socially concerned Christianity gives way to Soren Kierkegaards's existential pathos.

2. The Christian Dogmatics: The Spirit and the Word

As a preacher in Switzerland Barth severs his roots from his former university professors, such as Wilhelm Herrmann, who represent the subjective tendencies against which the two editions of *Romans* vehemently inveigh. As a German university professor himself, however, Barth begins to search for the deeper source of the inbred inclination to hominize God. Though it remains true that Barth's chief concern at this time is the very relationship of the divine and the human, another factor colors his understanding of how the two totally different realities become intertwined. Christian dogmaticians of the past seem too prone to allow man's experience of faith or man's life in the Church to take center stage in theology. They interject some other source of knowledge about the God-man connection which is patently independent of the Scriptural insistence on the strict tension between the eternal and the temporal. In attempting to pinpoint the genesis of this sovereignty of man over the Word of God, Barth lights upon the philosophical prolegomena to dogmatics which Schleiermacher, in close approximation to Catholicism, adopts as the measure of revelation's acceptability.[26] In the former a man's belief, in the latter the Church's holiness distorts revelation. Thus Barth must terminate his dependence on Schleiermacher's anthropocentrism and on Catholicism's ecclesiocentrism. Yet, in doing so, he realizes the need to depart somewhat from his own previous stress on God's Godness or otherness, since such a dialectical emphasis overlooks the Scriptural witness that God continually enters time through His Son and His Spirit. How to preserve the absolute distinction between God and man and still unite the two as the Bible manifestly does? The solution is to shift the focus from the chiaroscuro of the resurrection of the Christ to the softer shades of the incarnation of the Word.[27] God Himself overcomes the divine-human dichotomy by graciously choosing to address Himself to man in history, and by refusing to remain totally aloof. In the light of this truth the direction taken in *Romans* has to be modified.

Thus the writings either partially or totally on the Spirit which follow in the wake of the second edition of *Der Römerbrief* are on the one hand clearly stamped by its stark christological insights; on the other, Barth struggles between 1922 and 1927 to find a way of countering the philosophical pneumatology of Schleiermacher, as well as the ecclesiological pneumatology of Roman Catholicism, with the biblical solution: christological pneumatology. He is forced more and more to turn from a vague theology of the first article of the creed to explicit treatments of the connection between the second and third articles. What Barth openly admits later when he severs himself from his colleagues on the staff of *Zwischen den Zeiten* can be regarded as a summary statement of his own theological intention after the second *Romans*: "They were quite happy for my manifestos—which they were regarded as then—to speak in terms of the second and third articles of the creed (on Christ and the Holy Spirit), while insuring themselves with Gogarten, who spoke in terms of the first article (on the Creator)."[28] The Spirit confessed by Reformational literature is not the amorphous Spirit of the Creator, but the Spirit of the Word who necessarily convinces man that the incarnation is the key to anthropology and ecclesiology, not *vice versa.* Biblical pneumatology depicts the Spirit to be free over against man and the Church, and not determined by them. Only the sovereign Spirit of the Word can bridge the immense gulf between Christ and the Christian which modern Protestantism since Schleiermacher and Roman Catholicism since Augustine have sought to abolish by either a metaphysical or an ecclesiological means of identifying the Spirit of the Creator and man. Barth has first to separate the Spirit radically from the experience both of the individual Christian and of the worshipping community. But then he must restore the essential connection between the Spirit and Jesus Christ. For this union alone grounds Christian existence. Other theologies have indistinctly associated the Spirit with human spirituality or with Church tradition to the detriment of His primary relationship to the historical revelation of God's Word in Jesus Christ.

In 1926 Barth's stress on the absolute independence of the Spirit is evident in a short Pentecost meditation which appears in *Zwischen den Zeiten* and is entitled "Vom Heiligen Geist." Barth takes up the key theme of his new pneumatology: the difference between the Holy Spirit and the other "spirits" which man has created to describe the unaccountable dimension of either personal, cultural, political or religious phenomena. To make this distinction clear Barth turns from Paul to Luke. In the *Acts of the Apostles* the Holy Spirit exercises absolute sovereignty both over the apostles at Pentecost and over all who would join them thereafter; He comes as storm and fire, as transcendent force, to those assembled. Other so-called "spirits" do not claim the absolute dominance which the Holy Spirit, as the only agent of their rebirth, continually claims over the community's members. Nor do other spirits give men the power to live by a message which they cannot naturally arrive at, do not want to accept and yet freely believe and which others also gladly embrace once it is proclaimed to them. Barth's insistence on the otherness of the Holy Spirit is directed against Church preaching which confuses the Holy Spirit with an obscure religious spirit: "If indeed the account in *Acts* 2:1-13 concerns this "spirit", then the account is very incredible and the meaning of a *feast* of Pentecost very questionable. And again it is better to think *this thought* than, as it were, not to see the obvious difference and contradiction which the text implies. It would therefore be better, since in this way the possibility of seeing the true meaning of that account and of this text is at least left open."[29]

To make this contrast sharper, Barth suggests that the powerful, fearful and yet unifying presence of the Spirit at Pentecost can be better compared to man's experiences of senseless evil, incurable suffering and death itself. For such comparisons would not enable man to equate the Holy Spirit with the innocuous "spirits" which he can control because they make no demand on him and do not unite him with others who are confronted with the same dreadful experiences. Furthermore, such comparisons are more appropriate since the horrible realities of suffering, sin and death are precisely what the Spirit of Pentecost overcomes. For, the sole Redeemer proclaimed in biblical revelation is the Spirit of Jesus Christ Himself who in His person and work reconciled suffering, sinful and dying men with the Father. The feast of Pentecost celebrates the joy of being freed by the Spirit from ultimate meaninglessness. For this reason, theologians and preachers should describe the presence of the Spirit as an awesome happening and not as a static possession of an individual or an institution. Otherwise, the sheer sovereignty and liberating power of the Spirit is sacrificed for the sake of a more modern, comfortable and vacuous sense of Christianity. Barth's "actualist" understanding of the Holy Spirit is meant to preserve the freedom of God and also the dynamic notion of faith as encounter and not as consciousness alone.[30] Barth thus continues to choose categories of contradiction so as to offset what he now regards as Schleiermacher's and Roman Catholicism's categories of continuity. To describe the Holy Spirit as the *Gemeingeist* of the Church or as the soul of the mystical body was not in itself wrong, but to replace the contradistinguishing function of the Holy Spirit with the irenic one of fostering peace and unity in the Church would be inadmissible for Barth. The Spirit founds the Church in that He stands over against it, convicts it of its sinfulness and thus bestows on it genuine unity and unexpected joy.

To speak even more unambiguously about the centrality of the second and third articles of the creed, Barth next produces the most important work of this period and indeed the prelude to his future theology: *Die Christliche Dogmatik im Entwurf*. In 1927 Barth attempts to meet his new opponents on their own ground; he constructs a dogmatics, or rather prolegomena to an intended dogmatics, which is meant to counter Schleiermacher's systematics by situating God's Word and not man's consciousness at the center of theology; he also includes in this work what others regarded as the particularly Catholic approach to dogma, the doctrine of the Trinity. Both decisions are momentous. They indicate that Barth's opposition to his opponents rests on a hidden admiration. Barth writes to Edward Thurneysen that in a seminar at Münster he "bowed over Schleiermacher's *The Christian Faith*, in order to communicate the mystery of wickedness in these really thought-worthy runes."[31] As a Protestant professor in Catholic Westphalia, Barth deeply sympathizes with his Roman colleagues as he wrestles for the first time with the doctrine of the Trinity: "Indeed I am probably the only professor of theology (with the exception of the Catholics, of course) who is racking his brains over it."[32] In effect Barth is moving further away from a strictly dialectical or narrowly christological position to one that is expressly trinitarian. Existential strains are now being drowned out by the traditional wisdom of orthodoxy: "I had to change my own learning a second time. I simply could not hold to the theoretical and practical *diastasis* between God and man on which I had insisted at the time of *Romans*, without sacrificing it . . . I had to understand Jesus Christ and bring him from the periphery of my thought to the center. Because I cannot regard subjectivity as being the truth, after a brief encounter I have had to move away from Kierkegaard again."[33] Though *Die Christliche Dogmatik* is subsequently seen by Barth as a false start, it is determinative of all his later work.

The Spirit theology of this initial dogmatics finds its way almost entirely into *Die Kirchliche Dogmatik* (I/1) of 1932. There is no need to go into great detail concerning its content at this point. What is necessary, however, is to indicate some of its salient features within the context of Barth's own genesis as a pneumatologian. It is fascinating to watch the pneumatological themes of Barth's earlier works coalesce in this terse and lively volume. Here the eschatological role of the Spirit in the first edition of *Der Römerbrief* and the Spirit's christological role in the second are incorporated into a much broader schema. Barth's thought over the years induces him to adopt an explicitly trinitarian framework on which to secure his pneumatological insights. He harmonizes the apparently disparate biblical descriptions of the Spirit of the first creation and the Spirit of the recreation by naming the Spirit God the Redeemer, God as He comes to man and reveals Himself in man so that the work of the Creator Father and that of the Recreator Son become effective within him. Gone are the tones of *diastasis*. The Holy Spirit is no longer the Wholly Other but the gracious power of the self-revealing Godhead. Yet the third article of the creed underscores the Spirit's divinity and not man's divinization: "The propositions concerning the Holy Spirit and His action ought not to be interpreted as propositions concerning man on his own. They also speak of God and of His sovereignty, not of man."[34] Man thus assumes solely a receptive role in Barth's pneumatology, but it is a role nevertheless; only in this limited way does he nod to the anthropological starting point of Schleiermacher and Roman Catholicism. But there the acknowledgement ends. Barth insists that the solution to the contradictions of man's life is given to him by God's Spirit who comes to him as sheer grace and who makes it possible that he become a receiver of God's revelation: "The one God reveals Himself as the Redeemer, that is, as He, who in removing man's contradiction, is both with regard to man and in Himself the Lord. But He is such as the gift of grace, since He is the Spirit of the Father and the Son and is Himself from the beginning Holy Spirit."[35]

This stress on the free gift of grace, which tones down the harsher contrast of colors in *Romans*, must be protected from all misunderstanding. No blurring of God and man is implied here; even when man is encountered by the Word and His Spirit, he has nothing to show for it; he can only witness that something happens to him which gives him hope in what God can make of him: "Man, such as he is, receives the Holy Spirit, such as He is; even in his possession of the Spirit, man holds up empty hands before God. Though the Holy Spirit is poured out on all flesh, He remains the Holy Spirit, the Spirit of the promise of what man is to *become* . . . God remains the Lord, even in our grasping of His Word, even in our reception of His gift."[36] Barth realizes that, by conceding man to be the recipient of the Father's Word both in the person of Jesus Christ, in the Scriptures and in Christian preaching, the imminent danger is present that the gift will render the giver superfluous. Since the Holy Spirit assures that in all three forms the Word of God reaches the believer, the all-important distinction between the Holy Spirit and the graced person must be stated firmly. Repeatedly Barth asserts that it is not a question of man's elevation, deepening or enrichment, as Liberal Protestants and Catholics maintain. God alone is supreme; man knows only humility: "All that one ought to say about the man to whom the Holy Spirit addresses Himself and really gives Himself is said by the word hope, eschatology in the most strict sense . . . God gives Himself to us in His revelation in such a way that, rich in Him, we are and remain poor in ourselves."[37] The possibility of a relationship between God and man, which other theologies locate in man's inherent religious consciousness or transcendent nature, Barth grounds not in man, but in the Holy Spirit, God's own possibility of coming to man and existing in him and for him.

Barth discovers in the doctrine of the Trinity the means of allowing God's Word and Spirit to be totally free of the creature. God abides in eternal community; He contains in Himself a Thou, and thus does not have need of man's being to complete His own.[38] Yet this same doctrine also guarantees that God is free to communicate Himself to man through His Word and His Spirit, so that man can enter the divine community without either fracturing or complementing the unity of the Godhead. The Trinity thus grounds the freedom of God in His revelation on the freedom of God in Himself. Man cannot dictate the terms of his relationship with God; he can only participate in a freedom which comes as a liberating divine gift. This understanding of the Trinity permits Barth to make the distinctions which seem to be foreign to the then contemporary pneumatology. The Spirit comes to man, but He is not man's possession; the Spirit is identical with the Father and the Son, but He adds something distinctive, a third dimension, to the revelation of the Father and the Son. Determining the distinctive role of the Holy Spirit is not idle reflection, but important clarification of the very experience of being freed of the contradiction within one's own existence: "It is not sufficient that God as Father is the Lord over our contradiction; it is not enough that He as Son is also in the midst of our contradiction. We are still obviously outside of His power; His power is still conditioned and confined, in as much as He is not the Lord who removes our contradiction, as long as the 'Nevertheless' of His power does not have to do with us. Therefore the fact that it does have to do with us, that it has established itself in our existence, that God becomes our own Lord, that we ourselves, exactly as we are, are participants in His supremacy and in His victory, that we have been once and for all placed under His power as Creator and Reconiler—that is what it means when we speak of the Holy Spirit."[39]

The pneumatology of *Die Christliche Dogmatik* reveals that Barth finally settles on a backdrop against which the individual aspects of his Spirit theology come into clear relief. This backdrop is the comprehensive understanding of God's living Word. The role of the Holy Spirit is to relate the believer to the Word so that his entire existence is seen as taking place against its brilliance. The Spirit communicates this brilliance to the believer, since He emanates from it and belongs essentially to it. Man's contradiction is enlightened by the Spirit, but not totally removed. Although the incarnation of the Word, the Gospels and Christian preaching come alive for man through the Spirit's action on him and in him, the Word and the Spirit preserve their freedom over against the entire experience of the Christian.[40] There is thus a paradoxical closeness and distance between man and the triune God which Barth underlines on almost every page of this work. The affinity with *Romans* has been maintained. Yet God's objective existence as mysterious grace has also been recognized. Henri Bouillard notes that Barth's decision to place the Word of God at the center of dogmatics is parallel to the Catholic choice of "the supernatural" as the all-inclusive term by which to designate the mystery of God within which man exists.[41] Barth thus arrives at a very different form of Protestant dogmatics with his fresh accent on trinitarian theology, christology and pneumatology. Precisely christology stands at the center; from it the mystery of the eternal community within God and the mystery of the graced community of Christians are illumined. Though Barth himself later realizes that he must excise from this dogmatics everything "that might give the slightest appearance of giving to theology a basis, a support or even a mere justification in the way of existentialist philosophy,"[42] he senses that the greatest transition is behind him.

In 1930 Barth, in collaboration with his brother Heinrich, develops his pneumatology further in an essay entitled "The Holy Spirit and Christian Life." The circumstances under which this work was composed support the hypothesis that Barth's pneumatology is his response to those who insist on beginning theology with man. Barth's thoughts at the time centered on two issues: Erich Pryzwara's dialogue with him concerning the Catholic teaching on *analogia entis* and the tensions existing among the dialectical theologians over the first article of the creed. To answer the claim that the "ordinances of creation" are identical with the Word, or that the subjective experience of revelation rests on man's native character as God's image, Barth attributes man's being before God to the Holy Spirit alone. As the "sole reality" of the image of God in man, the Spirit struggles against man's hostility to grace. Divine sonship exists beyond the bounds of man's natural existence and is attainable only because the Holy Spirit constantly actualizes a connection between God and man from man's side. Man's likeness to God is not an innate power or an infused essence, but a promise.[43] There is no *analogia entis* between man's spirit and God's Spirit. Any similarity between the two is pure gift, is grace, is *dandum* not *datum*, is received not produced. Man is bearer of God's image, is hearer of God's Word, is freed from sin, is God's obedient, thankful and prayerful child not by reason of his nature; rather he becomes all of these by reason of the Spirit's action. As God the Redeemer, the Holy Spirit repeatedly bestows these privileges on man as gifts.

Barth's pneumatology seems at first to be built on a negative anthropology. Man is stripped of the ontic power to image and of the noetic power to know his Creator, let alone of the inherent ability to overcome the damage of his sin by a moral life. He becomes all of these only through the grace of the Holy Spirit. Barth so weds anthropology to pneumatology that man can only exist because of God's Spirit; man is not a being who is a "given" but whose very existence is a "gift of God." This apparently pessimistic stress on man's incapacity to acquire grace or to live an ethical life is counterbalanced, however, by a thunderous persistence on the fact that man is promised the ability to do so, and actually does so through the being and work of the Holy Spirit. Once the totally determinative role of the Spirit is firmly established, therefore, everything that can be said about man's place in theology is justified. Then Barth can agree even with the most apparently anthropocentric phraseology of Schleiermacher: "In the Holy Spirit we have a conscience. It is an amazing fact that theological ethics which concerns itself so much with this notion has never come up with the simple thought that conscience is to be understood in light of eschatology. Who should have *syn-eidesis, con-scientia*, a knowing together with God concerning what is good and what is evil, except a child of God who is continually reborn through His Word? . . . Even that great outrage of Schleiermacher's is true of this child: the God-consciousness in the self-consciousness of man is no longer an outrage, but the whole truth. This child gazes beyond the present and also beyond the dialectic of the *semper peccator et semper justus* to the coming kingdom of his Father."[44]

Even Schleiermacher is right provided that man is what he is only because the Spirit causes him to become such through eschatological grace! Here is the germ of Barth's future solution to the anthropological excesses of Neo-Protestant, Existentialist and Catholic pneumatology: an orthodox theology surely can begin with man, but with man as the graced receiver of the Spirit's promise, not as the natural possessor of a graced existence. Thus, the writings between 1922 and 1930 gradually clarify Barth's understanding of his present opponents and of his future work. The proponents of a so-called Christian theology anchored in the first article of the creed are the antagonists; they purport to know of God and man apart from the revelation of His Son and His Spirit. The task ahead is to prolong the manifesto that both God and man are unknowns until the event of divine revelation in its objective and subjective forms takes place. Furthermore, Barth is beginning to realize that the latter form of God's self-revelation, the work of the Holy Spirit revealing Himself in the Christian and transforming him into a recipient of grace, is to be the locus of his own anthropology. Man's status before God becomes clear not in the first but in the third credal section. Barth's later *Nein* to Emil Brunner, his continual wrestling with Schleiermacher and with Roman Catholicism, his disagreements with Bultmann and Gogarten are all intelligible in terms of one question. What comes first, pneumatology or anthropology? To put the second first guarantees the distortion of genuine Protestant theology: "How far is his (Gogarten's) anthropological basis for theology really different from the natural theology of Roman Catholicism and Neo-Protestantism?"[45] It is not far at all. A solution to the dilemma might be to interpret anthropology pneumatologically.

3. *Fides Quaerens Intellectum: The Spirit and Analogy*

How is Barth to free his dogmatics from the last remnants of an anthropological justification and explanation of Christian faith? How is he to posit, as the starting point of his theological epistemology, man pneumatically interpreted? This must mean that faith itself, the gratuitous experience of receiving the gift of the Holy Spirit, contains its own starting point. There must be a discernible correspondence between the truth of the faith which believes (*fides qua creditur*) and the faith which is believed (*fides quae creditur*). Once the resemblance between these two aspects of faith, the subjective and the objective, is established, Barth is able to settle on the theological methodology which will liberate him from reliance on other sources of verifying faith besides faith itself, the method his main opponents propose. To achieve this end, Barth turns to Anselm of Canterbury's phrase "credo ut intelligam," and in 1931 produces *Fides Quaerens Intellectum*, the book which he considers to be determinative of his entire thought system: "Only a comparatively few commentators, for example Hans Urs von Balthasar, have realized that my interest in Anselm was never a side-issue for me or—assuming I am more or less correct in my historical interpretation of St. Anselm—realized how much it has influenced me or been absorbed into my own line of thinking. Most of them have completely failed to see that in this book on Anselm I am working with a vital key, if not the key, to an understanding of that whole process of thought that has impressed me more and more in my *Church Dogmatics* as the only one proper to theology."[46] Given the importance which Barth attributes to this work, its pneumatological significance deserves careful consideration.

Though the content of the third, or for that matter of the second, article of the creed is not explicitly treated in the book, the thesis seems tenable that what Barth finds affirming in Anselm's method is its implicitly pneumatological character. Without labelling it such, Barth discovers that Anselm's methodology is pneumatic since its basic presuppositions have the power of God's Spirit as their only possibility; the man of faith, the Christian, is able to reflect on the truth of the creed by means of the inner intelligibility supplied therein. This can be the case solely because the Holy Spirit, God as He grants man faith, also assures faith's reasonableness by illuminating it from within. In other words, Barth understands this faith-giving and faith-illuminating work of God in the Christian as the work of the Holy Spirit. It is exactly in pneumatological terms that Barth describes Anselm's notion of theological proof: "It is a question of theology. It is a question of the proof of faith by faith which was already established in itself without proof. And both—faith that is proved and faith that proves—Anselm expressly understands not as presuppositions that can be achieved by man but as presuppositions that have been achieved by God, the former as divine *donare* and the latter as divine *illuminare* . . . God gave himself as the object of man's knowledge and God illumined man that he might know Him as object . . . Just because it is the science of faith about faith, theology possesses light, but it is not the light of the theologian's faith."[47] In short: the enlightening power which makes both man's faith and its object, God's self-disclosure of His own Truth, verifiable is not the ingenuity of the theologian but the grace of the Holy Spirit.

Barth comes to this conclusion by analyzing in detail Anselm's entire theological scheme. The believer seeks to understand his faith precisely because he presupposes its truth. For this reason, the theologian cannot abstract himself from the object of his belief as he searches its noetic intelligibility, that is, the human ability to understand the creed's veracity. Though the theologian's task is never totally successful, it is always privileged, since behind his efforts stands the *ratio veritatis*, the very Truth of God, which is contained in faith itself but which far surpasses the narrow limits of human comprehension. While the theologian's faith searches for knowledge, he not only examines, but participates in the supreme Truth of God, and thus does not seek to discover the subjective, natural reason for belief, but the divine reason given in the mystery itself which he is attempting to understand.[48] Behind Anselm's work is the conviction that the theologian is neither to lead man to faith, to confirm faith, nor to deliver faith from doubt. Least of all is faith itself to be questioned. Theology employs faith in order to penetrate into God's being: "For Anselm, 'to believe' does not mean simply a striving of the human will towards God but a striving of the human will into God and so a participation (albeit in a manner limited by creatureliness) in God's mode of being and so a similar participation in God's aseity, in the matchless glory of His very Self, and therefore also in God's utter absence of necessity. Thus, on no account can the given-ness or non-given-ness of the results of *intelligere* involve for faith the question of its existence. . . . It is not the existence of faith, but—and here we approach Anselm's position—the nature of faith, that desires knowledge."[49] Anselm's search for the *ratio fidei* is not a philosophical grounding of the truth of revelation, but a meditative probing into the incomprehensibility of God Himself. In other words, what Anselm's inquiry concerns is the rationality proper to the object of faith, not an extrinsic type of intelligibility.

The core of Anselm's argument is that the noetic *ratio* of faith is proven only as one discovers the ontic *ratio* of faith's object. For it is on the ontic *ratio* that the noetic rests. By the ontic *ratio* Anselm means the truth inherent in the creed apart from the belief of the Christian. This ontic truth (=*ratio fidei*) is an objective participation in the very Word of God (=*ratio veritatis*). Personal faith is rooted in revelation, which in turn is not self-sufficient: "But even the truth of the object's existence and nature is dependent not upon itself but upon the divine Word (and so on the real *ratio veritatis* strictly understood) through which it is created. This Word in creating it also confers upon it a resemblance to the truth which belongs to itself (as the Word spoken from God)."[50] But the ontic and the noetic reasonableness of faith are similar in that neither is independently creative or normative; they only become such because they participate in God's Truth which is conferred on them. They are different, however, since the ontic *ratio* enjoys a higher participation in Truth; the latter is conferred upon it with the creation of the object of faith of which it is the *ratio*. In contrast, the noetic *ratio* is more dependent on the insight of the believer and thus shares in Truth only imperfectly: "In the *Credo* and in the Bible it [ontic *ratio*] is hidden and must reveal itself in order to make itself known to us. It does this, however, only if and insofar as the Truth, God Himself, does it. Thus: from time to time in the event of knowing, it happens that the noetic ratio of the *veritas* conforms to the ontic and to that extent is or is not vera *ratio*—or (and this is normally the case *in praxi*) only to a certain degree. Fundamentally, the *ratio* either as ontic or noetic is never higher than the Truth, but Truth is itself the master of all *rationes* beyond the contrast between ontic and noetic."[51] Here for the first time Barth admits that the faith which is conferred on the Christian and the faith which is illumined within him are analogous to the truth in which the act of faith participates: the Truth of God.

Having arrived at this insight, Barth is able to grant the personal experience of the believer a part in God's self-revelation. For, if God's Truth were to remain in itself, its goal would not be obtained. Put differently, it can be said that the "outer text" of both the Scriptures and the credal confessions contains an "inner text." If the latter is not comprehended, then God's authority is not recognized and revelation itself does not occur in the full sense. Theology must unbare the inner text and thus create a noetic apprehension of the Truth which conforms, as much as the human mind can, to the nature of the self-revealing God: "One form of the revelation is obviously also the occurrence of *intelligere*, of the *vera ratione quaerere veram rationem*, the *intus legere*, to which even the inner text discloses itself, inasmuch as the conformity of *ratio* to truth depends neither upon the object nor the subject but on this same revealing power of God which illumines faith and which faith encounters as authority."[52] For Barth it follows that, though God Himself is not a necessary being, God's self-revelation must possess an ontic necessity, since otherwise God in Himself would be different than His self-disclosure attests, and the latter would not be a divine *self*-giving at all. Thus, just as the noetic *ratio* of faith presupposes its ontic *ratio*, prior to any noetic necessity, that is, antecedent to any assurance that what is personally known about God cannot be different, there is an ontic necessity: "The establishing of knowledge of the object of faith consists in recognition of the basis that is peculiar to the object of faith itself. Ontic necessity precedes noetic."[53] In this way, Barth maintains, Anselm, while preserving his belief that Truth itself is sovereign, argues successfully in his search for the *intelligere* of faith's noetic rationality; he arrives at the noetic necessity of faith by the "roundabout argument" for the rationality and necessity of faith's object; Anselm discovers the "hidden law of the object of faith."[54]

Finally Barth finds support for his own approach to theology in the work of a theologian whose search for faith's cogency is grounded not in a "shadow creed," not in general truths or in sources outside revelation, but in the ontic nature of the Christian creed itself. Both noetic rationality and necessity depend not on the philosopher's *Credo a priori*, not on natural theology or on a different level than the one on which the initial question is raised, but on the *Credo* itself. Anselm does not skirt faith to demonstrate its rationality, but "not mastering the object but being mastered by it, he achieves true noetic *ratio*, a real comprehension of the ontic *ratio* of the object of faith; he attains the *intellectus fidei*."[55] Thus Barth ascertains that Anselm bridges the gap between the veracity of the subjective experience of faith (noetic *ratio*) and that of its objective ground through a pneumatological and analogical method of theologizing which corresponds to the content and nature of faith itself. In other words, the Holy Spirit not only grants man an objective participation in God's Truth through faith, but also illumines faith's inherently analogous character for the theologian who is seeking after the inner intelligibility of the creed. The Holy Spirit can effect this intelligibility in man, since He is the very knowability of the God who gives His self-knowledge to man as gift. Thus the Holy Spirit creates a similarity between God's knowledge of Himself *(terminus a quo)* and the veracity of man's knowledge of God *(terminus ad quem)*. This correspondence allows Barth to assert with Anselm that there is contained in the creed itself (God is) the hidden basis of faith's veracity (God is known). The Holy Spirit is God turning towards man so that this self-impartation of divine truth takes on temporal form in Christian faith.[56]

It is precisely the discovery of Anselm's explicitly theological thought process which induces Barth to develop his own theological method in bipolar fashion: the revealed object of faith, Jesus Christ (the ontic pole), and the revealed subject of faith, the believing Christian (the noetic pole), are to be understood as analogous realities conjoined only by the mediating power of God, who both establishes the analogy and makes it known: the Holy Spirit. The correspondence between the ontic and the noetic *ratio* and *necessitas* of faith, or the resemblance between *veritas* and *vera ratio*, lie solely in the power of God Himself who is Spirit. He alone guarantees that Christian faith is a noetic participation in God's ontic Truth. For Barth, the one *Vermittlungsprinzip* between God's eternal Truth revealed in Jesus Christ and man's existence as a participant in this Truth is the Holy Spirit and not human ingenuity. Faith corresponds to its object both in the intradivine life of the Trinity and in the external manifestation of God's triune being in revelation. With this realization Barth comes upon an entirely new pattern of thought which is to pervade the *Church Dogmatics*, the concept of analogy. After his study of Anselm the concept as such no longer seems repulsive; it now becomes a characteristic feature of his own epistemological method. He understands that there is an analogy, a point of correspondence, between God and man, by virtue of which man is capable of knowing God. However, this point of correspondence is not given to man by nature, ontologically, as it were, but in faith *(analogia fidei)* since the only possibility of knowing God and His Word is to be found in the Word itself.[57] The Holy Spirit mediates between the Word and faith. For this reason, the point of correspondence is only given to man pneumatologically.

In Anselm's work Barth unearths a pneumatic understanding of theological method as well as of faith itself. This pneumatic insight provides him a biblical corrective to the purely ontological conception of faith and theology advocated by Neo-Protestantism, Christian Existentialism and Roman Catholicism. First faith and then theology have to be understood as the work of the Holy Spirit; their ontological significance, though it logically precedes, is only known through their pneumatic and analogical character.

Faith and theology have as their object not truth merely in the philosophical sense, but Truth both as the divine reality in which man participates through grace and Truth as it is in itself. Barth's tenet that man participates in Truth, but that he does not naturally possess it means that, ontologically speaking, man has the Truth only pneumatically—only as the gift of the Spirit of God comes to him and grants him a knowledge which corresponds to the Truth itself. Anselm convinces Barth that the truth of the *Credo* can only be arrived at *a posteriori*. The noetic reality of faith depends on the ontic reality which God creates in giving Himself as an object to be known by man.[58] In Barth's eyes, Anselm's argumentation is not philosophical but pneumatic, and therefore analogical. From the experience of the Spirit one is led to inquire into the truth of what one believes. The genuine correspondence between belief and revelation is then assured when the Christian realizes that the objective creed which he confesses contains within itself the necessary reasonableness on which personal faith can securely rest.

Besides offering Barth a distinctive theological methodology, the study of Anselm affords him an insight into the ontic and noetic absoluteness of God Himself. For the nature of faith's objective truth in its ontic and noetic form allows man to peer through the account of God's saving activity into the very being of God. Absolute freedom belongs to God's being since He possesses ontic and noetic self-sufficiency. God is sovereign both in His self-revelation and in the analogous faith of Christians because He is antecedently sovereign in Himself. This absolute freedom, however, not only undergirds the transcendence of God but also His immanence, His ability to express His divine being exteriorly in and with beings who are different from Himself. Thus the noetic activity of the Holy Spirit in Christian faith is not to be understood as perfecting the Godhead, but as creating an external correspondence between God's own Noetic and man's knowledge of God. The same is true of the ontic activity of the incarnate Word; God's self-expression of His being in Jesus Christ adds nothing new to the triune God, but reveals to man the ontic foundation of the intradivine life: grace itself. God relates Himself to man through grace which is the cornerstone of faith. God's grace is ontically present in Jesus Christ and noetically effective in Christian faith through the Holy Spirit. Thus grace and faith are analogous, even though a vast distance separates them. The correspondence is not man's creation or possession, but exists solely and totally in the relation of grace to faith bestowed on man by God.[59] It is precisely the Holy Spirit who permits human faith to be analogous to the ontic source of grace in the eternal and incarnate Word of God. As the divine Noetic, the Holy Spirit forms a similarity in man's being to the divine Ontic, the being of Jesus Christ. At the noetic pole there is faith, correspondence, redemption, knowledge; at the ontic pole there is revelation, being, reconciliation, grace. The Spirit mediates between the two because He is the divine Noetic with all the force of the divine Ontic. Since the Spirit is dependent on grace's ontic basis, He is for this reason grace's noetic efficacy.[60]

These insights are developed at length in the *Church Dogmatics* where they form the firm substructure of Barth's entire theological epistemology.

Here it can only be indicated how essential the Anselm book is not only to Barth's understanding of the analogous nature of faith, but also to his very conception of the prime analogate, God's triune being. Barth's work on Anselm represents, as he himself admits, the crowning work of the period before the appearance of his revised dogmatics in 1932. The development from the *Römerbrief* of 1919 to the *Fides Quaerens Intellectum* of 1931 indeed chronicles a shift from dialectics to christocentrism to analogy. What is more significant to this study of Barth's pneumatology, however, is that now the pneumatic reinterpretation of Neo-Protestantism, Christian Existentialism and Roman Catholicism, which forms the germ of Barth's Spirit theology, is more intelligible. If these thought systems could be regarded as covert theologies of the Holy Spirit, their entire christianocentric emphasis could be accepted as the first gropings towards a theology of the third article. Although Barth begins to reiterate this thesis more frequently in 1947, its origin can be found in the works discussed in this chapter.[61] It is undeniable that the Holy Spirit takes on growing importance in Barth's theology even during the early period and that pneumatology is the aspect of his thought which gradually opens the way for a full appreciation of analogy. Though traces of dialectics and christocentrism remain leitmotifs of his theological method, the influence of analogy—the work of the Holy Spirit—can be said to dominate the *Church Dogmatics*. Since Barth himself continually comes upon pneumatology as the corrective to natural theology, he understandably views a faulty Spirit theology as the root of his opponents' positions.

Having followed the genesis of Barth's appreciation of the third article by means of a more generic and a more specific historical overview, this study can now proceed to an objective presentation of the Spirit theology in the *Church Dogmatics*. Occasionally reference is made to issues which have already been discussed as Barth himself raises them in his major work. Though Barth is usually considered a christologist, pneumatology plays a key role in every aspect of his thought, and especially when it is a question of man's correspondence to the person and work of Jesus Christ. Barth clearly intends to write a theology of the Christian which is not christianocentric but pneumatocentric. For, once the unique role of Christ is firmly established in his theology, Barth is concerned that the Christian be taken seriously as the object of the Father's love in the Spirit of His Son. In short, Barth becomes more and more a pneumatocentric theologian. Barth's earlier thought is predominantly christocentric in order both to offset and to bolster the undeniably positive aspect of his opponents' theologies: their insistence on the role of man in theology. Barth becomes a christocentrist in order to support a valid christianocentrism. At heart Karl Barth is also a pneumatologian. Can this thesis be substantiated by examining the *Church Dogmatics*?

PART II

THE PNEUMATOLOGY OF
THE CHURCH DOGMATICS

CHAPTER III

THE SPIRIT, THE TRINITY AND EXPERIENCE

The exposition of the Word of God early in the *Church Dogmatics* (I/1) raises a key question which reveals the function of pneumatology in the structure of this major work. How is it that man does and thus can listen to the Word of God and actually believe in it? The starting point of Barth's most thorough presentation of pneumatology is that man's ability to hear and accept what God has revealed is not only an aspect of revelation, but its very goal. The revelation of the Word is not sufficient for the accomplishment of God's purpose. The Word must become accessible and must be imparted to man. That man hears God demonstrates from the start the active nature and spiritual power of the Word.[1] The first reference to the Holy Spirit in the *Church Dogmatics* is thus highly significant, since the spiritual quality of the Word is rooted in nothing less than the intrinsic power of the Word. The Word contains inherent spiritual power to reach man, that man might hear. The Holy Spirit is the power of God, inseparably linked to His Word, which goes out to draw men to the Word: "Moreover, the Holy Spirit (at least according to the Western notion of the Trinity of God) is inseparable from the Word and His power, therefore, not a power separate from that of the Word, but the power that lives in the Word and through the Word."[2] Not surprisingly, Barth's overture to a systematic pneumatology characterizes the Holy Spirit as the spiritual power which enables the Word to encounter man and bind him to Himself.

The Holy Spirit, as God Himself actually incorporating man into revelation through the experience of faith, is for Barth the last word in preaching and theology, because the Word's spirituality alone accounts for the fact that the Word is not only revealed to man, but also revealed in him so that he might believe. The Word of God is to be heard. The human person, once made open and ready for God's self-revelation, can accept it. But to be able to hear the Word is not a human possibility, for "The Bible and Church dogma and the entire older theology, when they come to say of this event whatever it is possible to say of it at all, speak of the Holy Spirit."[3] From the start, Barth clearly intends to distinguish the experience of faith from its source in the spiritual power of the Word—the Spirit. This pneumatology is rooted in a reaction to Schleiermacher's "anthropologizing of theology" and in reservations concerning Kierkegaard's and Pietism's "religio-psychological, existential thought." Barth maintains that theology must be concerned with more than mere experience of faith; it must search out the source and ground of the faith experience. Otherwise theology becomes a special instance of anthropology. Yet Barth cannot deny that pneumatology must take the experience of faith most seriously as its starting point, just as Anselm, Luther and Melanchthon did when they considered "*sensus* and *experientia* as the substratum of a proper theology." In pneumatology the *theologia regenitorum* or existential theology is a *particula veri* which must be kept in focus.[4] Faith itself must be believed; that there is existential faith in the Word of God is itself as much an object of human belief as is the Word. Thus Barth insists that faith is not man's work, but the miracle of the Holy Spirit: God concretely and historically imparts to man the power of His Word.

The God who speaks His Word (the Father) and the God who is the Word spoken (the Son) must also be understood as the God who makes the Word heard in man (the Holy Spirit). The God of man's hearing is not another God, different from the God who speaks and who is spoken, but the same God in a third way: "The Lord of the language is also the Lord of our listening to it. The Lord who gives the Word is also the Lord who gives faith. The Lord of our listening, the Word who gives faith, the Lord through those act the openness and readiness of man for the Word is true and real—is not another God, but the one God in this way—and that is the Holy Spirit."[5] As Lord of man's efficacious relationship to the Word, God manifests Himself in a third way, but is nevertheless the same Lord—God the Holy Spirit. The fact that there are actually men who hear the objective Word of God reveals that God acts in a third way. He is imparter of Himself, instigator of a relationship, intermediary between an objective self-disclosure and man's subjective acceptance of this divine act. God acting in this way, God accomplishing the goal of His self-revelation, this is God the Holy Spirit.[6]

All the implications at the core of Barth's pneumatology in the *Church Dogmatics* (I/1) are important. Even if Barth begins "existentially," as it were, from an analysis of the Christian's relationship to God through faith, he does not imply that faith springs from a native human capacity to hear and accept the Word of God, or that the Holy Spirit, as the Lord of man's believing, can be explained as a dimension of man's religious nature. That man believes is a fact, but a fact which he can only attribute to an experience in which he was met by the power of God. He claims to believe through an encounter with the Holy Spirit. The Christian knows, despite the existential character of faith, that the ground of belief is not found in himself, and that he is touched by a spiritual mystery. In order to maintain a distinction between man's spirit and the Holy Spirit, Barth stresses the strict spirituality of the attitude of faith and the thoughts of faith which result once one has heard the Word of God. They are not produced by the believer but by the Word, "because the Word of God is a mystery in that it really touches us spiritually, i.e., invariably only through the Holy Spirit, in full mediacy only immediately from God's side."[7] With this juxtaposition of the words "mediacy" and "immediately," Barth attempts to preserve two essential truths: man indeed believes since the experiences, attitudes and thoughts of faith are genuine human acts which mediate between man and God's Word, but also man's faith, as primarily a spiritual hearing of the Word which is beyond the realm of human experience, is not man's own work as such, but the result of an encounter with the Holy Spirit. This coming to man is attested by the Scriptures and by Church proclamation. The Lord of man's relationship to God's Word is at the same time necessarily the Lord of man's hearing of this transcendent Word in the context of his temporal existence. By designating the Holy Spirit the Lord of man's faith, Barth means that the Holy Spirit acts in history by relating man to the Word. Thus God's self-communication can be grasped in human terms.[8] The Christian comes to know his relationship to the Holy Spirit concomitantly as he comes to faith, since the Spirit is recognized as the initiator of the final phase of God's self-revelation at the moment when a man finds himself so evidently related to God that he believes. Suddenly discovering himself a listener and a believer, the Christian must ascribe his new state of existence not to himself, but to God who brings him to faith and forms a relationship with him. God leading man to the point where he is open and ready to hear the Word is God in His third form of existence, God the Holy Spirit. Barth's pneumatology begins, therefore, with the Christian experience of believing in and being related to God, but is impelled immediately to locate the source of this unexpected privilege in God Himself. This invariable progression from the existential experience of faith to its transcendent source affords Barth a way of correcting Schleiermacher's understanding of faith as an immanent capacity of the religious man. Barth's initial approach to a theology of the Holy Spirit in the *Church Dogmatics* is motivated by the desire to assure that "God in a third way" is the Lord of man's relationship to Himself and to insist that faith comes about through an encounter with God the Spirit and only through such an encounter.

1. The Lord of Christian Participation in Revelation

Barth moves directly from the Christian's subjective experience of hearing and accepting the Word of God to the divine spiritual ground of that experience. But how is it possible to specify that ground as the third mode of God's three-fold act of revelation? Why does Barth root the reality of faith precisely in pneumatology? Barth answers that he has consciously structured his theology by use of a scheme which attributes to the one God the functions of Revealer, Revelation and Revealedness, "only to make it clear to us that and to what extent we were led by revelation itself to the problem of the three-in-oneness".[9] This scheme corresponds to the logical and material order both of the biblical witness and the Christian tradition of the Trinity; it is vital to proper understanding and presentation of the distinctive aspects of Christian monotheism. Thus, when Barth considers the statement "God reveals Himself as Lord," he can legitimately indicate the grammatical object of the sentence, "Himself," as a third aspect which he calls "Revealedness" *(das Offenbarsein)*. There are men who do believe in the Revealer *(der Offenbarer)* and in His Revelation *(die Offenbarung)*. God's Revealedness, as the third and final facet of His being and as the accomplished goal of His self-disclosure, guarantees the Christian admission to true knowledge of the intradivine life. Thus the Christian shares gratuitously in the bounty of the one revealing God.[10]

Despite the prominent place which the Holy Spirit enjoys in this original scheme, it soon becomes clear that the three aspects of the one revealing God are from an historical point of view not equally important for Barth. God revealing Himself as Lord in a personal manner and at a definite point in time, stands out from the other aspects, and is the most determinative of them all, as both the New Testament and the history of trinitarian dogma attest. The central aspect of God's revelation as a triune community is His concrete self-unveiling in Jesus Christ: "Historically speaking, the three questions answered in the Bible as to Revealer, Revelation and Revealedness have not the same weight . . . And so, too, the doctrine of the Trinity historically considered in its origin and construction has not been interested equally in Father, Son and Holy Spirit; here also the theme was primarily the *second* Person of the Trinity, God the *Son*, the divinity of *Christ*."[11] Barth then proceeds to supplant his initial scheme with a new one which unquestionably places primary emphasis on the incarnation as the key to understanding the three distinct aspects of the one self-revealing God. Only through God's unveiling of Himself in Jesus Christ does the veiled Father, God as the one who by nature cannot fully reveal Himself to man, become known. Thus, through the historically manifest divinity of Christ men come to know the eternally hidden divinity of the Father.

The second article of the creed, however, does not say all. This self-unveiling of God must be perceived by men, if God's being is to be effective in, as well as formative and reformative of history. In this way pneumatology formally enters into Barth's now explicitly christologically-centered notion of revelation and of the Trinity. It is a question of the impartation of what God, though in Himself unveilable, in fact unveiled in Jesus Christ. Through the Holy Spirit men take part in revelation and are actually present at it. If the God unveiled in Jesus' resurrection is the same God who was veiled on the cross, He is also the same God who gives man a part in and makes him present at revelation on Pentecost Day: "The *pneuma* is the miracle of real men present at revelation . . . it really is a matter of Good Friday and Easter happening in the sense of a happening that touches *them*, befalls *them*, calls *them*, the fact that not only does Jesus Christ exist, but Jesus Christ is in the Church of Jesus Christ, is *in the faith* in Jesus Christ—precisely that is the distinctive thing about Pentecost and the Spirit in the New Testament."[12]

If in the concrete form of Jesus Christ (the Son) the same God is revealed who is also freedom from form (the Father) and if both in this form and in this freedom the same God becomes the God of specific men at a specific time, that is, if God's *historicity* in human experience is also a part of divine self-revelation, then this third sense is God the Holy Spirit. Like the Son and the Father, the Spirit is also a separate aspect of the one revealing God which cannot be reduced to the other two aspects, if the divine self-disclosure is what it is attested to be in Scripture. Revelation itself encompasses not only the self-unveiling of God to men *(die Selbstenthüllung)* and the veiling of God from men *(die Selbstverhüllung)*; it is not only form *(die Gestalt)* and freedom *(die Freiheit)* but also historical event *(die Geschichtlichkeit)* in many men, not just generally but at definite moments in time; it is not only Easter and Good Friday, but Pentecost as well. Revelation, according to Barth, attests to three "moments" in the one God, and delineates the one God as the Son, the Father and the Spirit in accordance with the three distinct aspects of His self-revelation.

The assertion that the Holy Spirit is God's own self-impartation in time, is Barth's reaction to a theological methodology born in the Enlightenment and influencing Hegel and Schleiermacher. By stressing the essential correspondence between God's being and actions Barth adamantly rejects the needless dichtomy between the "eternal content" and the "historical vehicle" proposed by the philosophical approach to religion. Biblical events are more than special instances of a universal idea, Barth repeatedly insists. The theological movement from Lessing by way of Kant and Herder to Fichte and Hegel, "must be described as the lowest depth of modern misunderstanding of the Bible."[13] Precisely through his own trinitarian teaching, which firmly defends the unity of God's economic and immanent being and activity, Barth counteracts every tendency to search for some mystical truth behind or beyond the revealed Word of Scripture. Such "existential" tendencies reduce the historical acts revealed in Scripture to symbolic expressions of what is eternally true and can be expressed in the mystical language of any religious community. Barth's conviction that God's eternal Spirit is His historical self-impartation *(geschichtliche Selbstmitteilung)* is incompatible with any mystical interpretation of the Bible or Christian faith. Barth's pneumatology expressly answers a theological question. How can the eternal transcendent God be present in the historical form of biblical language and human faith?

Once Barth has repudiated the proclivity of the existential approach to confuse the believer and the Holy Spirit, and to deny the latter as both the object and imparter of faith, he insists that the Christian's actual experience of faith is the apt starting point of pneumatology. In effect, Barth reaffirms his suspicion that Existentialism propounds a veiled pneumatology in the form of an hermeneutics and phenomenology of faith. Yet, in order to arrive in the *Church Dogmatics* at the divinity of the Holy Spirit, Barth takes from Basil the Great and Athanasius what has come to be known as the soteriological argument for the divinity of the third Person. Barth obviously finds similarities between this traditional argument and the phenomenological description of faith which all the followers of Schleiermacher employ. However, they do not rightly arrive at the divinity of the Holy Spirit as the ultimate explanation of the life of faith. Barth is thus compelled to adopt their methodology, but to modify it by means of a biblical and patristic understanding of the Christian's existential faith as the divine work of the Holy Spirit.

Barth's own version of the soteriological argument in defense of the ontological validity of the third aspect of the one self-revealing God begins with the fact that individuals living at a point in time find that they believe in Jesus Christ as Lord. They also believe that Jesus, as the divine Word spoken to them, reveals His very identity with the hidden God who has chosen to speak only in and through His Word. Further, believers know that they are related to the Word and to the Speaker of the Word in such a way that they cannot attribute this relationship fully to themselves except in that their own freedom was freed to say "Yes!" to the relationship. God's very power is here at work. Something has been imparted to them at a concrete place and time. They understand this impartation as a spiritual and historical event powerful enough to transform their lives. This experience is incomparable, irrepeatable. Christians find that they must be and in fact are the specific goal to which the spiritual intention of the hidden God who speaks and of the revealed God who is spoken is aimed. In short, they are called, and find themselves responding; a relationship is offered and they consent; an event of God is taking place and they concur with it; a surprising burden falls upon their shoulders, they allow it to happen, and are touched to the point where they are deeply involved. An effective meeting has taken place with God. For all its human elements, this meeting remains essentially a vertical encounter. God has become their God, the God of such men as they are. God, the eternal Speaker of the Word, and God, the Word spoken at a definite point in time, suddenly also becomes the God who speaks to them here and now.

The God who acts here and now does so in a way different from His eternal action or His action then and there in Jesus Christ. But, since God acting on Christians here and now brings them to faith in Jesus Christ and to the community of Jesus Christ, this faith and this community is the aim of God's self-impartation. This new and specific, this inviting and challenging, self-imparting and faith-bringing act of God in their regard is oriented towards making what has been objectively revealed a subjective reality. Since they know that they are not debating with themselves, Christians conclude that God is bringing revelation home to them. God wants to be revealed to them, and does in fact reveal Himself to them. God is actually concerned that there be a state of "revealedness" which has the mark of historicity. Individuals thus experience God's being-revealed to and in their existence. The God who meets them spiritually, who forms an historical relationship with them is God the Spirit, the self-imparting God, yet the same God as the Father and the Son. This same God acts in a unique way that touches them just as they read the apostles were touched at Pentecost.

Barth thus bases his own presentation of the Spirit and of the Trinity on a theological interpretation of man's soteriological encounter with the Lord of Christian experience, the being-revealed of the Father and the Son. But he also candidly admits that, by examining the roots of Christian teaching on the Trinity in scriptural revelation, he has not yet arrived at the fullness of the Church's doctrine itself, which is not directly or explicitly expressed in the Bible. Although the later doctrine of the Trinity is only implicitly contained in Scripture, the subsequent Church exegesis is justified in its interpretation of the biblical texts. For the statements of the doctrine of the Trinity answer the questions posed by revelation itself as clearly as any answer can confront a question. Barth is content to have established that the biblical understanding of revelation is implicitly, occasionally explicitly, an indication of the doctrine of the Trinity.[14] Such an indication that the Holy Spirit is inchoately grasped as the third mode of God's existence is found in certain questions which are put by Scripture itself. "Who is God?" "What does He do?" "What does He affect in man?" "What is His aim with regard to man?" These last two queries deal with the man to whom God reveals Himself. Revelation, therefore, asks about "the men who receive revelation, in view of what the Revealer intends and does with them, what His revelation *achieves* in them, what therefore His revealedness signifies for them."[15] This entire subjective aspect based on the revealedness of God for and in man comprises the inceptive pneumatology contained in revelation itself, which was then later supplemented by the doctrine of the Holy Spirit.

Barth concludes: "God reveals Himself as the *Spirit*, not as any spirit, not as the discoverable and arousable subsoil of man's spiritual life, but as the Spirit of the Father and the Son, and so as the same one God, but this time as the same one God in this way as well, namely, in this *unity*, nay, in this *self-disclosing* unity, disclosing itself to *men*, unity with the Father and the Son . . . that there is such a manifestation of the Father and the Son is what we mean when we say that He reveals Himself as the *Lord*. The fact, too, that according to *John* 4:24 God is a Spirit is God's lordship in His revelation."[16] This normative insight of Scripture should enjoy a place above the formal doctrine of the Trinity and the subsequent developments in pneumatology, but does not deny them. Later explanations with regard to the correspondence of the economic Trinity in revelation and the immanent Trinity in God Himself only confirm that Christian experience corresponds to the immanent nature of God's own historicity, the Holy Spirit. In his approach to understanding the Holy Spirit as the Lord of man's relation to the triune God, Barth argues "from below" or "experientially" to the divinity of the Holy Spirit. Reasoning based on the experience of salvation leads Barth to conclude that the spiritual quality of the Word of God who encounters man in faith is grounded in God's own being, and cannot be reduced to a mystical or psychological power in human nature. Man's existential experience of faith can only follow God's opening of Himself to man as historical self-impartation, as Spirit.

2. The Experience of the Spirit Discloses His Essence

The historical genesis of Barth's pneumatology is a reaction to the anthropologizing tendencies of Neo-Protestantism, Christian Existentialism and Roman Catholicism. This point cannot be overstressed. Thus the trinitarian dimension of Barth's pneumatology has the theological function of correcting the purely philosophical and anthropological tenor of the above-mentioned pneumatologies. As was already stated, Barth's soteriological argument for the divinity of the Holy Spirit concedes the validity at the core of Existentialism's method, but inherently implies a rejection of any purely philosophical or apologetical argumentation which reduces to a discoverable fact the absolute uniqueness of God's self-revelation as "three indissolubly different modes of being."[17] Such an attempt was exemplified for Barth chiefly in Roman Catholicism's notion of the *vestigia trinitatis* and its parallels in Protestantism, all of which he regarded as specific subdivisions of the broader Scholastic category of *analogia entis*.

Barth contends that his line of reasoning is based solely on revelation

itself, not on the *vestigia trinitatis*. All efforts to root the doctrine of the
Trinity either in nature, in culture, in history, in religion or in the human
soul are for Barth helpful but limited reflections of what Scripture attests
with the analogical concepts of Father, Son and Spirit.[18] These attempts,
however well motivated, cannot have the same power as the central analogy
which revelation itself supplies. If they did, there would be two main sources
of knowledge about God's own being. A question would immediately arise.
Which source is the definitive one, the knowledge derived from biblical
revelation or the knowledge attained by means of an *analogia entis* in the
form of a search for *vestigia* of the Trinity in human experience? Biblical
revelation would then stand in danger of being regarded merely as a subsequent confirmation of knowledge about God which could be gained quite
apart from this revelation. In the end one could never be certain whether
or not the *vestigia* were to be accepted as traces of a Creator-God tran-
scending the world. They could be just as well interpreted as determinations
of the cosmos in a strictly immanent sense or simply as determinations of
human existence. The speculation concerning the actual existence and
knowability of such *vestigia trinitatis* blurred theological clarity to Barth's
way of thinking and thus had the "greatest importance, not only for the
question of the root of the *doctrine of the Trinity*, but for the question of
revelation generally, for the question of basing theology solely upon revelation, and lastly and in particular for the question as to the meaning and
possibility of theology as distinct from a mere cosmology or an
anthropology."[19]

Barth rejects *vestigia trinitatis in creatura*, and chooses instead to invent
the phrase *vestigia creaturae in trinitate* since the latter seems more indicative of the real meaning of *vestigia* and thus more pertinent to the relation
of the Trinity to human experience. For, "traces of the creature in the
Trinity" leaves no doubt that things themselves are not capable of having
the Trinity immanent in them or of being reflections of the Trinity. Such a
modified rendition, as Barth proposes, would rightly affirm that the Trinity
is capable of reflecting itself in things. The power of revelation over reason
is protected, and the error that reason is capable of arriving at revelation
avoided. Remaining true to his intention to make theology theology and not
anthropology, Barth discovers a *vestigium creaturae in trinitate* in the fact
that God Himself has assumed form in man's language, man's world and
man's very humanity. His Word enters the world in the threefold form of
His self-revelation as Father, Son and Spirit, in the Scriptures which attest
to this revelation and in Church proclamation which continually makes this
revelation present for man. It is thus from man's experience in the Church
as a listener and a hearer of the Word of God that Barth discovers the true
meaning behind all the various attempts at locating a remnant of the Trinity
in the world. For, God alone creates a trace of Himself in His revelation,
and thus revelation itself offers the only access to the doctrine of the Trinity
fully respectful of the sovereignty of God's self-manifestation to men. If a
trace of God Himself can be found in human language and culture, it is
there because God has chosen to enter man's sphere, not *vice versa*. There
is a remnant of the creature in God's triune being which has imparted itself

to man's realm, not an independent trace of the triune God in the creature as such.

Barth grounds his insistence on a single source of man's knowledge about the Trinity on nothing less than the Holy Spirit. Biblical faith itself, as the work of the Holy Spirit, is the one source of man's knowledge about God's triune being which man can rely on with certainty. God the Spirit has formed such a relationship with man that man's own language and experience, his very lips and heart, may become capable of reflecting the inner-trinitarian being of God in the midst of the world. For, to comprehend all the implications of hearing the Word of God is not traceable to data lying within man's experience, but only to faith, to the Holy Spirit. Since the doctrine of the Trinity lies at the core of the revealed Word, and since the Word can only be known through the power of the Spirit, Barth links the knowledge of the Trinity to the mystery of the Spirit at work in Christian experience: "Thus: What is the nature of the Word of God? Answer: It is on our lips and in our hearts, in the mystery of the Spirit who is the Lord."[20]

By rejecting the *vestigia trinitatis*, Barth obviously puts a limit on the use of analogy in his trinitarian theology. In place of the analogy of being which underlies the concept of *vestigia*, Barth purposely substitutes what can be called a pneumatological notion of analogy, one rooted in the traces of God's presence to be discovered in the spiritual life of the believer alone. In doing so Barth develops the germ of what he will later call the *analogia fidei*, his own answer to Roman Catholicism's *analogia entis*. Barth also strictly limits his reliance on an existential method in pneumatology, since his concession to the experiential starting point of Spirit theology is substantially conditioned by his insistence that with the experience of faith—the work of the Holy Spirit in man—he does not mean the experience of man in general. Only by renouncing all attempts to ground the truth of revelation in the universal experience of man rather than in the explicit experience of grace, a gift from God, can Barth assure that the power of the Holy Spirit is the sole ground of any analogy between the being of God and the life of the Christian believer. Existentialism's methodology and Catholicism's notion of analogy thus play a limited role in Barth's pneumatology and trinitarian theology.

Barth now turns his attention to Schleiermacher's disturbing position that the doctrine of the Trinity can only stand at the conclusion of theology. Barth interprets this stance as a *de facto* admission that the doctrine of the Trinity has no constitutive meaning for the body of Schleiermacher's theology.[21] This understanding of the Trinity is for Barth only a further proof that Neo-Protestantism's theological method can only account for those aspects of revelation which are immediate to Christian self-consciousness. The very fact that Schleiermacher's theological method has no access to the Trinity, Barth views "as a sign that this matter should be noted and considered in the *first* place, at the point where real revelation is involved."[22] Thus, although Schleiermacher is right in asserting that the dogma of the Trinity is inconceivable to human consciousness as such, this very admission means that an accurate knowledge of revelation itself becomes most clear precisely in this doctrine. On the one hand, God's being is not in itself approachable by man, but on the other, man must go beyond his own consciousness to understand who God really is. Schleiermacher's unwillingness to allow the distinctions in revelation to correspond to the distinctions in God Himself is corroborating evidence that he limits the being of God to man's own conception of the divine, and thereby cuts man off from the real God and isolates him within the circle of his own being.

Barth, at first in full agreement with Schleiermacher, questions man's very ability to conceive the inner life of God on his own power. When man confronts the scriptural evidence for God's oneness and then the same source's evidence for the three ways in which He is one, he stands before the sheer mystery of God's Three-in-Oneness *(die Dreieinigkeit)*. This mystery is first and foremost not that of the essence of God in Himself but of the essence of God as He operates among men and reveals Himself to them in history. The distinctions in the unity of God which are recorded in revelation can become somewhat intelligible to man through faith. But, that the distinctions found in revelation actually correspond to real distinctions in God's own being apart from history is inconceivable to man. Thus, Barth maintains that the ability to conceive the threefold form of God's nature, as it is revealed implicitly in Scripture and defined explicitly in Church doctrine, rests in the native intelligibility of man. To comprehend the manner in which God exists in Himself, however, is completely different than arriving at the conceivability of historical revelation. Accurate knowledge about the inner life of God would thus seem to be impossible for man. On this point Barth and Schleiermacher fully agree.

Barth therefore admits that a gulf exists between man and God, for, if God's essence were totally patent to man's mind, there would be no sense at all in talking about God's self-revelation to man. Thus, the absolute mystery of God's inner three-in-oneness remains, despite any insight of revelation. For the human person should never confuse his own capacity to understand what is unveiled in revelation with the inner conceivability of God Himself. Furthermore, man's intelligence can grasp the three-in-oneness of God which is manifest in revelation, only because this mystery has become appropriately geared to human understanding by the very grace of God which has entered man's sphere through the event of revelation itself.[23] Yet, despite all that Barth concedes about the limits of man's ability to conceive the inner being of God, he argues against Schleiermacher that not to let the evidence revealed in Scripture hint at the actual existence of different relations within the being of God Himself would be a grave error. It would be just as serious a mistake to underestimate the data provided in revelation as to overestimate it. Barth, therefore, claims that scriptural evidence encourages man to speculate about the inconceivable, eternal distinctions within the Godhead. For theology's enterprise in this regard is based on the analogies contained in the language of revelation itself. God's entry into the sphere of human discourse by means of His self-revelation in history guarantees the theologian at least some access to God's interior being. While God always remains veiled, He has freely unveiled Himself in Jesus Christ, and continually imparts His own interiority to man in the Holy Spirit. Thus, whatever evidence revelation contains concerning God's three-in-oneness affords man reliable insight into what stands behind the words of revelation, that is, the truth of God in Himself.

God in Himself and God for us must be seen as one. There is thus a counterpart to what God enacts in His operations among men as Father, Son and Holy Spirit, a counterpart that is the very essence of God Himself: "God in His *eternal* truth and God also in the truth appointed and appropriate *to us* is one . . . to the involution and convolution of the three modes of existence in the *essence* of God there corresponds most completely their involution and convolution *(das Ineinander und das Miteinander)* in His operation."[24] This explains why, when Barth speaks of the proper work of the Holy Spirit in history, he must necessarily speculate about the nature of the Spirit's role within the Godhead, for the specifics of God's action in revelation demand a corresponding mode of existence in God's interiority. Thus, although Barth sets limits to man's ability to conceive the three-in-oneness of God totally for what it is, a mystery, he fully grants that it is at the same time a self-revealing mystery which is consistent with itself as it imparts itself to man. In His self-revelation God makes His own consistency appropriately intelligible to man's mind.

The Holy Spirit, God's own historical self-impartation to man, guarantees a correspondence between God in Himself and God as He is known by man. Clearly the solution to the problem concerning knowledge of the immanent Trinity must be for Barth a pneumatological solution. Only the Spirit, as the spiritual power of God's own eternal Word, can create through faith a human knowledge which substantially corresponds to the truth of God Himself. That man can know the immanent nature of God as the mystery which coincides with the economic activity of God on man's behalf is the work of the Holy Spirit. As God's own openness to man, He is both in God Himself and in the Christian the mediator between God's mystery and the mystery of man's participation in God. That Schleiermacher was not willing to make this last statement is for Barth the greatest weakness of his essentially self-contained theology of the Christian consciousness.

By reacting so decidedly against Schleiermacher's appreciation of the Trinity, Barth's chief concern is to guarantee that the God of theology corresponds to the personal God of the Scriptures, and thus to free God from the impersonal categories of an "He" or an "It", so that man's faith would be directed toward the God who is always a subject and whom he could address only as "You."[25] Barth's trinitarian teaching thus serves a hermeneutical function: it offers a human interpretation of God which corresponds to God's own self-interpretation in the Scriptures. In addition to correcting Schleiermacher, Barth is also attempting to lend his own understanding of the Trinity the same function which Bultmann later was to give to the process of demythologization, namely, that of comprehending God as "You." But, almost as a prefigurement of his subsequent disagreement with Bultmann, Barth prefers to allow God to interpret Himself rather than to employ extrinsic philosophical criteria to decide to what extent the God of the New Testament corresponds to God in Himself. Since God has interpreted Himself in revelation, Barth argues that Christian hermeneutics consist in a trinitarian understanding of the correlation between God as He acts through His Word and His Spirit and God as He is with His Word and His Spirit.

Barth is content that the theological derivation of the notion of three-in-oneness was able properly to signify what the Scriptures themselves reveal about the identity and the difference of God's actions among men. God always remains a single "I" who stands over against the "you" of man, so that, though His operations are different, He is only one God and not three. In this way Barth rejects any hint of Arianism in his admittedly triadic approach to God's revelation and to God's being: "In the doctrine of the Trinity we are speaking not of three divine 'I's', but thrice of the one divine I. The concept of the *equality* of essence *(homoousia, consubstantialitas)* in Father, Son and Spirit is thus at every point and pre-eminently to be regarded in the sense of an *identity* of essence. From the identity follows the equality of essence in the 'Persons' "[26] This means that God's revelation in His Son and His Holy Spirit must be considered as equal and identical to the Revealer Father. Thus Barth views the doctrine of the Trinity with its clear insistence on the essential equality of the three modes of God's existence as the only defense against a reduction of the thrice personal God to the world of objects, and therefore as the only defense against a theological denial of historical revelation. This, in Barth's opinion, is the primary hermeneutical function of the dogma of God's threeness-in-*oneness*.

On the other hand, the dogma also protects God's *threeness*-in-oneness, and thus guards against the opposite extreme of Sabellianism, according to which the absolute oneness of God makes it all but impossible to assert that distinctions in God's operation *ad extra* necessarily apply to God's essence. Barth considers this position just as much a violation of biblical revelation as the subordinationists' position. For, in modalism the ontologically real God stands behind the three modes of existence to which the Bible attests. This hidden "fourth" aspect of God once again reduces the divine to an object which man can speculate about, an It, instead of the indissoluble Subject of the Old and New Testaments.[27] The only way to escape this confusion of human and divine subjectivity is to acknowledge as normative the trinitarian formulation that the three modes of God's existence are in no way separate from His single essence. The one personal God, who reveals Himself and in this way communicates with man, must be seen concomitantly and necessarily as God in three distinct modes of being. Otherwise, revelation, man's only true source of knowledge about God, would not be a real self-description of the single divine "You" in three irreconcilably distinct forms, but simply an object of human conjecture. Only the God who speaks and acts as Father, Son and Spirit, as self-veiling, self-unveiling and self-imparting, as holiness, mercy and love is identical with the true God.

At the core of Barth's willingness not to underestimate the theological root of the doctrine of the Trinity which is found in the Scriptures is his appreciation of the implied correspondence therein between God's actions outside Himself and God's hidden essence. Only the God of the Scriptures, precisely in the threefold form of His self-revelation, is the God who can meet man and unite Himself to him. This God alone proves that He is identical with Himself in all His distinctly different, but invariably revelatory actions among men. Once this has been said firmly, Barth is ready to admit that there are limits to all forms of trinitarian speculation and thus to his own attempts at such in the *Church Dogmatics*. Barth concedes that the concepts which he employs, such as Revealer-Revelation-Revealedness, and self-veiling, self-unveiling, and self-impartation, both are and yet cease immediately to be of any use, for they are only useful to the extent that they point by their very uselessness beyond themselves to the problem as it is set forth by Scripture: "When we have said what is meant by Father, Son and Spirit in God, we must continue and say that we have said nothing. *Tres nescio quid* was the final answer which even Anselm could return to Augustine's query *(Quid tres?)*, indeed had to return."[28]

The doctrine of the Trinity is for Barth the eternal mystery which grounds the actual experience of the Christian since this doctrine preserves the biblical insight that God is, in His freedom for man, man's God. Christian existence, therefore, has its foundation in God's own being as Father, in the words He spoke to man as Son and in the actions which He still performs as Spirit. The Trinity guarantees that God is not any God, but the God of Christian experience: "And this Lord can be *our* God, He can meet us and unite us to Himself, because He is God in these three modes of existence as Father, Son and Spirit, because creation, reconciliation, redemption, the entire being, language and action in which He wills to be our God, is grounded and typified in His own essence, in His Godness itself."[29] In light of Barth's pneumatology, these words take on special significance. It is precisely the Holy Spirit, as the triune God's self-impartation to men and as God's continuous historical and personal effort to meet and be united with men, who is in this way the Lord of Christian experience. Yet, it is imperative for Barth that the Holy Spirit, as particularly the God of Christian existence, as their access to a real relationship with the Father and the Son, is such from eternity in the essence of God, in the Godhead itself.

Barth insists that the Spirit is always the divine "You" and can be reduced neither to an impersonal power which accounts for the historical continuity of the Church nor to a mysterious entity which cannot be properly distinguished from the God who stands behind the kerygma of the community. The Spirit is the divine "You" both in the economy of revelation and in the immanence of His own being. By saying that the Holy Spirit is the God of Christian experience, Barth agrees on the one hand with the efforts of Bultmann to talk about God only in personal terms, but on the other hand he criticizes both Bultmann's and Schleiermacher's tendency to divorce the Spirit of the Word or of the community from the essence of God Himself. With the statement that the Spirit is nothing less than the divine "You," Barth means that the Spirit is in Himself that which He is in His activity—the Lord of Christian faith. Barth in effect departs from Neo-Protestantism and Christian Existentialism and joins himself to Catholic and Reformational teaching on the Trinity, but he does so in such a way as to link God's essence and God's activity in history much more closely than had been done before.

3. *The Father and the Son Meeting Man from Within*

Per appropriationem it is God the Holy Spirit, God in His third mode of existence, who according to Barth makes the actions of the Father and of the Son become historical realities. The Holy Spirit is God completing His self-revelation in man, so that man can be united to the triune God in a new relationship called sanctification or redemption. This relationship is intrinsically linked to man's prior relationship to the Father and the Son through creation and reconciliation, but is still distinct from these mysteries. The Holy Spirit is God personally manifest to and in men; those who are met by the Spirit are men who themselves belong to revelation, "men who become what by themselves and of themselves they can neither be nor become, men who belong to God, who are in real communion with God, who live before God and with God."[30] Man's being-related to God, being-present before God and with God; God's being-related to man, being-related before him and with him is the distinct work of the Holy Spirit. To the objective givenness of the self-revelation of the hidden Father in the Son made flesh is added the special element of the subsequent manifestation of the same God which occurs subjectively in man. The Holy Spirit is God assuring the existence of the complementary subjective side of the event of revelation in Christians. That there are men who not only need to be related to God, but who actually enjoy such a relation, that there are men who believe in the Father through the Son is the work of the Holy Spirit.

When Barth first turns his attention to an explicit chapter on the Holy Spirit in the *Church Dogmatics*, he speaks of God coming to man, binding Himself to man, claiming man for Himself, becoming man's, making man His own. When this does happen, it can only be God's own reality at work; such a close union of God and man can lie only in God's power: "It is God's reality, by God being subjectively present to men not only from without, not only from above, but also from within, from beneath. It is reality, therefore, by God not only coming to man, but meeting Himself from man's end. God's freedom to be thus present to man and hence to introduce this meeting—that is the Spirit of God, the Holy Spirit in God's revelation."[31] Once the Christian experience has been described as the work of the Holy Spirit who, as God meeting Himself from man's end, is accountable for man's presence before, relation to and participation in God Himself, Barth immediately makes the claim that the Christian's temporal participation in the mutual love of God the Father and God the Son is grounded on the intradivine relationship between the three modes of God's existence from eternity. For these eternal relations within God Himself ground and typify man's actual meeting with God in time. How then, is the third mode of God's existence eternally related to the first and the second modes, so that the Spirit has the function in revelation of making man present, of relating and uniting him to God?

Barth approaches the answer first by considering revelation and then by appealing to the principle that what is true of God's action in revelation must be true of His eternal essence. The God of revelation and God in Himself are one. If there is a sharing, a relation, a presence between God and man through the Holy Spirit in revelation, there must be at least the possibility of such a sharing, relation and presence within God Himself. God must be previously in Himself what He is subsequently in revelation. Barth realizes that the dogma of the Holy Spirit, like the dogma of the Trinity, is not fully discernible in the New Testament; rather it results from an exegesis of those New Testament texts, which ascribe the work of the Holy Spirit to God Himself, and which therefore expressly unite the Holy Spirit from eternity to the being of God. The Holy Spirit does not first become God's Spirit in the event of revelation, but the historical event of revelation has a genuine subjective side, only because the Holy Spirit, who makes Christian experience possible, has a prior essential role in God Himself: "What He is in revelation He is antecedently in Himself. And what He is antecedently in Himself He is in revelation. Right within the deepest depths of deity, as the final thing to be said of Him, God is God the Spirit as He is God the Father and God the Son. The Spirit outpoured at Pentecost is the Lord, God Himself, just as the Father, just as Jesus Christ is the Lord, God Himself."[32]

Barth's reading of Anselm has already deeply affected his theological position and led him far beyond the prescribed bounds both of the Neo-Protestantism of Schleiermacher and of the Liberalism of his own early years. For, in making the statement that God is antecedently in Himself what He is in revelation, Barth actually applies the Anselmian principle that the subjective knowledge of the believer corresponds to the objective reality which he believes; the noetic rationality and necessity of faith corresponds to its prior ontic rationality and necessity. Furthermore, by employing this metaphysical principle within the core of his dogmatic theology, Barth is acknowledging his debt to Hegel's realistic metaphysics and at the same time achieving his goal of lending this impressive metaphysical framework its true content. Most interesting, however, is the fact that Barth sees the urgent need to assert God's correspondence to Himself precisely while he is developing his pneumatology. For the latter would indeed be vacuous if the Holy Spirit did not have the explicit function of correlating man's knowledge and experience of God with God's own being and inner life. The Spirit could only be capable of doing so if He were to effect in man the very relation to the Father and the Son which He causes to exist in the Godhead.

What, then, is the eternal inner relationship between the Holy Spirit and the Father and the Son according to Barth? The fact that *to pneuma* is a neuter noun in distinction to *ho pater* and *ho huios* makes it clear to Barth that the Spirit cannot be described as a "Person" in the modern sense of the term; He cannot be understood as a third I, or third Lord, alongside two others. He is, therefore, the one divine Subject in a third mode of existence which could be called the common factor or the communion between the Father and the Son. The Spirit is equal to the Father and to the Son since He is the act of their "communityness" *(die Akt des Gemeinsamseins des Vaters und des Sohnes)*. He is the mutual love and the reciprocal self-giving of the Father to the Son and of the Son to the Father. The Spirit is not simply an emanation that goes out from the Father and the Son; He is rather the intradivine effect of their love which remains inside God, even when the Spirit communicates this love to mankind. As the reciprocal love of the first two modes of God's being, the bond they produce between them is a third mode of divine existence, equal to the first two modes and belonging inherently to the single divine principle. The Spirit is thus the unique self-impartation of the Father to the Son and of the Son to the Father, and as such He is distinct from either of these two modes of divine existence but essentially related to each of them as their very reciprocity which is not an opposition *(Gegeneinander)* but an approximation *(Zueinander)*, a distinction *(Auseinander)* and a participation *(Miteinander)*. "This participation of the Father and the Son is the Holy Spirit. Thus, the *special feature* of the Holy Spirit's divine mode of existence consists, paradoxically enough, in Him being the *common factor* between the mode of existence of God the Father and that of God the Son, not what is common to them, so far as they are the one God, but what is common to them so far as they are the Father and the Son."[33] Thus, the Spirit is for Barth the two-sided communion within the one essence of God.

It is on the basis of these reflections that Barth proceeds to deepen his understanding of the correspondence between the intradivine essence and the *ad extra* actions of the Holy Spirit. Barth's argument is as follows: man can speculate concerning the intradivine nature of the Holy Spirit because the divine self-revelation attested to in Scripture points to a real relationship, or better, a real communion between man and the Holy Spirit as the very goal of God's revelation to man. There must be a corresponding function of the Holy Spirit within God's own essence which grounds and typifies His function among men in history. If the Holy Spirit is the love of the Father and the Son externally communicated and imparted to man, then the basis of this saving action or function must rest in the ontic constitution of God Himself. A communion and participation, an act of impartation and an act of love must exist in the very essence of God. That God can lovingly communicate with man and create in revelation a real relationship with him must have its source in a divine eternal truth, namely, in a divine and eternal loving communication and relationship in God Himself. This participation or communityness in God Himself Barth calls the third mode of God's existence, the Holy Spirit, who is at the same time for man God's own self-impartation *(Selbstmitteilung)* in revelation.

Not to accept this argumentation and thus to deny the eternal communion of the Father and the Son through the Holy Spirit as the necessary presupposition of the temporal self-impartation of the Trinity would constitute for Barth an emptying of revelation. Communion in the Spirit between God and man would then lack objective content and ground. Revelation would possess no warranty if the Spirit, in His proper and original reality, were not the only possibility of such a corresponding reality in history. It is thus clear why Barth hinges to this argument a defense of the *Filioque* of Western credal formulations. To deny that the Holy Spirit proceeds both from the Father and from the Son from eternity would in effect mean that the Spirit is not the divine ground of the temporal communion between the Trinity and mankind which takes place in faith, but is only a divine gift which originates totally from the Father. The Eastern Churches do not disclaim that the Spirit proceeds from both the Father and the Son in revelation, but deny that what is true of revelation must also be true of the inner being of God. Barth stands firm, however, by the premise that statements which theologians have made about the immanent Trinity have proven themselves to be just confirmations, underpinings and indeed hermeneutical and ontic explanations of the economic Trinity. By disavowing the *Filioque*, a separation is fostered between the immanent and the economic Trinity, and thus the belief that the Holy Spirit is the very ground of God's ability to communicate in an authentic way with man in revelation is jeopardized. "The *Filioque* is the expression of the knowledge of the communion between *Father* and *Son*, knowledge that the Holy Spirit is the love, which is the essence of the relation between these two modes of existence of God. And the knowledge of this communion is nothing else than the knowledge of the ground and confirmation of the communion between *God* and *man*, as a divine eternal truth, as created in revelation by the Holy Spirit. On the *intradivine* two-sided communion of the Spirit, which proceeds from the Father and from the Son, is founded the fact that in *revelation* there is a communion, in which not only is God there for man, but in reality—that is the *donum Spiritus Sancti*—man is also there for God."[34] Barth thus vigorously defends a univocal understanding of God both in Himself and in His self-impartation outside Himself, so that man is guaranteed in revelation a God-given participation in divine existence.

This insistence on the absolute consistency of the Holy Spirit both in regard to Himself and in regard to man is due to Barth's conviction that pneumatology has only rarely been properly understood in Christian theology as the sole explanation of man's relationship with God. It is the dogma of the Holy Spirit's divinity which convinces Barth that ". . . man can only be present at God's revelation as a servant is present at his master's action, i.e., following, obeying, imitating, serving and that this relation—which makes it different from any human relation between master and servant— is in no wise and at no point reversed."[35] Later failure to recognize the primary place which the doctrine of the Holy Spirit enjoyed in the patristic understanding of faith was the reason why controversies over grace and justification arose in the Western Church. Barth once again returns to the root of his own pneumatology in a now familiar theme: "Of course the real and full importance of the Holy Spirit was never understood in Catholicism (not even in Augustine!) and only very partially even in post-Reformation Protestantism. Modernist Protestantism in its entirety has largely been, quite simply, a reversion to the obscurities and ambiguities of the Ante-Nicenes regarding the Spirit."[36] Barth reiterates here that his presentation of the Spirit as the sole source of communion not only between the Father and the Son from eternity but also between man and God in revelation is intended to be a clear answer to the ambiguities of either an overly-philosophical, overly-institutional or overly-personal understanding of the Holy Spirit.

In order to avoid such confusion, Barth underscores again and again that it is not an *analogia entis* but an *analogia fidei* in the form of a trinitarian analogy which stands at the nucleus of his pneumatology. As the Spirit creates eternal community between the Father and the Son, He also creates temporal community between God and man. Barth rests the trinitarian aspects of pneumatology on the insight that God contains in Himself the possibility of an entrance into human experience precisely because He is Spirit who, prior and subsequent to any external self-revelation, perpetually creates community within His own being; the outward action of God in history actually enacts in the Christian the reality of communion with God which existed for all men from eternity in the Holy Spirit. In the act of faith, the Christian experiences through the power of the Holy Spirit that the communion which eternally exists between Father and Son becomes a communion for him. In historical revelation the Spirit lends a new potentiality to man by initiating him into the prepared communion between God and man which existed antecedently in the Spirit's own eternal communion with the Father and the Son. "Everything seems to us to depend on the thought of the complete consubstantial communion between Father and Son as the essence of the Spirit, originally answering to the communion between God as the Father and man as His child, the creation of which is the work of the Holy Spirit in revelation."[37]

Barth refuses to bracket the reality of God's self-revelation; one cannot say that something is true of God only in revelation, as if behind revelation itself there somehow stood another God; the reality of God which meets man in history is nothing less than His immanent reality from all eternity. The Spirit who unites man to God in space and time is no other than the Spirit who unites God in Himself, and who for this reason is able from eternity to bring man into such union. It is precisely through God the Spirit that man is already potentially present before, related to and in communion with the Father and the Son before Christian experience takes place. It now becomes evident that there is more than one level of meaning implied when Barth describes the Spirit as the Lord of man's readiness for, encounter with and participation in the mutual love of the Father and the Son. For Barth the very ground of man's relationship with God, as subjectively experienced "from below" in ecclesial life, is the personal mode of intradivine relationship, whom the Scriptures name *to pneuma hagion*. The Holy Spirit is therefore *Spiritus Dei et noster*, since He is both the third mode of God's one essence, which unifies the other two modes in love, and He is also the outreaching power of divine love which can become immanent in man and cause an interpenetration of God and man to take place in time.

To say that God is Spirit is to say that God is love and that love is God, for the Spirit is the mode of God's existence which creates the possibility that the real union in love between Father and Son becomes an analogous union between God and man. "God is thus—and to that extent He is God the Holy Spirit—antecedently in Himself the act of communion, of impartation, He is love, gift. For that reason and in that way and on that basis He is so in His revelation. Not *vice versa*! We know Him in that way in His revelation. But He is not so, because He is so in His revelation; but because He is so antecedently in Himself, He is so also in His revelation."[38] Thus, the doctrine of the Trinity, and especially the interior and exterior role of the Holy Spirit, serves as Barth's main hermeneutical principle for interpreting revelation in the *Church Dogmatics*. As mysterious to man and as unfathomable as God remains, revelation forces the Christian to envision Him as the one who is not only open to the Other, the Son, but who actually seeks communion through this Other with all others. It is therefore self-giving love which is the highest law in God, because from all eternity the Father has ceaselessly chosen to spurn loneliness in Himself by sharing His very existence with the Son and the Spirit: "By being the Father who brings forth the Son, God already negates in Himself, from all eternity, in His utter simplicity, existence in loneliness, self-sufficiency, self-dependence. Also and precisely in Himself from all eternity, in His utter simplicity, God is directed towards the Other, refuses to be without the Other, will only possess Himself by possessing Himself along with the Other, in fact in the Other. He is the Father of the Son in such a way, that with the Son He brings forth the Spirit, Love, and thus is in Himself the Spirit, Love."[39]

The fundamental premise of Barth's pneumatology, as it unfolds in the *Church Dogmatics* (I/1), is that the Spirit as Lord leads man out of isolation and separation from God into a relationship with and presence before Him. The Spirit is capable of introducing man into the mutual love of the Father for the Son because He is that mutual Love itself. Barth thus demarcates pneumatology from anthropology by insisting that the Christian's partnership with God through faith becomes an event when the Spirit initiates him into a life which transcends his own experience. Through the Holy Spirit God actually meets man from within: "Only that Spirit (in distinction to all created spirits) is the Holy Spirit, who is, remains and always becomes transcendent over man, by being immanent in him."[40] Only a divine Subject is at work in a genuine pneumatology; only a transcendent Spirit, who, as the reciprocal love of the Father and the Son, can give Himself over to man's intimate possession without losing Himself. Barth thus links the Spirit, the Trinity and Christian experience so closely together that the very life of faith is comprehended from the start as the goal towards which the triune God is oriented in His effort to bestow Himself generously on all others. God, insofar as He realizes this goal, both within and beyond God's community, is the Holy Spirit. While fully transcendent, the Spirit is restless until the immanent community of the Trinity which He perfects becomes through His own self-impartation immanent in the believer. When the Revealer so speaks His Word of revelation that it is spiritually powerful in man, the Spirit's function as initiator of divine and human communion is complete. These are the conclusions of Barth's explicitly trinitarian pneumatology.

CHAPTER IV

THE SPIRIT, JESUS CHRIST AND ELECTION

The focus of Barth's pneumatology shifts in the *Church Dogmatics* (I/2) to the Spirit's relationship to the eternal Word of God, to the there and then existence of the Word made flesh in Jesus Christ, and to the here and now life of the believer in Christ. This change of focus, however, does not substantially alter Barth's central insight that the Holy Spirit is God Himself reaching the goal of His self-revelation in man. Just as his previous reflections pivoted on a "trinitarian analogy" between the Spirit's role in the inner life of God and in Christian experience, his subsequent thought pivots on a parallel "christological" or "incarnational" analogy between the Spirit's activity in Jesus Christ and in the believer: as the Spirit was and is for Jesus Christ the power of God completely uniting His human nature to the Word, so He is for man. The Spirit's temporal mission is that of continually unifying in individual men what is already unified in Jesus Christ: divine and human nature. The Spirit carries out this unique role not only for but also in the Christian, by conjoining him to the risen Son of God. This union takes place when man hears, believes in and witnesses to the gracious self-revelation of God in Jesus Christ through a life of faith.

Moreover, as the Scriptures attest, the Spirit joins man to Christ in the particular community of the Church where the message concerning man's reconciliation with God is heard, believed and proclaimed.[1] Accordingly, the "incarnational" analogy at the root of Barth's pneumatology rests on the fact that in faith and in the Church the Spirit continually actualizes in man what was already an actuality both in the historical existence and eternal election of Jesus Christ. The Holy Spirit creates in the Church a community whose existence in fact corresponds to the divine election of all men in Jesus Christ. The ecclesial community is thus introduced by the Holy Spirit into nothing less than the eternal obedience of God's Word. Being related by the Holy Spirit to the election of the Word means personally being called to knowledge of and obedience to Jesus Christ in the Church. Only the Spirit can create a correspondence between Jesus and the believer since He is the very power of Jesus Christ Himself; the Holy Spirit, God's Revealedness for and in man, is the Spirit of Jesus Christ who is in turn the Revelation of the self-revealing Father's will for man. The Spirit's function in the world is to guarantee access to Jesus Christ, the historical manifestation of mankind's eternal election by the Father's Son. Thus, the Spirit is primarily the Spirit of the elected Son, His power to reach human persons in history so that they can hear, believe in and witness to the Father's eternal compassion in the community of the Church.

"In the Spirit" is for Barth the subjective correlate to "in Christ." Being in the Holy Spirit is consciously sharing in the being of Christ. The Christian's relationship to Jesus Christ is facilitated by the Holy Spirit, God present to man and accompanying him in saying "Yes!" to the Word. The Spirit secures what man cannot secure for himself, a personal participation in God's self-revelation. "The act of the Holy Spirit in revelation is the *Yes* to God's Word, spoken through God Himself *on our behalf*, yet not only *to us* but *in us*. This yes is the mystery of *faith*, the mystery of the *knowledge* of the Word of God, but also the mystery of willing *obedience*, well-pleasing to God. All of it exists for man 'in the Holy Spirit,' to wit, faith, knowledge, obedience."[2] Consequently, whatever Barth asserts in his christology about the unique relationship of the Word of God to the man Jesus, he also asserts in his pneumatology about the analogous relationship of the Word of God to the Christian.

It is decidedly an incarnational, not a philosophical analogy which stands behind the close correlation of Barth's pneumatology and christology. Thus, before a detailed exposition of this correlation under the headings of faith, Church and election is undertaken, Barth's use of the incarnational analogy must be examined more closely; it offers the pattern which will later serve to illustrate his treatment of the Christian's hearing, believing and witnessing in the Church. The origin of the incarnational analogy can be found at the end of the christological section in the *Church Dogmatics* (I/2), where the miracle of Christmas is understood as the work of the Holy Spirit. By defending the Church's teaching on *conceptus de Spiritu Sancto*, Barth reaffirms not only the Spirit's prior and unequaled role in uniting the Word of God to the human nature of Jesus, but also the Spirit's subsequent and parallel function of uniting human nature itself to the Word of God through the faith of believers.

On the grounds of his understanding of the incarnation, Barth can affirm that the very union between God and man is the Holy Spirit. This is true primarily of Jesus Christ, but also of the believer. "It is this freedom of the Holy Spirit in the incarnation of the Word of God, in the assumption of human nature by the Son of God, in which we have to recognize the real ground of the freedom of the children of God . . . The very possibility of human nature's being adopted into unity with the Son of God is the Holy Spirit. Here, then, at this frontal point in revelation the Word of God is not without the Holy Spirit of God. And here already there is the togetherness of the Spirit and the Word. Through the Spirit flesh, human nature, is assumed into unity with the Son of God."[3] Just as the Spirit is the only possibility, the only real ground of the Word's becoming man in Jesus of Nazareth, the Spirit is alone responsible for the Word's union with the believer in and through faith. The Holy Spirit, the same divine power at work in the incarnation of the Word of God, is at work in the believing Christian. This insight forms the base of the incarnational analogy underlying all that Barth will aver about the miracle by which the Spirit of the Son truly becomes the Spirit of man.

Essential to Barth's understanding of Christian existence in the Spirit in his repeated insistence that solely the incarnation offers a paradigm of Christian faith; in both cases something foreign to God can exist in communion, even in union with God: "What is ascribed to the Holy Spirit in the birth of Christ, is the assumption of human-ness in the Virgin Mary into unity with God in the Logos mode of existence. It is the work of the Holy Spirit in the birth of Christ that this is possible, that this other thing, this human-ness, this flesh exists for God, for communion, in fact for unity with God, that flesh can be the Word by the Word becoming flesh. This work of the Spirit is *prototypical* of the work of the Spirit in the becoming of the children of God; thus in fact we *become*, only not directly but indirectly, *per adoptionem*, in faith in Christ, what we are not by nature, namely children of God."[4] The incarnation is therefore the prototype of faith; man becomes through faith what Jesus is by nature: Son of God. The Holy Spirit brings God and man into communion, just as He binds the Father and the Son, and the Word of God and the human flesh of Jesus into one. Barth thus views faith, life in the Church and the vocation of the Christian as works of the Holy Spirit worthy to be ranked with the incarnation itself. The Spirit takes men as they are and allows their humanity to experience union with the Word of God in a way comparable to the birth of salvation.

The Holy Spirit offers man the gift of relationship to God. Even more, He renders man the recipient of this gift, in that He brings him to the point where he can hear the Word and be transformed by what he has heard. Through the Holy Spirit the Father makes His Son's definitive claim on man existentially effective; thus Barth elaborates here on the central tenets he had developed in his trinitarian pneumatology. The fulfillment of the Father's self-revelation is attained precisely because of the christological foundation of pneumatology. The Spirit of the triune God makes real in man what was and still is real in Jesus Christ. Men become partakers by grace— which for Barth is always man's reception of the Spirit's self-gift—in the divine sonship which is proper to Jesus Christ by nature. Barth first describes this participation as faith, which is nothing less than a renewal of revelation in man; through faith the triumph of free grace rooted in the incarnation becomes a reality for the believer. The Holy Spirit integrates the Christian into Christ, so that he can personally hear and receive the revelation of the Father, and can freely know and obey the God desirous of communion with him through His Word. This correspondence between the incarnation of the Word and the faith of the believer is the guiding principle of Barth's pneumatology as it relates to christology; this development does not at all contradict the main thrust of Barth's trinitarian pneumatology, but reasserts it. The Holy Spirit is the self-impartation of Father and Son to the believer: "Through the Holy Spirit and only through the Holy Spirit can man be there for God, be free for God's work on him, believe, be a recipient of His revelation, the object of divine reconciliation."[5] Barth's pneumatology is, as the necessary complement of his christology, concerned with the very foundation of Christian existence.

1. Faith: God's Ontic Revelation Assuming Noetic Form

After assuring that the christological dimensions of his pneumatology are solidly built on the incarnation itself, Barth proceeds to delineate the implications of such a pneumatology for Christian existence. He does this in a lengthy section of the *Church Dogmatics* entitled "The Outpouring of the Holy Spirit" which closely parallels the key christological section which precedes it: as Jesus Christ is the objective, so the Holy Spirit is the subjective reality and possibility of revelation. If God says yes to man in Jesus Christ, man can say yes to God in the Holy Spirit. If God is free for man in Jesus Christ, man is free for God in the Holy Spirit. God's revelation creates a human freedom for Himself; human existence takes on a capacity foreign to itself. This new freedom and capacity is the gift of God's Holy Spirit, His Revealedness for and in man. What historically occurred at the incarnation is reproduced in the faith experience of the Christian. There exists through grace an actual correspondence on man's side to the divine act of reconciliation in Jesus Christ. The Scripture recounts the event by which man becomes free for God in the story of the outpouring of the Holy Spirit at Pentecost, not in a treatise on the innate freedom of man. Barth insists that the theologian must first consider the sheer reality of faith which the Christian receives as unexpected gift before he can attempt to speculate about the conditions of possibility which form the basis of this faith. The central fact of the New Testament witness is that God the Holy Spirit converts men into recipients of the divine self-revelation; at the reception of the Holy Spirit man does hear the Word of God, and the power of the Word does become effective in him.

If the theologian begins by asking how it is at all possible that man can be free to hear God's Word, instead of discovering how it is that man is actually free to do so, the invariable danger exists that theology will lay down the conditions under which the way from God to man or from man to God is traversable. Barth is persistent in declaring that the way is already traversable through the outpouring of the Holy Spirit. First this reality must be examined, and only then can one find its cause to lie solely in a possibility rooted in God's own freedom. God can create a freedom in man which corresponds to His own fredom for him; this freedom of God is the Holy Spirit. The power of God able to establish a state of revealedness in man, to bring man to the point where he can hear God's Word, receive it and live it is God the Holy Spirit, the subjective reality and possibility of man's being related to God.[6] It follows that the Epistles of the New Testament are equally as important as the Gospels; the subjective is as significant as the objective account of revelation. To be able interiorly to appropriate Jesus Christ, the exterior reality of revelation, is due to nothing less than God's own freedom operative in human persons. This can only happen as the result of the presence of the Holy Spirit in the men who do believe and live the truth. The Holy Spirit reveals Himself as the subjective reality and possibility of revelation in Christians by directing them towards and integrating them into the objective revelation in Jesus Christ.[7] Once the Holy Spirit is poured out, God's Revealedness exists both invisibly in the inward rebirth of individual Christians and visibly in the tangible human signs, words and actions of the Church.

Revelation's assumption of temporal form is thus the work of the Holy Spirit in two primary ways: through faith and through the Church. The

Spirit's temporal activity through these two channels enables what is eternally true of the Father and the Son to become the Christian's personal truth. This work of the Holy Spirit takes place in the individual believer through the witnessing community: "We have only to accept the witness about Jesus Christ, and we have then only to look to Jesus Christ—and it is indeed the work of the Holy Spirit, it is indeed the nature of true faith and of the true Church that this happens—to see the man to whom God is knowable, to see and understand ourselves as those to whom God is knowable. And then we can go on to speak in truth of man in his relationship to God, and there can and will actually be a Christian anthropology and ecclesiology."[8] Only the reality of the Holy Spirit accounts for the unexpected relationship to the self-revealing God in which believers find themselves both individually and corporately. Christians united in community are in possession of new ability not only to be addressees of God's objective self-revelation, but also its real recipients. Christians hear God's Word and confess that they know it, that they in fact personally apprehend it. This realization is the germ of Barth's anthropology and ecclesiology.

The obvious, yet mysterious, reality of the conscious faith of the Christian induces Barth to investigate the various observable aspects of this faith before he can adequately explain their possibility. The first of these concrete aspects is that the individual Christian is in fact capable of acting publicly as a man who has heard the Word of God addressed to him and accepted that Word with the trust of a child. The believer discovers that he both is and acts in a way which his own powers could not account for. He has become the recipient of a new capacity. This central fact of Christian existence constitutes for Barth the subjective reality of revelation, the work of the Holy Spirit, God present in man creating in him the freedom to become obedient to the Father through faith. When a man believes, God receives a new son through the power of the Holy Spirit who alone makes it possible first that a man is a child of God and thus that he can subsequently become so: "The concept of being children of God declares materially that when the Scripture speaks of the Holy Spirit as the force in revelation, it is a matter of a *being* of that man to whom such freedom, such ability belongs. Such men are what they *are* able for. They are able for what they *are*. Thus and therefore they are real recipients of revelation, they can have faith. Once again, how does *homo peccator* become *capax verbi divini*? . . . He does not first *become* so, in order to be so, but he *is* so, and in that way, because of his being, he becomes so. He is God's child. As such he is free, able to have faith. And he is God's child by receiving the Holy Spirit."[9] The Holy Spirit is God effecting the being-in-faith of the Christian by assuring that he is free to become such; He is God being revealed to and in men by allowing divine revelation to assume a temporal form in the new freedom of the Christian.

In light of the historical perspective which serves as the backdrop of this entire study, it is important to note that Barth's understanding of the Holy Spirit as the sole possibility of man's hearing and believing the Word of God represents his most radical attempt to counteract Schleiermacher's immanentist theology, in which faith is viewed as a natural component of man's consciousness. Barth cannot but agree with Schleiermacher that faith is essentially a relationship of a son to his Father and that this relationship is one of complete dependence. But Barth understands the source of the relationship called faith to lie in the power of God's Spirit and not in the dynamism of man's inner life. In the end Barth judges Schleiermacher to be concerned not with the Spirit-led man of the New Testament, but with the self-sufficient man of the Enlightenment. Neo-Protestantism accepts the pneumatological determination of faith as it is described in the Scriptures only "conditionally, that is to say, upon the parallel presupposition that there is another and primary witness in respect of a revelation in man *per se*, a witness which is self-given, and in light of which the Scriptures have now to be understood."[10] Faith is surely a relation to the Father which the Christian experiences as a real possession, but for Barth this relation is to be attributed to the Holy Spirit alone, as Augustine maintained against Pelagius and Luther against Catholic Scholasticism.

Faith is not only a relationship to God; it is also a knowledge of God in the fullest sense. If Barth's decidedly pneumatic understanding of faith as a relationship to God is his answer to the subjective tendencies of Schleiermacher, his stress on the pneumatic ground of man's knowledge about God is his answer to the natural theology of Catholicism. In order to counter the metaphysical arguments of the natural theologians, Barth develops within his pneumatology a unique metaphysics by which the believer is given a share in God's ontic truth through the noetic activity of the Holy Spirit. In this way, Barth makes it clear that man can only know God through God's own Noetic. Just as God the Father knows Himself in His Son through the Spirit, the man of faith can come to know his Father in Jesus Christ through the Spirit. Only a metaphysics rooted in divine reality guarantees that man can mediately know God as God immediately knows Himself. Faith's pneumatological access to knowledge of God is Barth's reply to Catholicism's stress on man's natural ability to comprehend the divine. The Holy Spirit alone makes the Father and the Son knowable to man, just as He makes the Father knowable to the Son and the Son to the Father. Through the Spirit the Father communicates to man the ontic knowledge which He has of Himself in His Son. This is the central tenet of biblical revelation. The triune God crosses an enormous chasm between Himself and man when He allows the Christian, by nature an enemy of grace and a fugitive from truth, to be led from the realm of lies to Himself. This movement from false towards true knowledge of God is not the product of any innate human potentiality. It is the work of God's Spirit, God's own Noetic, who brings man to a new metaphysical state by introducing him to Jesus Christ, God's ontic self-revelation.

Thus Barth speaks of God's readiness for man which alone can explain man's readiness for God. The former is Jesus Christ; the latter is the Holy Spirit. For in Jesus Christ man's lie is overcome, and God's readiness for man becomes man's readiness for God. When the Logos becomes ready and open for humanity in Jesus of Nazareth, man becomes ready and open for God because God meets him on his side; the readiness of man included in the readiness of God is Jesus Christ.'[11] According to the guiding principle of Barthian pneumatology, however, it is only the Holy Spirit who allows what is ontic in Jesus Christ to become noetic in man. To achieve this end, God first makes His own readiness for man an object capable of being known by man the subject. This is the objective act of grace in Jesus Christ, the person in whom God makes Himself present in history. Secondly, God makes Jesus Christ, who is His own self-knowledge, accessible to man through His Holy Spirit, His own knowability. The Father establishes what Barth calls a two-way communication between Himself and the human person. This divine communication is necessarily bipolar since otherwise it would not preserve the distinctness of God and man while it joins them to each other through the medium of true knowledge: "The reality of our knowledge of God stands or falls with the fact that in His revelation God is present to man in a medium. He is therefore objectively present in a double sense. In His Word He comes as an object before man the subject. And by the Holy Spirit He makes the human subject accessible to Himself, capable of considering and conceiving Himself as object. The real knowledge of God is concerned with God in His *relationship* to man, but also in His *distinction* from him."[12] The Spirit lets God's Ontic assume noetic form through faith without, however, blurring the duality between the divine Revealer and the human believer.

Though the duality between God's truth in itself and man's apprehension of it always remains, faith "already" overcomes this duality, since faith, as the gift of the divine Spirit is eschatological. However, faith must itself believe that the Holy Spirit guarantees the Christian the full truth despite the eschatological tension between the "already" and the "not yet": "In the Holy Spirit this 'already' is valid; for the Holy Spirit is the temporal presence of the Jesus Christ who intercedes for us eternally in full truth. Therefore for us life in the Spirit means 'already' even in the midst of the 'not yet,' to stand in the full truth of what, considered from our 'not yet' is pure future, but on the strength of this 'already' pure present, in which therefore we can already live here and now expecting the annulment of the duality . . . This is man's truth believed by faith. And it is the work of the Holy Spirit that the eternal presence of the reconciliation in Jesus Christ has in us this temporal form, the form of faith, which believes this truth."[13] In accord with his theological understanding of metaphysics, Barth describes the being-in-faith, the work of the Holy Spirit in the Christian, as a temporal expression of the eternally present event of God's reconciliation with man in Jesus Christ. Faith, man's noetic participation in the ontic nature of this event, is the concrete realization of the Holy Spirit's mission to make the "not yet" manifest "already". Thus, Barth's pneumatic understanding of metaphysics is rooted in the eschatological dimension of the work of the Holy Spirit.

Faith is essentially promise. This means that the temporal form of the Spirit's presence to and in men can only be fully understood from God's side. Faith is a gift which man can possess, but which he possesses only as promise. Christian faith entails futurity, since even Spirit-given knowledge about God is necessarily shrouded in hope. The action of the Holy Spirit in man does not result in man's possession of God, but in man's guaranteed present and future portion in the eternal being-alive which always exists fully only on God's side. Faith, the new way of being through the work of the Holy Spirit, is man's anticipatory share in the fulfillment promised to him by God. The Holy Spirit is God presently granting man an ontic part in His own being and making him cognizant of this gift in the noetic sign of faith. By insisting that ontology, pneumatology and eschatology are intrinsically related in the New Testament, Barth intends to preclude any confusion of the revealed truths of pneumatology with the abstract speculations of anthropology: "Everything that is to be said about the man who receives the Holy Spirit, is driven and filled by the Spirit, is in the New Testament sense an *eschatological* pronouncement. Eschatological means not 'with an improper or unreal intent,' but related to the *eschaton*, i.e., to what from our point of view is still in arrears for our experience and thought, to the eternal reality of the divine fulfillment and completion . . . The New Testament speaks *eschatologically*, when it speaks of man's being called, reconciled, justified, sanctified, redeemed. That is the precise way in which it speaks *really* and *properly*."[14] Christian faith is the future of man, already assured in Jesus Christ, reaching the Christian in the temporal form of a transforming experience through the power of the Holy Spirit.

By subsuming faith itself under the aegis of revelation, Barth attempts to repudiate the claim of natural theology that man can come to faith on his own. Faith itself belongs to the content of revelation. It is a miracle which is no less gratuitous than the miracle of the incarnation and no more comprehensible than the eternal intradivine communion of the triune God. Faith reveals the miracle that through His Spirit God does not exclude man from union with Himself.[15] Far from destroying the independence of anthropology, Barth's understanding of the miracle of faith aims at preserving man's humanity while it opens up a new ontological possibility for him. In no way does Barth intend to transform the human person into "a sort of Holy Spirit."[16] Man remains man, but he becomes a witness to revelation—a miracle of free grace—through the power of the Spirit who comes to him. Through faith man's freedom becomes Spirit-encountered freedom since the Holy Spirit introduces man's being to a new possibility. But since man as such is always called to this new possibility, and possesses it objectively in Jesus Christ, the Spirit grants the Christian a rebirth which makes him a conscious recipient of the sonship and freedom guaranteed for him in Christ. The Spirit does not create but recreates man through faith; He does not establish but reorients his freedom. The Holy Spirit makes the ontic *assumptio hominis* of the Word a reality in the Christian by uniting him noetically to Jesus Christ. "This can be shown very clearly in *John* 3: birth of the Spirit is a *new* birth, a *re*birth, and the man to be born of the Spirit to be a child of God is already there, by the fact that this happens to him. He is born of the Spirit to be a child of God. But clearly it cannot be said that the child of God which this man becomes is created or begotten by the Spirit. The child of God is what he is in communion with Jesus Christ, the eternal Son of God."[17] Through faith the Holy Spirit achieves the creation of a new being who is now in conscious communion with Jesus Christ, but this new being is the very man, whose freedom for such communion is already assured ontically by the eternal Son of God. It is the Holy Spirit who renders man subjectively free to hear and to say yes to God's self-offer to him in the Word made flesh. In the Christian's experience of faith the Spirit makes noetic the ontic freedom man always enjoys in Jesus Christ.

2. Church and Sacrament: Divine Sign-giving in Process

Faith, the temporal sign of the work of the Holy Spirit among men, is only the secondary manifestation of the Spirit's activity. The primary sign is decidedly the visible community of believers, the Church.[18] By the action of the Spirit the subjective reality of revelation, which is the experienced faith of the individual believer, springs from something outside the believer himself. This fact leads Barth to the more central insight that the subjective reality of revelation is rooted in objective signs. Barth then develops all the many aspects of his ecclesiology under the heading of sign-giving. The faith of the individual is indeed a sign of revelation, but the Church is its prior visible sign to which every individual believer is bound. Furthermore, Barth views the "sign-worlds" which exist in the Church as immanent expressions of the central truth that the transcendent Word once entered the world of man's experience. After the resurrection of Christ, however, the Church remains in the world, and consists of symbols for the benefit of men who continue to require sign-giving from God. "The New Testament sign-world belongs to that revelation just as strictly as the earlier sign-world of the Old Testament. The Church, the body of Christ, and therefore Christ Himself exists and exists only where there are the signs of the New Testament, that is, preaching, Baptism and the Lord's Supper, in accordance with their institution fulfilled at the inauguration of the apostolate."[19] Barth's pneumatology thus necessarily includes a thorough discussion of these signs in accord with his understanding of the incarnational analogy. Since the Spirit continues to work among men as He had done in the Word made flesh, the sign-giving so essential to the incarnation is the ground of the sign-world of the Church.

The Spirit keeps the transcendent mystery of the Word available to the world only through the immanent sign-giving of the Church; in this way, the Church's sign-world becomes the channel by which the divine sign-giving in Jesus Christ is present to men. Thus any pneumatology based on a kind of unmediated spiritism or anti-ecclesial Pentecostalism which repudiates the need for preaching and for sacrament is suspect for Barth, since such thought systems fail to include the divine sign-giving essential to a genuine Spirit theology: "It forgets that the Holy Spirit is not only the Spirit of the Father but also the Spirit of the Word. It forgets that the Holy Spirit certainly comes to us, not by the independent road which bypasses the Word and its testimonies, but by the Word and its testimonies. We remember that the Word of God is not bound to the sign-giving. But we also remember that we are bound to the sign-giving. We cannot know anything or say anything about any other Word or Spirit except that which comes to us through the divine sign-giving."[20]

Barth, branded as the "Word of God theologian", proceeds to place the sacraments before preaching since, as visible signs, the former make it clearer than the preached Word that divine sign-giving rests not on an idea, but on an event; the origin and model of God's sign-giving is the *et incarnatus est*. This aspect of Barth's thought is often overlooked, but the centrality of the Word become flesh induces his pneumatology to stress the Spirit's role of making the unique event of the incarnation a continuing reality in the sacramental life of the believing community.[21] God has not only entered the world of man, but has also willingly made Himself an object of man's knowledge and experience through the mediation of human actions and language. Barth's initial treatment of sacramental theology in the section entitled "The Outpouring of the Holy Spirit" in *Church Dogmatics* (I/2) clearly links the revelatory character of the sacraments directly to the action of the Holy Spirit. He enables repeated human actions to correspond to the uniqueness of God's action for man in Jesus Christ. The interconnection between Spirit and human action is thus firmly established by Barth, even though later in *Church Dogmatics* (IV/4) he will make a distinction between the external action of the Church and the invisible action of the Holy Spirit with regard to the sacraments. With time Barth comes to appraise his earlier treatment of the sacraments as exaggerated, in that a clear demarcation is not made between the primacy of the Spirit's activity in the work of sanctification and the secondary, merely corroborating function of the Church's external signs. In contrast, this original presentation of the sacraments is more integrative, and serves the purpose of pointing out how essential pneumatology was and would remain in Barth's specifically ecclesiological thought.

Barth stresses the objective presence of grace in the sacramental signs themselves. The Holy Spirit causes the Word of God to reach men interiorly through the external signs of Baptism and the Lord's Supper; they allow the transcendent Word to become immanent in the lives of men. The sacramental signs are concrete, historical events which objectively signify the inner action of the Holy Spirit who alone makes them means of grace: "It is in this living and concrete way, as a creative event in history, that revelation comes to us and seeks to be received and adopted. It comes in exactly the same way as in a sacrament, stressing the objective quality of grace which it possesses. It is no mere matter of the water in Baptism or of the bread and wine in the Lord's Supper. For we have also to remember *John* 6:63: 'It is the Spirit that quickeneth; the flesh profiteth nothing.' "[22] The sacraments, as objective yet personal contacts with the Word, belong to the subjective reality of revelation, and are understood in the New Testament as the work of the Holy Spirit, who allows the Christian community to be receptive to and to accept revelation's recreative power.

Barth comes to the same conclusion with respect to the Church and the sacraments as he did with respect to faith in and knowledge of God: their reality includes their possibility. Like Christian faith, ecclesial community and sacramental signs are not within the scope of man's possibility. Rather, they rest on the gracious decision of God to enter the realm of the human and to assume human reality. God, insofar as He enters the world of man, creates a human community, endows it with a sign-world, and thus fashions new paths to communion with the Word, is the Holy Spirit. The Spirit is not only the ground of the Christian's participation in subjective revelation, but also its only possibility: "The work of the Holy Spirit means that there is an adequate basis for our hearing of the Word, since He brings us nothing but the Word for our hearing. It means that there is an adequate basis for our faith in Christ and our communion with Him because He is no other Spirit than the Spirit of Jesus Christ. He is therefore the subjective possibility of revelation, because He is the process by which its objective reality is made subjective, namely, the life of the *body of Christ*, the operation of the prophetic and apostolic testimony, the hearing of *preaching*, the seeing of that to which the *sacraments* point."[23] The Holy Spirit, who alone was responsible for the *assumptio carnis* of the Word of God, is likewise solely responsible for the Word's ability to assume form in human knowledge and symbols.

Having established that revelation, in its objective and subjective forms, is always a divine possibility, Barth then juxtaposes revelation to any native ability of man to be religious. Concretely, this means that biblical revelation serves as the divine abolition of all human religion, even of Christianity itself, if the latter departs from the objective content of revelation and asserts a righteousness of its own. If any form of religion, including Christianity, is to become true religion, it can only do so with the aid of grace and not independently. Barth thus includes in his pneumatology the entire phenomenon of human religion in which the Spirit of God is actively present both as Judge and Reconciler of man's own efforts. As Barth understands it, all religion is concerned with the core of pneumatology, that is, with man's encounter and communion with God. Since God enters the history of human religion through the incarnation and the outpouring of the Holy Spirit, He is both the determiner of this history and at the same time the sole initiator of the many religious manifestations which men consider divine. Thus, God's presence in the world of religion is a self-revealing presence and as such a sovereign action which puts all human religion into question. For this reason, Barth understands God's revelation not as the fulfillment of human religion, but as its greatest challenge. God's self-disclosure is Jesus Christ, who makes the absolute claim on man that He is the only way by which the true God can be reached. Religion must therefore find its real identity in the person Jesus Christ, through whom God Himself has definitively intervened in the world of man's religious experience. The christological doctrine of the *assumptio carnis* annuls the very validity of human religion as well as its independence.

Barth's position is based on his conviction that only the incarnation makes it possible that there can exist a religion founded on the gracious intervention of the God who has made Himself known as He truly is. God does attain this goal in the world of human religion precisely through the outpouring of the Holy Spirit and through the existence of the Christian community in which the Spirit allows the grace of the incarnation to be embodied in a true religion: "That there is a true religion is an event in the act of grace of God in Jesus Christ. To be more precise, it is an event in the outpouring of the Holy Spirit. To be even more precise, it is an event in the existence of the Church and the children of God . . . It is of grace that the Church and the children of God live by His grace. It is of grace that they attain the status of the bearers of true religion."[24] Clearly, Barth views the very existence of Christian religion as a sacramental event which comes about by the Spirit's work of lending the grace of God in Jesus Christ a concrete reality among men. The Spirit's role in the domain of human religion perfectly parallels His function in faith, in the Church and in the sacraments. He guarantees that revelation can continue to speak to man, so that he can hear it amid the tumult of his manifold efforts to find the true God through religion. The Spirit alone permits God's true self-disclosure continually to reach man's deafened ears. In this way its reconciling message can both expose and judge man's inadequacy, while it assuages him and grants him the unexpected possibility of attaining genuine communion with the God whom his human efforts at holiness could never have discovered. Thus, the sanctification of man which becomes event in Christian religion was indeed accomplished once and for all in Jesus Christ, but it must be continually acknowledged and reaffirmed as such in the course of history through human obedience. The Holy Spirit makes this obedience a human reality and therefore a real human possibility through the sacramental sign-world of Christian religion. "The Christian religion is the sacramental area created by the Holy Spirit, in which the God whose Word became flesh continues to speak through the sign of His revelation. And it is also the existence of men created by the same Holy Spirit, who hear this God continually speaking in His revelation . . . and that is the sanctification of the Christian religion."[25] In Barth's view, it is the function of pneumatology to explain how the reality of the incarnation becomes a source of holiness in the idolatrous man who stubbornly clings to his own conception of the divine.

It is imperative at this point to anticipate the conclusion of this chapter on the christological aspects of Barth's pneumatology by introducing the concept of divine election. For, free grace, the gift of the Holy Spirit, is anchored in the free election of all men in Jesus Christ. Only this election is the source and prototype of the temporal and eschatological work of the Holy Spirit. Thus, the ultimate justification of Barth's assertion that Christian faith is the true religion is his prior tenet that the free election of man by God, and not the inborn spirituality of man himself, accounts for the existence of genuine religion. The Holy Spirit is the source of true religion because He alone realizes in time the free election of Jesus Christ from eternity. All genuine spirituality is a gift of the Holy Spirit: "If the alleged spiritual element is genuinely of the Spirit, then it is only by the Holy Spirit who breathes as He will, it is only because of a free and merciful turning on the part of God, it is only by election and not by any immanent aptitude for genuine spirituality."[26] Clearly, the two central realities dominating the christological aspects of Barth's pneumatology, free grace and *electio continua*, are not products of any human potency, but are pure gift. Both are rooted in the eternal action of the Word of God who, in the one person Jesus Christ, chose all humanity as the object of His covenant of compassion. The Holy Spirit affirms this act from eternity, and His particular function in salvation history is to make the covenant of grace effectual among men. Through the outpouring of His power and authority, the Holy Spirit can transform men in the course of time into actual recipients of the divine election.[27] Barth's radical No to mysticism and to all forms of self-justification is grounded precisely in his pneumatological understanding of every relationship of man to God. The unrelenting vigor of Barth's rejection of all immanentist notions of religion has as its source the conviction that the Holy Spirit is the sole bearer of the free grace of election. In this capacity, the Holy Spirit acts to insure that the historical revelation of this election in the person and work of Jesus Christ is a continual revelatory event in the existence of the Christian Church.

In keeping with his preference for the Johannine Word Christology, Barth dedicates a key section of his pneumatology to a discussion of the ongoing revelatory event of Christian language itself as it is recorded in Scripture and reworded in preaching. Barth also applies the incarnational analogy to the language of the Church, since in the Bible and in Christian proclamation the Word of God assumes human words. Again, it is the Holy Spirit who alone has the power to make human language capable of receiving the Word of God and thus of transmitting God's own self-revelation to men. That human language can make the objective Word of God present to actual individuals is as much the work of the Holy Spirit as is the subjective reality and possibility of faith, community, sacraments and spirituality. In fact, since revelation itself is for Barth nothing less than the Word of God turned towards man, the linguistic record of this objective revelation grounds all the other forms of subjective revelation. For, the Holy Spirit, as God's self-attestation to the resurrection of Jesus Christ and therefore to His true identity as the incarnate Son of God, allows His own witness to this central event to be captured in the very words of the Scripture's authors. By the power of the Spirit human words become revelatory of God Himself. This insight forms the core of Barth's argument in defense of the divine inspiration of Scripture. The original Spirit-inspired witness of the biblical writers becomes an historical event for men of all time, so that they can attest to the risen Christ by the power of the same Spirit.[28]

Barth's pneumatological understanding of Scripture is rooted in the term *theopneustia* (2 *Tim*: 3:16) which means that the whole of the Bible is "of the Spirit of God." This concept is explained by Barth in accord with his teaching on the miracle of the incarnation, since divine inspiration did not involve the destruction of the authors' freedom but its full use, just as the incarnation respected Jesus' full humanity. The Spirit made their human freedom capable of being free for God's Word. The Scriptures contain in human words a genuine account of God's self-revelation. Yet they can be subject, like all language, to inevitable misunderstandings, and can likewise give offense because of the blatant inadequacy of their literary form. In treating *theopneustia*, as he had done in his treatment of the incarnation, of faith and of the Church, of religion and of sacraments, Barth rigorously defends the human element in the Scripture which the miracle of the Holy Spirit did not abrogate but respected. It was precisely the authors' human concepts which the Spirit related to and made revelatory of the Word of

God. Real men can thus speak to other men in the name of the true God: "Moreover, what we experience elsewhere of the work of the Holy Spirit on man in general and on such witnesses in particular, and our recollection of the *conceptus de Spiritu Sancto* in christology, does not allow us to suppose that we have to understand what we are told in the teaching of the *theopneustia* about the authors of the Holy Scriptures, as though they were not real *auctores* . . . That as such their action acquired this special function, was placed under the *authoritas primaria*, the lordship of God, was surrounded and controlled and impelled by the Holy Spirit, and became an attitude of obedience in virtue of its direct relationship to divine revelation— that was their *theopneustia*."[29] Once again, Barth shows the Holy Spirit to be the divine empowering of men to speak the Word. The Spirit is the only means by which men can be related to the Word, so that it comes to their lips as truth, and so that the chasm between divine infallibility and human fallibility is bridged. Through the Holy Spirit human language can become the language of God.

This leads Barth to the further realization that the Bible itself, like faith, the Church and the sacraments, is a sign of promise. The source of the promise is not the parousia but the incarnation, at which God first entered the actual history of humanity. For Barth, promise is rooted in the past. The miracle that took place in Jesus Christ is continually a source of hope for men in and through the sign of the biblical witness as well as the other signs which are constitutive of the Church.[30] The Holy Spirit makes the reality of God's unique entrance into the world of man a lively promise in the works and words of the Church. Thus Barth's concept of the Holy Spirit is thoroughly christological and for that reason alone eschatological. Where the Spirit is present, the new possibility once made available to man in Jesus Christ is embodied in human persons, signs and language. Barth has clearly distanced himself from the eschatological excesses of 1919 and thus grounds his pneumatology solidly on the incarnation itself. It is the eschatological Spirit of the incarnate Word who establishes the whole sign-world of the Church's sacraments and language. Due to the eschatological force of the incarnation, Barth describes the historical work of the Holy Spirit as that of assuring that human signs are tangible conveyors of divine promise.

It is also apparent here that Barth's ultimate answer to Schleiermacher's vague notion of the Spirit as the *Gemeingeist* of the Christian community is the christological character of his own pneumatology. For Barth, the Holy Spirit continually fashions the Church into the contours of the incarnate Word; the Bible is a sign of promise since it rests on the eschatological power of the Christ-event. Furthermore, Barth's stress on the supremacy of the Holy Spirit in the realm of man's language about God forms the germ of his later controversy with Rudolf Bultmann over the proper nature of Christian hermeneutics. Barth's hermeneutics has already been called pneumatic. Now the trinitarian and christological roots of his distinctive hermeneutics are laid bare. The Spirit is God's own power of relating Himself to man and of committing His self-revelation to human signs and language.[31] With his insistence on the concept of *theopneustia* Barth nullifies any purely philosophical hermeneutics. Pneumatology is from now on to afford him a specifically Christian tool of interpretation which corresponds to his trinitarian teaching and to his christology.

3. Calling: Eternal Divine Compassion Confessed by Man

The conclusion of the previous chapter concerning the trinitarian aspects of pneumatology in the *Church Dogmatics* described how Barth grounded the temporal activity of the third mode of God's existence on the very intradivine life of the Trinity. The communion with the Father and the Son which the Spirit realizes among men in history is consonant with the Spirit's eternal function within the Godhead as the common factor, the "communityness" between Father and Son. Now at the close of this treatment of the christological aspects of Barth's pneumatology, a similar thought process is discernible. Barth grounds the Spirit's function of creating the subjective appropriation of revelation in the Church, that is, His role as Lord of man's hearing, believing in and witnessing to Jesus Christ on the Spirit's eternal relation to the Son within the Trinity. Barth does this by allotting the Spirit an essential role in the eternal election of man by the Word of God.

In the doctrine of predestination or election, which Barth calls the summary of the whole Gospel, the Spirit's temporal activity of allowing man to respond to the Word through faith and through the Church is rooted in His immanent role of concurring spontaneously with the Word's intradivine decision to choose man and to unite Himself to him eternally. Barth thus proceeds by extending to the election the principle that there is a correspondence between God's revealed actions and God's ontic nature, a principle which can now be called a hallmark of the *Church Dogmatics*. Since the Holy Spirit plays a key part in man's faith in and acceptance of his election by the Word, the Spirit must have a corresponding part in the Word's eternal election of man. If the latter function of the Spirit were not assured, not only would man be deceived by God, but also the Spirit's role in revelation would not be grounded in His being. For, if the Holy Spirit acts in the Church to make the gracious turning of God to man in Jesus Christ an event in time, He must implicate the Christian in the Word's election of men from all eternity. Otherwise, Christians would not be from eternity what they are in time, united to the Word by the Holy Spirit. Just as Barth can claim that the election of man from eternity is an "act of divine life in the Spirit," he can also assert that the knowledge and acceptance of his election on the part of man is an eternal act of divine grace for him in the same Spirit.[32]

Barth bases his understanding of the Spirit's eternal role in the election of grace on His spontaneous approval of the primal decision of the Father and the Son before the creation of any being outside the Godhead. The triune God decided that He would be gracious towards, would unite Himself to man. This choice was made concomitantly by the Father, the Son and the Spirit, and constitutes what Barth calls the triune God's *opus internum ad extra*, or His original act of love on behalf of the men whom He would create. This awesome election of man from eternity rests on the free decision of God by which He determined that His merciful dealings with not yet extant human persons would be the primary *interna actio* of His own being. The eternal election of man, therefore, is an incomprehensibly generous act of the three divine modes of existence. Yet, Barth insists that the primary subject of the election was the Son, though certainly in company with the Father and the Spirit. The Son chose to be obedient to the Father's loving will, and elected to take upon Himself all the consequences of man's freedom. The Son did so by identifying Himself eternally with one man, Jesus of Nazareth, who was to assure that man's rejection of God would not end in perdition but in a new bond of love. The Son of God is for this reason the main subject of the divine election: He is the electing God. Jesus Christ is its main object; He is the one elected to be reconciled to God in the name of all men.

Nevertheless, that this could happen at all, that the Son of God could totally unite Himself with the rejected and elected Jesus Christ, and not destroy the unity of God within Himself in doing so, is explained by Barth precisely through a consideration of the Holy Spirit's part in the Son's election of man. In the beginning it was the choice of the Father Himself to establish a covenant with men through His Son, and it was the Son's choice to guarantee the full realization of this covenant. The Spirit too pledged to make it possible that the generous covenant of the Father and the Son would be subjectively actualized in time so that their loving will would be confirmed: "In the beginning it was the resolve of the Holy Spirit that the unity of God, of Father and Son, should not be disturbed or rent by this covenant with man, but that it should be made the more glorious, the deity of God, the divinity of His love and freedom being confirmed and demonstrated by this offering of the Father and this self-offering of the Son."[33] The Spirit's distinctive role in the covenant of grace was to insure that the Son's already accomplished election of all men in one man be known in time by the actually graced recipients of this election, the Christian community chosen in and with Jesus Christ. Realization of the Son's eternal choice of all men in Jesus Christ would be noetically impossible if it were not revealed to particular persons in the course of history by the miraculous power of the Holy Spirit.[34] In order to do so, the Holy Spirit first empowered the incarnate Son, Jesus of Nazareth, to perform His gracious act of obedience on man's behalf in such a way that it is known and appreciated by him. Because of what the Spirit accomplished in this one instance, He is in every instance the Spirit of obedience to the divine act of election. For this reason, the Holy Spirit can truly be the power behind Christian faith, man's conscious and free obedience to the identity he already possesses from eternity in and through the Son's election of Jesus Christ.[35]

The pneumatological aspect of Barth's doctrine of predestination is clearly based on the Holy Spirit's pivotal task of actualizing the Son's eternal decision to become man. The election of man would not have become an historical reality, had the Spirit not kept His pledge to respect the unity of God and yet to allow the Word to assume flesh. At the center of salvation history, the Spirit actually carried out His eternal resolution to secure the self-offering of the Son by joining Him to Jesus of Nazareth. Barth thus maintains that the execution of the eternal election was only possible by the action of the Holy Spirit, who alone can make God's graciousness an event. Jesus of Nazareth became the elected man in the fullness of time only when the Holy Spirit acted in accord with His eternal pledge to fulfill the election of the one man. What was eternally real became actual in time through the mediation of God's Spirit. Thus, the predestination of all men in Jesus Christ was always ontically real, but the historical realization of the incarnation and the subsequent entrance of individual men into the eternal mercy of God on their behalf is the work of the Holy Spirit. In the Christian that takes place which once took place in Jesus Christ: a Spirit-filled man emerges who gives witness to his brothers concerning the endless glory and goodness of God. In and through Christ, the one predestined for all, the Christian becomes a conscious participant in divine compassion, or as Barth says, "man made usable to God by the Holy Spirit."[36] Through the ongoing work of the Holy Spirit believers become what they already are in the eternal plan of God: sons not servants, elected together with Jesus Christ. Here in his teaching on predestination, Barth once again makes use of the distinction between the objective reality of man's reconciliation achieved in the mission of Jesus Christ and the subjective reality of man's incorporation into Jesus Christ achieved in the outpouring of the Holy Spirit.

The intriguing quality of Barth's unique understanding of predestination is not only that it departs from the long tradition from Augustine to Calvin but also that it does so at a particular point in Barth's development. If there is any one aspect of Barth's theology, which is more directly aimed at correcting the religious subjectivism he found in Neo-Protestantism, then it is certainly his treatment of predestination. This fact is no mere coincidence, since Barth believed that the very cause of Schleiermacher's individualism was the distorted individual view of predestination which was taught by the Protestant Churches for centuries. Such an individualistic interpretation of what for Barth was clearly God's predestination of all humanity was a factor which paved the way for Rationalism and the other forms of secular individualism so hostile to biblical faith.[37] Puzzled by this fatal development Barth asks why there were not other serious protests against this distortion of Christian faith than the occasional objections which were voiced. His answer is that the secular individualism of the previous two centuries was so permeated by "the conviction that the beginning and end of all the ways of God, and even the essence of all divine truth, are to be recognized and honored in individual human beings"[38] that it could make no really earnest objections to the aberration of double predestination. Furthermore, a strangely misguided pneumatology seemed to be the hotbed of such human autonomy.

Barth's pneumatology arises out of an attempt to correct this rationalistic and individualistic tendency in Christian theology. It is thus understandable that the corporate christological element, which he so strongly underlines by stressing the Spirit's role in affirming the universality of predestination in Jesus Christ, is geared to reintroducing objectivity and collectivity into pneumatology, an area of theology which had been reduced to the most private of Christian doctrines. Barth is thus reacting to what he calls Neo-Protestantism's tendency "to separate itself from the New Testament Church by setting over against the knowledge and life of faith in Christ an autonomous knowledge and faith deriving from the Holy Spirit."[39] Barth realizes, however, that this subjective tendency of Neo-Protestantism was itself a reaction to an earlier objectivism which had become lifeless. To stress the subjective side of election once again would have been a laudable matter in itself, if in doing so christology had not also been subjectivized to the point of non-recognition. Given Barth's desire to rectify this far-reaching subjectivism, the concrete and collective aspects which he attempts to reintroduce into the theology of election, through an objectively grounded pneumatology, can be interpreted as aiming at one goal: the restoration of classical christology to its central place in dogmatic theology. For this reason, Barth cannot consider the Christian's election to life in the Spirit apart from the objective instance of this election in the incarnation. Jesus Christ is the elector and the elected.

And from eternity! Barth feels obliged to plant the christological foundation of human existence before God deeply within the very intradivine life as a sure guarantee that the personal experience of being elected to faith is anchored in nothing less than the being of God. Barth fashions his teaching on predestination in such a way that any possibility of understanding the divine election of all men in Jesus Christ as an individual favor would be excluded from the very start. The grace of God in Jesus Christ is extended to every man and forms the core of the universalism which marks Christian proclamation. The graced existence of the Christian is good news to every man since all are objectively included in the divine election from eternity. The ontic foundation of Christian evangelism is so firmly secured in Barth's eyes that he views any individualistic interpretation of the destiny of the human person as sheer departure from the truth. Once this has been said, Barth can then admit the need for the individual's personal acceptance of his destiny. This noetic apprehension of the divine election is the task of the Holy Spirit. God's Spirit so fully committed Himself to the actualization of the eternal election of all men that His work in salvation history can never be severed from the person of Jesus Christ, the incarnate manifestation of the Son's self-gift on man's behalf. By welding pneumatology to christology, Barth removes even from the subjective appropriation of the Christ-event by the believer every trace of subjectivism. Thus, the existential experiences of Christian consciousness, which are the direct result of the Spirit's presence, are ultimately rooted in the objective election of Jesus Christ which alone lends their noetic quality ontic significance. The strict christological framework in which Barth situates his pneumatology in the *Church Dogmatics* is proof enough that he is struggling against subjectivism with as much force as he can assemble.

With the doctrine of predestination Barth firmly sets into place the two main poles around which his theology will circle, and thus unbares the objective-subjective scheme of his dogmatics. Although Barth himself is always aware of the danger that the christological and pneumatological poles could be regarded in isolation, he nevertheless treats the two separately at times. Yet Barth constantly insists that there is one revelation with two different aspects, which have to be distinguished only for the sake of theological clarity. Thus the revelation in Jesus Christ and the revelation in the Christian are one. The Holy Spirit assures this unity by pledging from eternity that all men will be included in the election of Jesus Christ: "It is not that there are, as it were, two different points: at the one the Son of God assumes humanity; and then, at quite different point, the question of our destiny is necessarily raised and answered. In the one reality of revelation He is, in His assumed humanity, the Son of God from eternity as we, for His sake, are by grace the children of God from eternity. Therefore the 'perfect' of the truth of revelation already includes the conception of its existence for us. . . . Subjective revelation is not the addition of a second revelation to objective revelation."[40] In this way, Barth incorporates the subjective experience of the believer into the objective reality of the divine election; pneumatology is included in christology; the work of the Holy Spirit, God revealed in the Christian, is one with the work of the Son, God revealed in Jesus Christ.

Reflection on the Spirit's unique function in the divine election, however, allows Barth to attribute to the Spirit's temporal mission a distinctive character. The Spirit is to translate the divine calling of all men into the believer's personal experience of being called. This notion of vocation, as the special task of the Holy Spirit, succinctly summarizes the christological aspect of Barth's pneumatology.[41] For through faith and proclamation the Holy Spirit causes men to hear of, believe in and witness to their own individual participation in the calling of all men which took place in the eternal election of Jesus Christ. The Holy Spirit executes in and for the Christian the objectively necessary expression of their election, that is, their calling to life in the Church. To be called by the Spirit is to know what has already occurred on man's behalf in Jesus Christ, and in this way to live and witness the truth. Not to be called is to consider the truth of Jesus Christ a lie; for those not called invariably accept as true what has already been declared false in the death of Jesus Christ, at which the Father made His own Son the only rejected man, and rendered the eternal rejection of all other men an impossibility. Thus, Barth consistently maintains that even the man who refuses to hear the witness to his calling is not rejected; he too belongs eternally to Jesus Christ, and is, despite his isolation from the Father, loved and called by Him. The man who believes in his calling can only know it, live it and proclaim it by the grace of the Holy Spirit: "It is only by their calling, by the twofold work of the Holy Spirit (faith and proclamation) that their election is accomplished in their life . . . Without the Holy Spirit and therefore without their calling they would necessarily be the same as others in all respects in which they are distinguished from them. Apart from their calling they, too, would be godless, and the witness of their lives could only be the false witness by which the divine election of grace is denied and blasphemed . . . And so there is none who has any reason at any time to see anything other than the expiating grace of Jesus Christ even in his calling and in the gift of the Holy Spirit."[42] So as to avoid every trace of subjectivism, Barth firmly holds that Christian vocation, the very work of the

Holy Spirit in the Church, is a result of the eternal decision which has been graciously made by the Father and the Son about human life.

The Holy Spirit, by calling individual men to knowledge of their election in Jesus Christ, accomplishes and actualizes the goal of the good news intended for all mankind. What is already *extra nos* in Jesus Christ is made effective *in nobis* through the gift of the Holy Spirit. In the intradivine life of the Trinity the Spirit allows the Son's election of man to become, without fracturing the unity of God, an eternal self-determination of the being of the Father. The Spirit permits the Son to demonstrate His eternal self-offering on man's behalf by temporally becoming man and by taking on Himself the entire plight of those rejected by the Father. Similarly, in His work within the Church the Spirit, as God's self-impartation to men, assures that their election is seen by them as a loving self-gift of the Son and as a gracious self-determination of the Father for their salvation. When Christians believe in the Father's compliance with the self-offering of Jesus Christ on their behalf, and when they find new life with the Father through Jesus Christ, the work of the Holy Spirit both in eternity and in time attains its end. The Holy Spirit not only brings Christians to a share in the mutual love of the Father and of the Son, but He also calls them to proclaim before the world the loving decision for all men made in Jesus Christ before the beginning of time. These insights summarize Barth's reflection on the christological dimensions of pneumatology.

CHAPTER V

THE SPIRIT, HUMAN EXISTENCE AND ETHICS

In the *Church Dogmatics* (III) Barth embarks on yet another dimension of his Spirit theology; it concerns the movement from the Spirit-filled man to the Father which forms the core of Barth's anthropology. Barth conceives this movement as one proceeding from the Spirit's actual presence in Christian freedom and love to the ultimate source of these gifts, the free and loving Creator. Just as the substructure both of Barth's trinitarian and christological presentations of pneumatology proved to be a correspondence between the self-revelation of God in history and the eternal being of God in Himself, the treatment of the antropological dimensions of pneumatology likewise rests on an analogy. The Christian knows, through the revelatory work of the Spirit within him, that his new freedom to love makes him an image of God and that this is only possible since God already freely loves him. This insight leads to what Barth calls the analogy of relation: as God is related to man, so man is related to God. In his presentation of the Spirit's activity within man, Barth makes use of this analogy so as to ground human freedom in divine freedom: as God is free through His Holy Spirit to reflect Himself in man, so man is free, through the same Spirit, to be the likeness of God.[1]

This further dimension of Barth's pneumatology follows logically on what has preceded it. For, having considered man's "being related" through the Spirit to the triune God and man's "being-called" by the Spirit to the elected community of Jesus Christ, Barth now centers on man's "being-freed" by the Spirit obediently to fulfill the demands of the new relationship to the Father which has been granted him through Christ's Spirit. Thus, Barth's pneumatology is to encompass not only the Spirit's role in man's relation to God and in his vocation to faith but also in his responsibility to love. Barth is now prepared to understand Christian existence as action; in doing so, Barth enters the area of theological ethics, which he claims cannot be separated from dogmatics, for "without ceasing to be dogmatics, reflection on the Word of God, theology is ethics."[2] As the likeness of God, the Christian is led to an ethical existence which reflects the very being of the Father in whose image he has been recreated by the Son and the Spirit. The Christian must be free to become what he is and to do those things which correspond to his role as copartner in the New Covenant. Just as the Spirit made his coexistence with the triune God a reality, so too the Spirit empowers him to live out his co-responsibility as covenant partner both in his individual and social life.

When the Christian examines his new life in the Spirit, he finds that he is more than just a passive believer in his union with the Father through

Christ. He finds that he acts, that he loves *in concreto* both God and his neighbor, that he confesses his love in public through his life-style and his human decisions, that he worships and prays—in short, that he feels constrained by love to obey the commands of God which the Spirit makes clear to him. Not only does he feel free to obey, he actually does so. His freedom as a child of God is paradoxically experienced as a claim which summons him, since the Holy Spirit not only liberates him, but captures him as well, so that his new participation in the life of God is seen as a genuine impulse to walk according to the law of the Spirit of life (*Rom.* 8:2f.). The Spirit thus sets him free by binding him to a life of loving obedience as the only fit response to the call of Christ which he has been offered and has accepted. For the Christian, being-real is now being-in-love, because he has been placed by the Spirit in the sphere of the divine covenant of grace.[3] His faith necessarily takes on the character of obedience since he has been called not only to hear but also to act out what he has heard by the power of the same Spirit who is the Lord of his listening.

Barth's anthropological pneumatology thus begins with a phenomenological description of Christian existence. Faith is not only an invitation to knowledge, but also an impulse to action. Faith is both the freedom to know the content of what has been revealed and also the freedom to obey the demands which this content places upon the whole range of one's human actions. In this way Barth characterizes as a false dichotomy the separation of faith and works. Faith consists of both divine content and divine demand at the same time. The entirety of a man's life is suddenly so determined by his new ability to believe that Barth can say: "as we come to faith we begin to love. If we did not begin to love, we would not have come to faith."[4] The new life of the Christian in the Spirit is clearly one of freedom, yet this freedom cannot remain noetic, in that the Christian rests in knowing of it; it must become performative; the Christian must act out his freedom through love both for the God who called him to faith and for his fellow men. There is thus a dual determination contained in his Christian freedom; he is to exercise his new responsibility both to be a man of faith and to act as such in the world to the glory of the God whose image he has become. Put differently, it can be said that two concentric circles, with the circle of the love of neighbor included in that of the love of God, now delineate the Christian's existence. By solidly situating Christian freedom within the confines of both revelation's content and command, Barth deliberately assures that the freedom which comes from faith necessarily includes the "sacramental" dimension of works.

1. Christian Freedom as Outward Sign of the New Creation

In a fashion reminiscent of his treatment of the Church's sign-world, Barth employs the image of erecting signs to explain further the twofold love required of the Christian. Called by the Spirit to a new existence, the Christian responds by the "obedient erecting of a *sign*" which indicates that God alone has inaugurated the life of grace which he now enjoys. Concomitantly, however, the erecting of another "*sign* of love for his neighbor" is demanded of him as a consequence and pledge of the first sign.[5] This setting up of signs springs from his thankfulness that he can now coexist in peace with God and with other men. Yet once again Barth insists that the new reality of Christian freedom as well as the very possibility of erecting such signs of love in the world are not within the power of the Christian himself. They reflect the force of God's love within him, and thus it is to the Holy Spirit Himself that the Christian attributes not only his initial hearing but also his subsequent obeying of the Word of God who has now encountered him personally. Even in the face of his own freedom to set up signs of obedience, the Christian acknowledges the Spirit of God as the Lord of his personal existence-in-love for God and man. Barth's theological anthropology thus rests on the tenet that Christian life is nothing other than the constant recognition of the Holy Spirit's power drawing the believer to be what he already is, a child of God. The whole of Barth's ethics, rooted as it is in his anthropology, falls under the heading of freedom as gift of the Holy Spirit. This is the case, since the subjective freedom of the Christian is not independent of the objective freedom of God for him in Jesus Christ. Man in the Spirit lives from the new freedom won by Jesus Christ, and "as he lives in this freedom he lives in the Spirit, and as he lives in the Spirit, he is one with the Lord."[6] The Christian's subjective experience of revelation is continually joined by the Spirit to the objective reality of revelation, Jesus Christ. Through the Spirit, Christian freedom actually accomplishes here and now the command to love given by the incarnate Word of God there and then. As the Lord of Christian obedience, the Spirit enables the circle of God's freedom for man in Christ to intersect the circle of man's own personal freedom, so that what was in fact accomplished, demanded and promised in Jesus' "there" becomes a reality or a realized promise in the Christian's "here."

It is impossible within the confines of this study to investigate Barth's ethics in detail, but, by considering his treatment of prayer and marriage, the decidedly pneumatic character of his entire approach to Christian morality can be illustrated. Since prayer is for Barth the free encounter of man and God and since marriage is the free encounter of man and woman, Barth notes that the very actuality of these forms of Christian existence is by no means self-evident. For, the reality of such encounters rests on the one real encounter between man and God and between man and his fellow man which was historically achieved in the life of Jesus of Nazareth. His union with God and man is realized again by the Christian in whom a divine command receives a human response, an eschatological promise finds temporal fulfillment. That this can happen at all is due solely to the work of the Holy Spirit in the sphere of man's activity, that is, amid the signs of love which he erects for God and for his neighbor. Like the Church and the sacraments, Christian love is a fully human sign which the Spirit transforms into a means by which the Christian is united both to God and to neighbor. Human words and human affection become in prayer and in marriage the Christian's path to obeying a divine command and to realizing a divine promise. Christian ethics deals with actions of love which are guaranteed to bring man to an authentic holiness. This guarantee is the presence of the life-giving Holy Spirit.

The Christian finds that he can pray, despite all the objections to a dialogic meeting with God which his inbuilt skepticism and his secular culture can raise. He discovers to his own surprise that he is free to address God with the certitude that his words will be heard. It is not so much that he is able to pray as that he is enabled to pray, even pressed to do so, that he is led to an unexpectedly fresh sense of God in the course of his prayer. His actual experience teaches him that a power beyond his own is at work enabling him to assert the right to address God which he had been promised by Jesus Christ. In the act of praying the Christian knows that the Holy Spirit Himself is speaking through him the one decisive Word which can be heard by the Father and is heard already by Him even though it cannot be uttered by man alone. Through the action of the Spirit, the Father recognizes in man's words the Word of His Son spoken on man's behalf: "as the Spirit who frees us for prayer and incites us to it is the Spirit of *Jesus Christ*, the power of His Word and promise and command, the power in which we are with Him children of God and addressed as such, so that, irrespective of what we ourselves can offer and perform, we can call God our Father and go to Him with our requests."[7]

The Christian realizes that he possesses Spirit-given freedom because in prayer he can act so as both to fulfill a divine command and actualize a divine promise along with Christ whose power becomes his own through the Spirit who binds them. Barth understands prayer as a participation in the power of Christ's resurrection from the dead, and therefore in the power of the Father's justification of sinful man. Since he can pray, the miracle of Easter Day reaches the Christian and ushers him into a new existence as redeemed son of the Father with Christ. The mission of the Redeemer Spirit is accomplished and revelation reaches its intended goal, when there is real prayer.[8] The anthropological task of the Holy Spirit attains its apex, according to Barth, when the objective self-offering of Christ and the subjective response of the believer meet at the point where the latter can address the Father as a brother of Jesus Christ through His Spirit. The presence of the Spirit accounts for the spirituality of the Christian—that interior experience of a movement from God to him, and from him to God. By examining the phenomenon of Christian prayer, Barth discovers the existence of a cycle of divine action in man through the intercession of Jesus Christ and His Spirit: "We may again think of the intervention of Jesus Christ and the Holy Spirit which makes our human asking a movement in the cycle which goes out from God and returns to God."[9] In Christian prayer the Holy Spirit enters into the sphere of man's existence, only to return again to His origin in the intradivine life. In this way, God accomplishes in His *opera ad extra* a loving movement which corresponds perfectly to His *opera ad intra*: the Spirit of love proceeds from the Father and returns to Him in the Son; through his spirituality man can stand with the Son, receive the Spirit from the Father, and return the Spirit to the Father, as a concrete sign of his own share in obedient love.

Yet, Barth does not fail to mention that the sign of his love for God which the Christian erects in prayer is always a sign of promise. Thus Barth's anthropology has an eschatological dimension. The movement of man back to the Father in the Spirit of the Son, which is his privilege in prayer, is granted to him as a sign of what is to come at the end of time. Barth extends the geometric analogy at the core of this understanding of prayer as movement: the circle of God's movement to man and man's movement to God never ends; God is continually the *terminus a quo* and the *terminus ad quem*, the Whence and Whither, of all human activity in time. God's Spirit breaks into man's world, eschatologically realizes in the Christian's temporal existence the fullness of His own eternal life, and thus promises man an unending share in this movement: "As God turns to the creature, there is also a turning of the creature to Him, not on its own strength, but in virtue of what God does in and with and to it. Thus when it reaches its goal, the divine movement returns to its origin. The *resurrexit* follows the *conceptus* and *natus*, the *mortus* and the *sepultus*. An *ascendit* follows the whole *descendit*. The faith, obedience and prayer of the Church and of Christians follows the outpouring of the Holy Spirit. The only thing is that the cycle does not end as it were; the last word again becomes a first: *unde venturus est*."[10] In prayer the Christian finds himself caught up in God's inner act of love which has turned towards him, and his response in the form of a sign of love is a return of this movement back to its origin. The Holy Spirit extends to man the love which eternally exists in the Godhead and assures his response in kind through the love which existed historically in Jesus of Nazareth. Through the Spirit man becomes free to enjoy the right which he is eternally promised as a child of God. To pray is to experience the eternal freedom of the Spirit as a promise realized in time.

Just as Barth views prayer as an inward sign of man's being-in-freedom which is granted to him by the Holy Spirit, he also views love of neighbor as an outward sign of his acting-in-freedom which is the gift of the same Spirit. Thus, like true prayer, true love lies beyond man's possibility. The freedom genuinely to love one's neighbor begins for Barth only when the native freedom to love, which man thinks he has in his power, is proved to be hollow. True relationships first commence when men ground their love for one another on something beyond either the idealistically or realistically conceived ordinances of human potentiality. Christian love is not an exercise of an innate talent, but an event which happens each time anew; it is the miracle by which the Holy Spirit constantly founds love in man. Since man can love only in response to the love of God which disclosed itself in the concrete history of Jesus Christ, there is for Barth no love *in abstracto*. That the Christian in fact experiences the essence of his life as love, is no less a work of the Holy Spirit than the virgin birth and the incarnation. Barth thus stresses that love is founded on God's inclination towards man, His "manward" self-communication through His Spirit: "It is the work and gift of the Holy Spirit that the fact of God's love speaks to us."[11] The Christian loves because he is loved; he is willing and able to determine himself as a lover of others only because God predetermined Himself to love all men in Jesus Christ.

Love of neighbor is a continual promise for which man must yearn since his hope is God Himself, and it is a continual command since God demands of man an outward sign of the divine fulfillment of his created nature. According to Barth, it is a miracle of the Holy Spirit that this promise and this command can be realized by self-determining human acts: "Love must be a description of the human self-determination which occurs in the sphere and light of the divine pre-determination."[12] Only God's decision to bestow the gift of freedom on man through the Spirit can cause him to overcome his inability publicly to bear witness to divine love for other men: "That it is not in my power to give this work of love the efficacy by which it is to the neighbor the fulfillment of revelation, the imparting of the Word and Spirit of God by which therefore his need takes on that other side—this limitation belongs to its very nature as witness."[13] The Holy Spirit allows the Christian to experience that his human capacity for love surpasses the limitations natural to it, and serves to bring others directly into contact with God's revelation. Christian love allows others to experience on their side the gift of love from God's side. Human encounter can thus give testimony to the actual fulfillment of revelation among men. This can only be the work of the Holy Spirit, who is Himself the self-impartation of God's love to man.

Barth sees revelation's completion in love particularly symbolized in marriage. When a man and a woman decide to live in harmony and to surmount the conflicts which are inherent in all human encounter, they actually walk in the Spirit. By curbing their hostility instead of allowing it to boil up into a destructive force in their relationship, they experience in themselves not only the unity of the Christian community to which they belong, but also the presence of the very Spirit of God who brings about this unity. They become a microcosm of that unity between God and man which is promised to the whole Christian community.[14] Since their married love is a gift of the Spirit, He alone discloses the meaning of their union, and makes the meaning of manhood and womanhood clear for the first time. By experiencing the Spirit dwelling in them, they discover the power of Jesus' resurrection operative in the fulfillment of their relation as man and woman. They are freed in principle from the ultimate victory of conflict, and are set on the way of overcoming in practice whatever conflicts may exist between them. The Spirit assures the Christian couple that all strife was resolved on Golgotha, and that the peace of the risen Lord is already theirs.

Married love is for Barth a concrete sign that the Spirit has not been given to man in vain. Christian spouses openly witness to the new possibility for harmony won for all men and women by the death and resurrection of Christ and by the outpouring of the Holy Spirit. The union of bride and bridegroom, as a sign of the union of Christ and His Spirit-filled community, becomes a sign of the extraordinary freedom which the Father's self-revelation has procured. In their marriage Christians are free because they are made by the Spirit sharers in God's own freedom which is expressed through this special relationship as husband and wife: "Marriage is a matter of freedom. It is a matter of the Holy Spirit freeing man for this in no way ordinary, but highly extraordinary fulfillment of the relation between man and woman."[15] Human love stands under the power of the Holy Spirit who makes men and women free to proclaim the paschal mystery to others as the answer to their search for a relationship which lies beyond their grasp, one that will bring their manhood and womanhood to fulfillment.

Barth concludes that true prayer and true love are possible for the Christian only through the work of the Holy Spirit. Although this rather arbitrary and brief sketch of Barth's ethics fails to do justice to the many areas treated extensively in the *Church Dogmatics* (III), it does, however, indicate the essential role of the Holy Spirit in Barth's ethical reflections. Only from the actuality of Christian freedom in the Spirit can Barth argue to its possibility. That there is a new coexistence of man with God, that there are signs set up in the Christian's existence which are reflective of divine revelation is not due to himself, but to the Spirit of God. Only this new human freedom, which comes to man as a gift of the Holy Spirit, enables him to be faithful to the covenant offered to all men by Jesus Christ. In short, the Christian discovers that he lives the life of a real man, since the Spirit of the one ontically real man, Jesus Christ, awakens in the Christian the possibility of being what he is meant to be. According to Barth, the new reality of Christian morality which expresses itself in prayer and love, is the work of God revealed in the Christian, the Holy Spirit: "The free decision of man, the act and work of man, the life of real men is revealed as the fulfillment of revelation at the outpouring of the Holy Spirit . . . It acquires this character 'from outside,' that is, from God . . . But it is the hidden reality of their existence. It is He, He who is the reality. He is not I. He is not we. Only indirectly is He identical with us and we with Him . . . There is always this eschatological frontier between Him and us."[16]

To be morally free is to exist in the Spirit, but not to become identical with the Spirit; the loving Christian is privileged to share in any given time the eschatological breakthrough of God's time into man's, but not to cross the eschatological frontier between himself and God. Barth can therefore assert that to be morally able to live in the Spirit is to possess a personal share in the ontic, eschatological freedom of Jesus Christ. Something happens to human life itself through the outpouring of the Spirit at Pentecost which matches the marvel of the resurrection. A new possibility is created for man. His life is now not only objectively but also subjectively a new creation; he is free to pray and to love in virtue of the freedom given to him by the divine Spirit, God revealing Himself in him. At Pentecost the sub‑jective possibility is given to man of loving God and neighbor as Jesus Christ did objectively. The Christian's moral self-determination actually corresponds to God's pre-determination for him in Jesus Christ. The freedom-giving Spirit of Pentecost creates this similarity between Christian morality, revelation's subjective fulfillment, and the morality of Jesus Christ, revelation's objective source.

2. *Spirit Christology and the Potential of Soul and Body*

Jesus Christ is for Barth the model of the new freedom which the Christian acts out in the Spirit. At this point in the *Church Dogmatics* reflection on the work of the Spirit in the Christian induces Barth to allow Jesus' relationship to the Holy Spirit to come to the fore. Jesus, Barth claims, had an absolutely unique relationship to the Holy Spirit. By being totally filled and governed by the Holy Spirit, Jesus owed His very existence to His presence and power. The freedom of Jesus to be and to act was not a partial and temporary, but a total and lasting freedom, since He possessed the life-giving Spirit without measure. Something new happens to the life of all men in the Spirit-filled Jesus; a potency is given to human flesh which it would otherwise be incapable of. Flesh becomes quickened by Spirit and thus becomes liberated; chaos becomes cosmos. For, Jesus did not live only *kata sarka*, but also *kata pneuma* which privilege made His resurrection from the dead a divine necessity: *"Jesus has the Holy Spirit lastingly and totally*. He is the man to whom the creative movement of God has come primarily, *originally* and therefore *definitively*, who derives His existence as soul and body from this movement, and for whom to be the 'living soul' of an earthly body . . . is not a mere possibility, but a most proper reality. He breathes lastingly and totally in the air of the 'life-giving Spirit.' He not only has Spirit, but primarily and basically He is Spirit as He is soul and body. For this reason, and in this way, He lives. This is His absolutely unique relationship to the Holy spirit."[17] Jesus' paradigmatic freedom is grounded by Barth on the unprecedented relationship of the Holy Spirit to His living soul and earthly body. The whole of Barthian anthropology rests on the correspondence which the Spirit creates between Christian freedom and the unsurpassed freedom which was proper to Jesus. The Spirit alone, and not anthropology or ecclesiology as such, can bridge the gap between Jesus' unique ability to overcome the conflict of the flesh and the spirit and the parallel victory of Christian love. Only the miracle, by which the life-giving Spirit of Jesus liberated Him for the sake of all, is able so to liberate the Christian that he can tread the path of Jesus' real freedom.[18] At the core of Barth's anthropology stands the Spirit-filled Jesus; thus anthropology cannot be severed from soteriology and pneumatology.

Neither can Barth's anthropology be divorced from eschatology, which is also linked inseparably to the work of the Holy Spirit. For, the Spirit is no other than the Spirit of the risen Lord whose presence and power alone lend ultimate hope to Christian liberty. Thus Barth maintains that, at Pentecost, Easter becomes a present reality at the center of Christian existence: "It is clear that Pentecost is the result of the resurrection achieved in the time of the apostles, yet not by the apostles, but in them and to them. It is the *result of the revelation* of the fullness of time accomplished in His life and death. It is the bridging of the gulf between His past and their present; the assumption of their time into His."[19] At Pentecost, God's time breaks into man's, and man's present time takes on the character of the end time. Wherever the Spirit is at work, Jesus is present not merely as the recollected Messiah but as the living Lord of man's deliverance; the efficacy of the New Covenant is neither past nor future but present.[20] The Christian community already shares in the Parousia which is the future of Jesus made accessible through His Spirit in the midst of time. Whereas the community's past was laden by slavery to the flesh, its present is quickened by the Holy

Spirit who raised Jesus from death to life. The direct temporal presence of the risen and glorified Christ is thus made possible by the Holy Spirit. As Barth turns his attention to the new freedom of the Christian, which the Holy Spirit realizes in time as the human response to the New Covenant offered by the risen Christ, his pneumatology becomes decidedly eschatological. Christian life in the Spirit is the tangible guarantee of the full liberty of man which is to come: "Hence, even the presence of Jesus in the Spirit, for all its fullness, can only be a pledge or first installment of what awaits the community as well as the whole universe, His return in glory."[21]

Barth's understanding of the Christian and of his new life of freedom is therefore not primarily an anthropological, but a Messianic one, since the life-giving Spirit responsible for the Christian's new freedom is none other than the Spirit who anointed the Messiah, accounted for His unique existence and raised Him to new life. First the Christian comes to know the Spirit as the Lord of his redeemed, eschatological existence in and through the Spirit-filled Jesus. The Spirit is thus above all the Lord of man's recreation, of his ability to love and to obey, to live from the hope that the Spirit of the risen Lord will quicken his soul and body and make him free to praise the Father in all his human actions. Theological anthropology, normally understood to deal with man's creation, is for Barth rooted in man's recreation, that is, in soteriology and eschatology. The anthropological dimension of Barth's pneumatology does not rest on the first, but on the second article of the creed. The starting point of Barth's theology of man, which considers the similarity fashioned by the life-giving Spirit between God's freedom and that of the Christian is not creation but recreation, not man himself but the Spirit-filled Messiah, His resurrection and future coming. As the Christian lives from these mysteries through the power of the Spirit, he is created anew; the new life of grace and freedom, of faith, hope and love is thus the key to the very meaning of man. Grace alone unlocks the meaning of nature; soteriology of anthropology.

When the *Credo* of the Church calls the Spirit the Giver of life *(to pneuma zoopoioun)*, Barth interprets the meaning of this title soteriologically in accordance with the New Testament understanding of the life-giving Spirit in *Jn.* 6:63 and 2 *Cor.* 3:6. A major factor in this interpretation is, of course, Barth's insistence that life in the Spirit is a subjective possibility for Christians only because it was an objective possibility for Jesus Christ. Thus Barth's Christian anthropology is grounded in the uniquely Spirit-filled existence of the Messiah, the bringer of salvation. Given the prominence which a Logos Christology enjoys in the Barthian corpus, the stress which Barth places here on the role of the Spirit in the life of Jesus of Nazareth is significant. In effect, Barth provides the outline of a Pneuma Christology in the explicitly anthropological sections of the *Church Dogmatics*. This fact is extremely significant for Barth's development as a pneumatologian. As it became evident to Barth that, if he intended both to counteract and to do justice to Schleiermacher's veiled pneumatocentric theology, he would have to modify his own Logos Christology, he took definite steps in the direction of a Pneuma Christology. This development supports the contention that Barth's sincere efforts towards a genuine theological anthropology first led him to pneumatology, and especially to a pneumatological understanding of man. In the process, moreover, it became evident to Barth that the necessary model for his understanding of anthropology, Jesus Christ, had also to be understood pneumatologically.

Once the christological foundations of his anthropology are laid, Barth makes it clear that behind many New Testament texts on the life-giving Spirit "stands the recollection of the significance for the *regnum naturae* assigned in the Old Testament to ruah and neshamah of *Gen* 2:7 where Adam does not, like Christ the second Adam according to 1 *Cor*. 15:45, himself become the *pneuma zoopoioun*, but rather a 'living soul' *through* the 'living breath' of God."[22] Barth thus argues that the true meaning of the original creation of man by God the Father can only be understood in the light of man's recreation in Jesus Christ and in His Spirit. The life-giving breath of the Creator is made fully manifest when that same breath raises Jesus from the dead; in turn, Jesus becomes a life-giving Spirit who gives new life to men and recreates them by uniting them to Himself. There is a theological distinction to be made between the Spirit of the Creator and the Spirit of the Recreator, if the self-revelation of the Father through Jesus Christ is to be respected. Those who receive the Spirit of Christ know they are united with God; those who live from the Spirit of the Father include even the godless: "As the Spirit of Jesus Christ, who proceeding from Him, unites men closely to Him *ut secum unum sint*, He distinguishes Himself from the Spirit of God who lives as *vita animalis* in creation, nature and history, and to that extent in the godless as well. And just because He is Christ's Spirit, the work of Christ is never done without Him. Nor is it done except by Him."[23] Such a fresh distinction, moreover, between the Spirit of the Father and of the Son is no doubt a mark of Barth's mature thought.

For, when he comes to treat the doctrine of creation, Barth recognizes that the Spirit's action on behalf of all men at time's dawn is similar to His action in the Church on behalf of those recreated through faith in Jesus Christ. In both instances the Spirit executes in history a covenant which God the Father initiates with man. At Pentecost, the Spirit of the New Covenant continued what He had always done from the beginning of time— bringing men to life as the creative breath of the Father who offers them a gracious covenant with Himself: "If, then, in the New Testament especially the Spirit's activity in the historical execution of the covenant of grace is described as the *zoopoiesis* of the creature subjected to death, as the divine power of the work and witness of Jesus Christ, and therefore as the power of the new birth and faith, of salvation and hope, we do not find it difficult to recognize in this activity the character which is already peculiar to Him in that first work of His."[24] Though the two works of the Holy Spirit are distinct, they so closely correspond that Barth finds himself compelled to make an equation between them. There is only one Spirit of God who manifests Himself in revelation quite consistently whether He acts generally in all men or specifically in Christians. Thus, Barth at times makes his readers aware of the more fortuitous than confusing overlapping of the Spirit's functions as they are described in the New Testament: the Spirit's work as Yahweh's breath of life and His work as the guarantor of Christian hope.[25]

Just as the need to consider the uniqueness of Jesus' humanity led Barth to depart somewhat from his Logos Christology and entertain the advantages for a Christian anthropology which a Pneuma Christology affords, so the need to allow room for the work of the Creator's Spirit leads Barth in a new direction. He must both distinguish and yet unify the concepts of *Spiritus Creator* and *Spiritus Redemptor*. Yet Barth does this in such a way that he begins with the latter concept so as to comprehend the former. He imagines two concentric spheres, the larger of which depicts the work of the Spirit of Christ; the narrower sphere, contained within the larger one, depicts the work of the Spirit of the Creator. Thus, though "the *same* Spirit who is there the principle of his renewal, is here the principle of his creaturely reality,"[26] rebirth clarifies creation, and the new life of the Christian illumines the meaning of the natural state of man. The Spirit is for Barth the *sine qua non* of man's existence in both the soteriological and the anthropological sense of the word, and thus he makes an analogy between the two ways by which man's life stems from an encounter with the Holy Spirit. The prime analogate, however, is the soteriological one, for it is only in Jesus Christ and in His Spirit that the Father fully completes His initial creative movement towards man: "The relationship between the Spirit and man even in its anthropological sense is to be represented on the analogy of expression used in the soteriological context. He is poured forth upon man, laid upon him; but He is not to be thought of as changing human nature into divine nature, against which Paul twice (1 *Cor.* 15:45, 2 *Cor.* 3:17-18) ventures the equation *kurios = pneuma*. These passages tell us that this man, because in His humanity He was also Son of God, accomplished and still accomplishes in His own person the mighty quickening action of God in relation to all other men."[27] It is Jesus Christ who definitively reveals, because He alone possesses, life in the fullness of the Spirit.

Barth concludes that passages in the New Testament which deal with the Spirit and man, although they are meant soteriologically, that is, with primary reference to the saving Spirit of Jesus Christ, have at the same time an indirectly anthropological significance. Barth understands *John* 6:63 and 2 *Cor.* 3:6—"It is the Spirit that gives life"—to refer not only to the Spirit of Jesus given to the Church at Pentecost, but also to the Spirit given to all men, insofar as they live from the breath of God. With regard to 2 *Cor.* 6:19, Barth remarks: "the primary reference is of course to Christians as members of the body of Christ, but it has also a more extensive anthropological truth and significance."[28] This double meaning of the texts concerning the Spirit as Giver of life in the New Testament leads Barth to understand the Spirit in general as God Himself engaged in a creative movement to His creatures; whenever God breathes His Spirit on men, they partake of His life and become living beings. This turning of God's Spirit towards man is described in two ways in the Scripture: as a creative turning which establishes and conditions man's free being through the free gift of breath at creation, and as a redemptive turning which fulfills man's created being by continually recreating his freedom through the free gift of redemption at Pentecost. However, Barth maintains that man's "natural" or created being is not known simply from nature; it first becomes evident that man "has" Spirit and therefore shares in God's life from a knowledge of the "new" being recreated by Christ's Spirit in the community of salvation, the Church.

Barth admits of the Spirit's anthropological work in all men only because of a prior knowledge, derived from revelation, concerning the Spirit's work in the Christian as the totally unexpected flowering of something which existed previously in a general and incomplete form. Pentecost sheds light backwards onto creation, the life of the prophets and the public life of Jesus, and forwards onto the life of the Christian community in time and onto its promise of fulfilled life at the last coming. The experience of new life at the outpouring of the Holy Spirit and its continuous effect in the Christian community elucidates what the natural man was actually capable of becoming before the dawn of redemption. Barth thus appreciates the anthropological significance of the original creation of man only after considering the soteriological significance of Pentecost which is limited neither forwards or backwards: "However are we to take *John* 2:11, if future is not also here thought of as future, and likewise as already present? And *John* 20:22 and the Pentecost account in *Acts* 2 must of course be regarded as the express and solemn testimony of an event which chronologically was *not limited*, either forwards or backwards, to the precise day of Pentecost."[29] As Barth views God's self-revelation at Pentecost, the redemptive turning of Christ's Spirit towards the Christian reaches back to the original turning of the Father's Spirit towards all mankind at creation, in the prophetic life of Israel and in the public life of Jesus. For, if scriptural revelation is to be heeded, neither the redemptive nor the creative movements of the one Spirit can be understood without the other.

Furthermore, just as Barth insists elsewhere that the acknowledgement of grace precedes that of sin, and the force of the Gospel reveals that of the Law, he argues in his treatment of creation that it is only in the actual fulfillment of man that his human potential becomes clear for the first time; Pentecost is the key to creation, and not *vice versa*. As the Christian is brought to the goal of revelation by the Spirit and as his being is made free to love, he startlingly confronts his potential to be so from creation. The burgeoning of Christian freedom alone discloses the root of this possibility in creation; the New Covenant uncovers the meaning of the Old. Barth's anthropological pneumatology is, as it were, the thread which his soterio-eschatological pneumatology gradually discovers to have been woven into the fabric of creation from the start. The Spirit of the Old Covenant, while He is and remains chronologically such, is from the point of view of faith known first as the Spirit of the New Covenant. Through the gift of grace, the Spirit sheds light on the gift of creatureliness. Only through the new freedom given by the Holy Spirit to the Christian community can the believer come to realize that the same Spirit has been there for him from the beginning. The Christian's freedom reveals the hidden existence of what Barth calls the "may" *(das Dürfen)* of his freedom, or his "transcendent enabling" *(die transzendente Ermöglichung)*, that is, the activity of the divine Spirit in him as the basis of his very existence as body and soul.[30] The work of the Spirit of Christ in the Church concomitantly divulges His nascent work as the Spirit of the Creator in all men. The Spirit of Pentecost allows His patent activity in the Church to betray His veiled activity as the Spirit of man's transcendent enabling, and thus as the Spirit by whom man's entire life is already graciously constituted.

Since it was precisely the issue of man's native ability to comprehend, accept and live the Word of God which inaugurated Barth's pneumatology as a reaction to Neo-Protestantism, Christian Existentialism and Roman Catholicism, Barth proceeds very carefully as he accounts for man's inexplicable potentiality, or transcendental enabling, to hear the Word of God. That man can do so is a pure gift, a divine enabling, a "may" granted to him by the Spirit of God. The form which this gift takes is man's creatureliness, his natural existence as soul and body. Man's very ability to exist as a potential believer is not something native to him which he can control, but something given to him for which he can only be thankful. Thus, any precondition, any explanation of his capacity to be saved by the Word of God is sheer creation of the Holy Spirit: "His creatureliness, what he is through the Spirit, is itself and as such this ability . . . Soul and body, as the essence of human nature, are in any case the presupposition and precondition, the potentiality which underlies the actuality of his being in the Word of God."[31] Christian existence in the Word through the power of the Spirit discloses that the same Spirit made of his creatureliness the prerequisite foundation of what he was to become through grace. For this reason Barth underlines the close affinity between the creative and the prophetic work of the Spirit in man. The Spirit in His creative capacity sustains the soul and the body of man so that he can become a covenant partner of God, which is the very goal of the Spirit's prophetic role: "The Spirit given to man, and grounding, constituting and maintaining him as soul of his body, has *per se* an affinity to the prophetic Spirit, by whose operation the actuality of his being in covenant with God arises out of the potentiality of his creatureliness."[32] There is, then, a native ability in man to which God appeals when He offers him a covenant relationship, but this very ability is also the work of the Holy Spirit who establishes the creature's being as body and soul.

Barth can therefore confidently acknowledge that the Holy Spirit is not only the Spirit of God but also the Spirit of man. But Barth immediately qualifies the latter description by insisting that man does not possess the Spirit in the way he possesses his soul and his body; the Spirit always stands in a dialogic relationship to man. Insofar as man is met by the Spirit, he has Spirit as a gift. Man is what he is as he has Spirit, the divine quickening factor of his soul and therefore of his body; he is what he is as he is gifted by the presence of the Creator Spirit who from the beginning enables him to exist as a potential covenant partner with the Father through His Son. The meaning of the statement that man actually has Spirit, or that the Holy Spirit is also the Spirit of man can only be that "whatever else can be said about the Spirit of man, the reference is always to the center of his being and existence which is not a third thing beside soul and body, but is to be sought in soul and body and at the same time *above* and *beyond* them, being understood as the representative of the divine grace of creation over against the whole being and existence of man."[33] Even though Barth concedes that the Holy Spirit is also the Spirit of man, he makes every effort to assure that the Spirit's gracious immanence in no way threatens His unqualified transcendence. Despite the closeness of God's Spirit to man, even to the point where the Spirit becomes man's Spirit as well, Barth is persistent in defending the dialogic quality of man's spirituality; Barth's anthropology is not a neutral but a pneumatic concept of human nature. In effect, Barth's anthropology is a treatment of the pneumatological dimension of creation.[34] Thus, when he considers the meaning of *Gen.* 2:7—"God breathed into man's nostrils the breath of life, and man became a living being"—he does not identify man, and especially man's soul, with the Spirit of God, so that the soul itself effects life, but calls the soul the "life of man in being." The soul is not the quickening breath of God Himself, but "that which lives by it," "man's answer to the breathing of the Creator."[35]

Consequently, Barth maintains that the human soul is directly present to the Spirit, and therefore enjoys a likeness to the Creator by whose Spirit it was made. Furthermore, Barth understands the Spirit to be the principle of man's corporeality; the Spirit is, through the soul, indirectly present to the body of man. Barth's anthropology can be summarized by the statement that man is body and soul in that he has Spirit. Through the power of the *Spiritus Creator*, the soul is awakened and made soul, and the material body is "besouled" and thus becomes and is maintained as an organic body. The Spirit which man has is not something; rather the Spirit is the dynamic personal action and attitude of the Creator at the core of His creation. The Spirit is the very presence of God to man, the life-giving principle bestowed on him so that he is and remains a subject. Human reality is soul and body, but it is not Spirit. "Yet it is soul and body as Spirit *comes* to it, as it *receives* and *has* Spirit, as Spirit *has* it and will not leave it, but grounds, determines, limits it."[36] As a subject, man is inchoately capable of a free and loving response to his Creator. For this reason, Barth concludes that man is already at his creation nothing less then the revelation of God's own freedom and love. Through the power of the Holy Spirit at work in his being, man partakes in divine self-revelation. His spirituality and corporeality can, because the Spirit acts upon them, function as revelatory of God's gracious design that man be created as His free partner.

The Spirit whom man receives at creation is not only the creative force of his natural life, but also the prophetic force of his renewed life as God's covenant partner. Since man is able to encounter and relate to God, the creative Spirit within him proves Himself also to be the prophetic Spirit who allows man freely to cooperate in the covenant of grace. By giving man His Spirit, the Father guarantees that the covenant is the inner basis of creation. As God's creative and prophetic movement towards man, the Spirit insures that within man's being the principle of his relationship to and fellowship with God will remain central. The Spirit thus lends man a divine basis for renewal and freedom, and the transcendent ability to recognize Himself alone as the initiator of this new life and freedom. "The covenant is the inner basis of creation . . . Spirit in His *fundamental* significance is the element in virtue of which man is actively and passively introduced as a partner in the covenant of grace, in which he is installed in his position as God's partner in particular stages and decisions of the history of this covenant and in which he is equipped for his function as such . . . Whoever is given the Spirit of God becomes, as the man he is, another man—a man of God, the kind of man whom God uses, and who as he is used by God begins to live a new life."[37] When the Spirit of God permits man to "take place" as an image of God, man becomes genuinely capable of a free and loving union with the Father as a hearer and doer of His Word.

Barth's reflections on the anthropological role of the Holy Spirit clearly lead him to the same insights which he developed in the context of his trinitarian and christological presentations of pneumatology. The key words which characterize Barth's previous treatment of Spirit theology, such as relationship, hearing, believing and witnessing, all come together here under the heading of God's free and loving movement towards man through His Spirit. Thus, Barth's anthropological pneumatology deals with the very presupposition of all that was to be fulfilled in the history of God's covenant with man. Just as the soteriological aspects of pneumatology are essentially eschatological, so are the anthropological. Since man possesses the Spirit of God from creation, he is already determined by the promise of God which was to be initiated in Israel and fulfilled in the Church.[38] By understanding the covenant as the inner basis of creation, Barth refuses to sever the creature in any way from the divine promise anchored in the Spirit's acquiescence to the election of all men in Jesus Christ. The Spirit who breathes on man is the Spirit bound to carry out in history the realization of the divine decree of grace. At creation God not only makes man a living soul and body, but also predetermines that he is to have a future share in His own life. Though it is only Jesus Christ who uniquely realized the promise of eternal life, since the Spirit rested fully on Him, by the outpouring of His Spirit, Jesus allows the Father to fulfill His love intention towards all men by bringing them to an actualization of the potential they are given at creation. That potential, Barth's anthropology insists, is rooted in the eschatological power of the Holy Spirit who can not only bestow natural life but also eternal life on man. God's "may" or predetermination of man for glory at creation, "can" become, through the work of Christ's Spirit, man's own self-determination.

3. Pre-existing in the Holy Spirit as the Creator's Image

The correspondence between God and man from creation, which the Spirit establishes as the basis of all further correspondence to take place in the history of redemption, is the germ of what Barth terms the analogy of relation. God chose from the beginning to cause a similarity to exist between Himself and man by which man might mirror, through his own acts of freedom and love, the free and loving act of God towards him from all eternity. God thus willed that His image become man's. This is the promise which the Father begins to fulfill by endowing man from creation with His life-giving Spirit. The Spirit completes the promise, because He allows man's freedom and love to reflect the free and loving Creator. Through the cooperation of the Holy Spirit the creature calls upon the Creator; uncreated freedom is worshipped by created freedom. Thus at the very basis of Barth's theological anthropology stands the Holy Spirit, God creating an analogous relation between Himself and man. The option for the *analogia relationis* is meant to preclude the possibility that it is an *analogia entis* which brings man to appreciate God's gracious action of fashioning him in His likeness. It is only when the man of faith comes to perceive the work of the divine Spirit within him that he simultaneously recognizes his similarity to the God who calls him: "Is it of ourselves, in virtue of our decision and action, by reason of our suitability, that we are this mirror? No, but *kathaper apo kuriou pneumatos* (2 *Cor.* 3:18). This *object*—the Lord and His glory— *makes* us mirrors in this way, bringing about the change in which His image becomes ours and by reason of which we become bearers of the image of the heavenly. He can and does do it because according to 1 *Cor.* 15:45 He is the *pneuma zoopoioun*, and as the quickening *Spirit* He is the Lord."[39]

The analogy of relation ultimately rests on the only analogate which the believer can find for the act of creation: the inner life of God Himself. Creation is God's willingness to externalize in time that which He already is in Himself from eternity. The relation which God creates between Himself and His creatures is a mirror of His own intradivine existence, the mutual giving of the Father to the Son in the Holy Spirit. What God does outside of Himself in His gracious act of creation is not alien to His own being: "God *repeats* in this relationship *ad extra* a relationship proper to Himself in His inner divine essence. Entering into this relationship, He makes a *copy* of Himself. Even in His inner divine being there is relationship. To be sure God is One in Himself. But He is not alone. There is in Him a co-existence, co-inherence, reciprocity. God in Himself is not just simple, but in the simplicity of His essence, He is three-fold, the Father, the Son and the Holy Spirit."[40] Thus Barth states that it is the Father *per appropriationem* who is the Creator, but that the Father fashions the cosmos along with the Son and the Holy Spirit in accord with the eternal decision of the triune God to manifest His inner life externally. There is, despite all the disparity between God's relation to Himself and His relation to man, also a great similarity. Barth adds that, where variations exist among God's individual actions for man in the course of the covenant's history, these variations are themselves signs that God as Father, Son and Spirit is acting on behalf of man in a way revelatory of the real distinctions within Himself.

As the Father is related from eternity to the Son through the Spirit, so He is related in the course of time to man through the same Holy Spirit. This correspondence is most perfectly reflected in the man Jesus in whom the inner divine relationship of the Father and the Son through the Spirit realizes a matchless copy of itself in the creaturely world. The primary instance of the *analogia relationis*, and therefore of the *imago Dei*, is for Barth the christological one, in which the union of the Father and the Son becomes a temporal reality in the man Jesus.[41] But the analogy of relation applies to all men as well, in that their relationship with God is patterned on God's relationship to Himself: "There is an *analogia relationis*. The correspondence and similarity of the two relationships consists in the fact that the freedom, in which God posits Himself as the Father, is posited by Himself as the Son and confirms Himself by the Holy Spirit, is the same freedom as that in which He is the Creator of man, in which man may be His creature, and in which the Creator-creature relationship is established by the Creator."[42] The Holy Spirit, as the self-confirming freedom of God's relationship to Himself, accounts for the similarity of the relationship between the Creator and the creature by confirming the free reciprocity of God and man. The Holy Spirit enables man to be the extra-divine object of God's free love, just as He allows the Son to be the intra-divine object of the Father's free love. Man receives his similarity to God from the same Spirit who assures God's interior self-sameness.

By locating the source of man's likeness to God in the intradivine life of the Trinity, Barth in effect proposes a theology of man's pre-existence in the Holy Spirit from eternity, which perfectly parallels his understanding of Christian faith as pre-existing in the eternal divine election of Jesus Christ. Just as Barth's doctrine of predestination roots Christian existence solely in the free choice of God the Son, his doctrine of man's pre-existence roots Christian anthropology solely in the eternally free love of the Holy Spirit. If, on the one hand, anthropology is not to dominate pneumatology, and if, on the other, pneumatology is to remain the Christian doctrine which includes a theology of man, Barth has to insure that the confusion which can easily occur here between the Holy Spirit and man's spirit is avoided once for all. Given the historical genesis of Barth's pneumatology, his doctrine of creation is countering a monistic concept of the cosmos. Instead of viewing man's creaturely existence as standing over against God, "Christian monism, the synoptic view of God and the world, God and man and sin and redemption classically represented by Schleiermacher and Hegel, comes up against a frontier where it either ceases to be Christian or must cease to be monistic."[43] Despite the positive attempts of Hegel and Schleiermacher vigorously to counteract the materialism of their time and consistently to defend the unique content of the Scriptures within the framework of their theological systems, Barth discovers in them the trace of an extremely uncertain Christianity. Once Christianity becomes uncertain, a confusion takes place between the truths which Christianity must proclaim and the cosmological theories of a given historical period. As a result, Christianity "is led at once to the discovery and assertion of Ludwig Feuerbach, that at the bottom it too is nothing but concealed anthropology."[44]

The origin of this uncertainty and of the ensuing theological distortions which were advocated is, in Barth's opinion, the failure of Christianity to allow the doctrine of creation to be God's own self-demonstration of the relationship of human to divine being. Instead, Christianity adopted a concept of man which independently accounted for his relationship to God; the doctrine of creation thus became an effort on the part of the theologian to inform himself about creation instead of allowing himself to be informed.[45] Such an attitude degrades the Christian creed to a "definition of human existence" and reduces the doctrine of creation "into statements about the inner life of man." When this occurs, it is no wonder that theology finds itself in the "anthropological straight-jacket" which constrains Bultmann's thought as well as that of Wilhelm Herrmann, Albrecht Ritschl and Friedrich Schleiermacher.[46] Any attempt at a cultural Christianity, which seeks to explain faith in the divine creation of the world in terms of a prevalent cosmological view, is rebuffed by Barth's insistence that faith has something unique to say about man. That man is different from God and can only be encountered by Him is proved by the failure of every synoptic view of God and man, whether it was that of 2nd-century Gnosticism or Catholicism's acceptance of Aristotelianism, that of 18th-century Rationalism or Schleiermacher's cultural Christianity and its aftereffects in German theology. No world-view has the power definitively to undermine the structure of Christian belief in creation: "the confession of faith always showed that it had its own meaning and function in face of cosmology, and its own continuity in face of cosmological developments."[47]

In order to buttress the threatened doctrine of creation, Barth turns to a pneumatology which contains an explicitly Christian anthropology, understood as a soterio-eschatological presentation of the re-creation and creation of human existence through the Holy Spirit. Barth's pneumatology contests against the apologist's perennial tendency to distinguish between what is generally known and what is specifically revealed about man's nature. For this reason, Barth cannot tolerate any kind of syncretism between nature and grace. Man has to be understood totally in terms of God's being if theological anthropology is not to be limited to the "mere content of man's pious consciousness," man's transcendent nature or man's self-understanding.[48] Both Barth's understanding of the *analogia relationis* between human and divine being and his insistence on the eternal ground of this analogy in the Holy Spirit are the means he employs to confront any synoptic monism, by which a particular view of the world and of man becomes determinative of Christian theology. The tyranny of philosophical cosmology is thwarted by the Holy Spirit who is the power of God's creative freedom in the world, since He is such in God Himself. The Spirit is God as He realizes in time His eternal redemptive and creative turning to man. In doing so, the Spirit reveals Himself as the God who transcends the world of man and who nevertheless intimately encounters man and lends him the ability to be what he is called to be from eternity: the free and loving covenant partner of God. Rather than a natural, there is a pneumatological cosmology behind Barth's understanding of man: the freedom of matter itself is grounded in God's free decision to establish a correspondence between Himself and the world. When this correspondence is made manifest in Jesus Christ and acknowledged in Christian faith it is the achievement of the Holy Spirit, the divine Giver of life in the soteriological and anthropological sense.

Since the Church confesses that Jesus Christ, the man fully free to love the Father because He possessed the Spirit in a unique way, manifests and personifies the eternal free and loving decision of the Creator for man, Barth arrives at the truth of the first acticle of the Christian creed from the third via the second. It is only through the noetic realization of the Father's freedom and love in the Spirit-filled Christian, whose faith is based on the ontic embodiment of this freedom and love in the Spirit-filled Jesus, that man can come to genuine knowledge of the Creator: "We believe in Jesus Christ when we believe in God the Father Almighty, Maker of heaven and earth. These words of the first article do not make sense if for all the particularity of their meaning they do not anticipate the confession of the second and third articles."[49] Barth further argues that, since Christian faith in the Creator rests on the authoritative witness of scriptural revelation, the Spirit, the guarantor of the Bible's credibility, brings the believer to knowledge of the Creator through the Word. This important reversal of the usual order of approaching the doctrine of creation, by which the third article in conjunction with the second leads to the first, is indicative of the centrality of the Holy Spirit's function in Barthian systematics. Knowing the Father at all first depends on knowing the Spirit who leads the believer to the perfect image of the Father, Jesus Christ. The Holy Spirit enjoys the pivotal temporal function of imparting to Christian consciousness and of carrying out through Christian freedom the Father's eternal decision to copy His own existence outside Himself.

On some of the most profound pages of the *Church Dogmatics* Barth discusses the intradivine beginnings of all things, and in doing so grounds his entire pneumatology on his understanding of the role of the Spirit of God before the act of creation. The intradivine decision to create the world is made by the triune God in such a way that the Father's original decree and the Son's willingness to carry it out coincide in the Spirit's assurance that what is fashioned will reflect the free and loving creative will of the Father and the Son. The Spirit pledges, before the actual enactment of the divine consensus, that in the relationship between the uncreated and the created world the Father and the Son will meet in Himself as is the case from eternity. The historical unfolding of the relation between God the Creator and His creatures is perpetually secured by the Spirit, and as such pre-exists: "There pre-exists in the Spirit the whole reality of the fatherly compassion of God, His self-expression, His own glorification in His Son, the whole truth of the promise, the whole power of the Gospel, and therefore the whole order of the relation between God the Creator and His creatures. Because God is also the Holy Spirit in His will and activity toward and with the world and man, God becomes possible and supportable for the creature and the creature for God . . . We may say in a word that it is in God the Holy Spirit that the creature as such pre-exists."[50] This speculation on the pre-existence of all creatures in the Spirit is of course fixed for Barth in the actual role which the Spirit performs in salvation history. The Spirit acts out in revelation what He is from the beginning; as the life-giving Spirit of man from eternity, the Spirit provides warranty that man will actually exist as body and soul once he has been created and that his creaturely existence will be maintained in its essential relationship to the Creator.

In the course of time the Spirit is directly present to man not only as the divine ground of his creatureliness but also as the wise and loving power leading him to the achievement of the pre-existent decree of grace on his behalf. The Father externalizes this decree by creating the world of man;

the Son re-establishes its validity by reconciling the world to the Father, and the Spirit pledges its effectiveness by awakening man to faith and to obedience.[51] When the Spirit is at work in the sphere of creation, He aims at fulfilling man's spiritual and corporeal existence by allowing him to return through Himself to the origin of his being. It is in the faith, obedience and prayer of the Christian that the fatherly lordship of the Creator and the childlike obedience of the creature take place together through the Holy Spirit.[52] The historically subsequent work of the Spirit among men in the Church is possible because it is grounded in the pre-existence of all men in the eternal being of the Spirit. This insight forms the germ of what Barth means by the Spirit's role in the divine accompanying or divine providence. Through the faith and obedience of the Christian the Spirit elicits free human cooperation in His task of fulfilling the covenant of grace in the domain of world-occurrence and world-governance. All of human history already pre-exists in the benevolent disposition of the Father, the Son and the Spirit, "and indeed in the form of contingent history in His eternal decision regarding this creaturely history, in His election of grace as the eternal beginning of all His ways and works."[53] Only through faith and love, and thus through the power of the Holy Spirit, can man both understand the gracious operation of God among His creatures, and participate in the success of this operation. For, the Father's intention in all that He does through Word and Spirit is that, in everything which happens, no matter how great or small, there occurs both an objective movement from Himself to man through His Word and a subjective movement from man to Himself through His Holy Spirit. That the Christian through his Spirit-led activity can realize a correspondence between the Creator's will and world-occurrence convinces him that divine providence is not a form of tyranny, but a call to freedom and love.

The Creator's provident governance of the world both reflects and reveals His own interior freedom and love. As the Creator who has fully chosen to love man, the Father does not coerce man into a free and loving response, but commits Himself to solliciting such through the activity of His Word and His Spirit in the affairs of the world. The Father makes a claim on man through His Word and awaits a response from him through His Spirit; He speaks to man through His Word and is heard by him through His Spirit; He commands obedience from man through His Word and receives it through His Spirit. The Creator thus works among men objectively through His Word and subjectively through His Spirit. In this way men take part in the operation of divine providence, for when they are invited and go, when they hear and say yes, when they are given a command and obediently respond, they concur with the power of God's Word objectively given to them through the power of God's Spirit at work subjectively within them. Having accepted His Son, Christians return the Father's movement towards His creation back to Him through His Spirit: "Every time that God shows forth His power to the men of His choosing, and through them to others, every time, then, that He acts, He does so in the following way: His *Word* goes forth to these men, to be received by them in the power of His *Spirit*; His *Spirit* is given to these men, to receive His *Word* of power."[54]

The Spirit is operative not only at the origin of the intradivine decree of grace, but also during its temporal unfolding in the form of divine providence. The Spirit is God eternally grounding the very life of His creatures so that in time their free and loving existence in Christ can return all things to the provident Father.

By arriving at the core of Barth's anthropology with the realization that the Spirit assures among men the efficacy of the Creator's Word, this chapter concludes where it began, that is, with a consideration of the free and loving existence of the Christian as a child of God. Barth's reflections on the anthropological role of the Spirit inevitably lead back to his soterio-eschatological pneumatology. The Holy Spirit is active in a general way among all men with the intent purpose of leading them in a specific way back to their Creator through His Word. The *Church Dogmatics* (III) thus centers on the Spirit as the Lord of man's realized promise of life in freedom and loving obedience as a son of the Father. All human life and human history are determined by the free and loving turning of God to man through the Spirit of creation who is no other than the Spirit of redemption. The one Spirit of God acts in two ways: as the Creator Spirit He gives man the breath of life as the presupposition of that new life which as Redeemer Spirit He will bring about. When man as body and soul responds to the awakening and vitalizing power of the Spirit in him through free acts of loving obedience, the goal of God's self-revelation and the temporal fulfillment of God's eschatological promise is achieved. In the uniquely Spirit-filled Jesus of Nazareth, whose life's breath was transformed into everlasting life, the model of man, the source of salvation and the hope of glory appeared within creation's bounds. The perfect likeness of the Creator, which the Spirit fostered in the freedom and loving obedience of Jesus Christ, He now fosters in the analogous existence of the Christian. This is the central theme of the anthropological aspects of Barth's pneumatology.

CHAPTER VI

THE SPIRIT, THE CHURCH AND ONTOLOGY

The *Church Dogmatics* (IV) marks a pneumatological turn in Barth's theology, since the person and work of the Holy Spirit emerge as its dominant theme. Within the doctrine of reconciliation Barth intends to treat the renovating work of the Holy Spirit and man's participation in it in great detail and at great length.[1] As a response to the critics who find in his theology a disproportion between the descent of God to man and the ascent of man to God, Barth counters that his ensuing pneumatology, by underscoring the latter, unites these two aspects of Christian revelation and forms a correspondence between them. In attempting to understand both the root of the mystery of reconciliation within the history of the triune God and its fruit within salvation history, Barth is compelled to a new stress on the Holy Spirit as the material "coincidence" between these histories: "More and more the Holy Spirit has forced Himself upon us as the true theme of this section, and He must now be our constant theme as we try to penetrate the matter at this dimension of height and depth."[2] Barth turns to the Holy Spirit as the one in whom the Reconciler, Jesus Christ, continues to exist among the many who believe in Him. The expressly ecclesiological aspects of Barth's pneumatology result from the conviction that the Holy Spirit unites Christ and man, thus rendering incomplete either a christomonistic or an anthropomonistic solution.

The framework on which Barth's ecclesiological pneumatology rests is already familiar since it is essentially the same which he employed earlier: the Holy Spirit is God Himself creating the new being of the Christian community; He alone is the divine possibility and power of the coexistence of Jesus Christ and man; the Holy Spirit brings God's freedom and man's freedom to true encounter; all communication between God and man is the work of the Holy Spirit, God as He bridges the gap between the objective divine change of man in Jesus Christ and the subjective human response to this unexpected alteration of his being. Yet now Barth says all of this with an air of definitiveness: "From God's standpoint, and therefore with final seriousness, we have to do with the totality when we are dealing with the unity between the man Jesus and other men, and therefore with the being and operation of the Holy Spirit."[3] With pneumatology one grasps the totality! Through the power of the Holy Spirit man's free decision for God echoes God's free decision for him. This happening represents for Barth the totality of theology which surpasses the partial truths of either christomonism or anthropomonism.[4] The definitiveness with which this is stated corroborates Barth's admission that the human response to reconciliation, which the Holy Spirit initiates, must now come to the fore: "That man *can* and *must* and *actually does respond* with his own life and work, that he makes his own free decision corresponding to the divine change, is something which he cannot do by his own wisdom and power or in his own freedom . . . The divine change and act in virtue of which this happens— seen now from the standpoint of the freedom, ability, willingness and readiness of man—*is the work of the Holy Spirit*."[5] The Christian community exists through the Spirit's power. He brings human persons to the free decision which makes their existential lives in fact correspond to the historical givenness of the Christ-event.

Though pneumatology has come to the fore, it may never stand alone. The existential being of the community is secondary; it is grounded in the primary being of the God-Man. Only the admission that Jesus Christ exists in the community by His Holy Spirit, gives ontological significance to the converse statement that the community exists in Jesus Christ by His Spirit; the order of divine grace depends on the order of divine being. Otherwise, the life of the Church would not be implanted in the life of God; it would lose vitality and wither. The Holy Spirit assures that the being of Christ and the being of the Christian community are historically coordinated and unified: "Itself excluding a misunderstanding, the second, pneumatological statement tells us that the relationship of the being of Jesus Christ to that of the community is not static or immobile, but *mobile* and *dynamic*, and therefore *historical*. As the act of the Holy Spirit which underlies the existence of the community takes place in the order of the being of Jesus Christ and His community, the latter existing as Jesus Christ *causes it to exist* by His Holy Spirit."[6] Barth thus maintains that the Holy Spirit does not act independently of Jesus Christ. Nor does the Christian community exist independently. The Holy Spirit guarantees that His own allegiance to the ontological order of being, established by the Father through Jesus Christ, will be reflected in the noetic appropriation of revelation by the graced community. To assure that the Christian community can exist as Christ exists, the Holy Spirit coordinates and conjoins the order of being and the order of grace. The temporal form of Christ's being, the Church, forms one entity with the being of Christ Himself.

This one entity is what Barth calls the *totus Christus*, the coexistence of the glorious Christ and His Body, the Christian community. The Spirit can perform this unitive function between Christ and the Church since He only repeats in this work His eternal function within the Godhead. As the Spirit of the Father and the Son, He assures the unity of divine community. As the Spirit of Jesus Christ and of the Church, He assures the coordination of the *totus Christus*, of the heavenly and earthly forms of the being of Jesus Christ; "Just as the Holy Spirit, as Himself an eternal divine 'person' or mode of being, as the Spirit of the Father and the Son *(qui ex Patre Filioque procedit)*, is the Lord of peace between the two, so in the historical work of reconciliation He is the One who constitutes and guarantees the *unity* of the *totus Christus*, i.e., of Jesus Christ in the heights and in the depths, in His transcendence and in His immanence. . . . He is the One who constitutes and guarantees the unity in which Jesus Christ is at one and the same time the heavenly Head with God and the earthly body with

His community."[7] With this statement Barth not only links the ecclesiological aspects of his pneumatology to those he had developed when he considered the Spirit's role in the Trinity, in the incarnation and in creation, but he also reveals the main themes of the pneumatology of the *Church Dogmatics* (IV): the Holy Spirit is Himself the unity between the objective and subjective dimensions of reconciliation, between the ultimate and penultimate glory of the community and between the ontic and noetic self-communication of God's being. Soteriology, eschatology and ontology, not simply as theological doctrines but as experiences of Christian faith, are functions of pneumatology.

1. Ecclesial Existence: Predicate of Jesus Christ's Being

When Barth speaks of the existence of the Christian in Christ and in the Spirit, he does not mean man's natural, but his redeemed, altered existence. The lordship of Christ and of His Spirit accounts for man's peace with the Father, for his new state of knowing that he is a son of the Father. Through His self-communication in Jesus Christ, the Father guarantees man's objective participation in His own community, and through His self-impartation in the Holy Spirit He guarantees man's subjective participation as well. The salvation of the Christian community thus has a twofold basis in the two different ways in which the Father graciously turns to man while he is at enmity with Him: in Jesus Christ and the Holy Spirit. Both names are indispensable to the community's existence, since the historical event of mankind's reconciliation with the Father through Jesus Christ at one point in time becomes an existential event in the course of time through the Spirit's work in the community of Christians. Existence in the ecclesial community rests on the Spirit's ability to make the community itself a predicate of the being of Jesus Christ, the Reconciler of God and man: Jesus Christ's being is the community's being. The Spirit can do so since He is the Spirit of Christ. Thus, "Jesus Christ in the power of His Holy Spirit" or "The Holy Spirit as Jesus' Spirit" are two complementary and distinguishable, but in the end identical statements: "The power of Jesus' calling is the power of the living Word of God spoken in the community. And the power of this Word is the power of the Holy Spirit. As Jesus Christ in the power of the Spirit, or the Holy Spirit as *His* Spirit, creates recognition, establishes knowledge, calls to confession and therefore quickens the dead, the existence of the community begins and endures. Hence its existence is absolutely given, imparted and presented to it by Him as the One who in the power of His enlightening Spirit, the *Creator Spiritus*, is at work in it."[8] When Barth considers the creative work of the Spirit, he understands it primarily in the soteriological sense: the Holy Spirit brings men to new birth in the salvific community of Jesus Christ, the Church.

As Barth promised, he does highlight the role of the Holy Spirit in the renovating work of raising man to true participation in the being of the God who has freely chosen to be gracious to him. At least Barth makes perfectly clear his intention to give pneumatology an indispensable function in his theology. He returns again and again to an explicit reminder of this aim throughout the *Church Dogmatics* (IV). This point is essential to any evaluation of Barth's pneumatology, which one might readily accuse of being secondary to his christology. For Barth, however, there can be no question of primary or secondary when it comes to the being and work of God in any of its aspects. To neglect the lordship of the Holy Spirit in the Christian community as it awaits the final coming is to reject belief in God's powerful presence among men: "As the Spirit of the Lord (2 *Cor*. 3:17), the Spirit is Himself the Lord. To restrict His dignity or depreciate His work is thus to question God Himself. To reject Him in this time between is to reject God, i.e., the God who in this time acts and speaks in the Son through the Holy Spirit. Hence the famous hard saying in *Mt*. 12: 31 about the sin of blasphemy against the Holy Spirit which cannot be forgiven because it denies the presence of God as the source of a life of forgiveness."[9] This could not be more unambiguous. Barth unequivocally states that the Holy Spirit is Lord of the new being of the Christian community and that God's action in the time of the community takes place in the sphere of the Spirit's lordship. Moreover, to diminish the Spirit's role is to question whether God's being has any salutary relevance for man.

What does the Holy Spirit do? He alters man's being by bringing peace and forgiveness. These two realities, more powerful than the anguish and hatred they replace, epitomize the ecclesiological dimension of Barth's pneumatology. Since the Spirit gathers the community through faith (*CD* IV/1), directs it in love (*CD* IV/2) and sends it out in hope (*CD* IV/3), He turns men from enmity with God to peaceful coexistence with Him through the forgiveness of sin. The Spirit alone realizes in the subjective experiences of the community the objective justification, sanctification and calling of all mankind in Jesus Christ. "So, then, man can have 'peace with God' (*Rom*. 5: 1). But how and on what basis? We can only answer: by the Word of God, in Jesus Christ, by faith in Him, by the Holy Spirit who awakens faith."[10] The Holy Spirit makes the verdict of the Father, His "No!" to sin in the death of Jesus Christ, a "Yes!" for the believer. The new direction of the world attained in the resurrection of Jesus Christ can thus instigate the Christian to love. The new promise of the world proleptically realized in the Spirit's presence among men can induce the Christian to witness to Jesus Christ and to hope for himself and for all others. In all these works the Holy Spirit guarantees man the ability to recognize the thorough alteration of his human situation: his sin is pardoned; his struggle with God is resolved into peace. But the passive voice does not express all. The Holy Spirit incites man to an active confession of this alteration through a life of lasting gratitude.

By describing the Holy Spirit as the gracious power of Jesus Christ and by stressing the Spirit's role in making forgiveness of sin the hallmark of ecclesial existence, Barth is directly countering Schleiermacher's view of grace as an immanent power of the community and his view of sin as an obstruction in the determinative power of the human spirit. For Barth, the Holy Spirit is the dynamic power of Jesus Christ at work in man leading him first to a personal realization of grace and only then to a proper understanding of personal sin. In the Christian self-consciousness the Spirit permits the objective nature of grace, revealed in Jesus' victory, to be existentially effective; the Spirit likewise permits the objective nature of sin, revealed in Jesus' death, to be seen as the antithesis to grace.[11] It was precisely in the course of clarifying Schleiermacher's notions of grace and of sin that Barth first came upon his pneumatological interpretation of Schleiermacher's entire theology. The latter was correct in illuminating the existential character of sin and grace, but if Schleiermacher's theology were a true pneumatology, the role of the Holy Spirit would have been seen as making subjectively real in the being of Christians what is already objectively real in the being of Jesus Christ: God's No to sin in His Yes to grace. According to Barth, the redeemed man grasps the reality of sin as the antithesis to grace only through his encounter with the Spirit who makes dynamic and historical in him the reconciliation of all men in Jesus Christ.

Once again Barth is compelled to agree with Luther's later thought, with Pietism, with Kierkegaard's and with Hermann's stress on the *pro me* of Christian faith and on the experience of the Spirit's powerful presence in the individual. But Barth points out that this power and presence are rooted in the *propter nos homines* of the christological article of the creed.[12] Barth finds room for the *pro me* of "I-faith" in his pneumatology since the Spirit causes the individual Christian in the community to experience his redemption as an interior happening. Yet the transcendent power active in man's personal awareness of grace is no other than the Spirit of Jesus Christ who gives man a real share in the one source of grace, the incarnate Word: "It will be acknowledged that Christian faith is an 'existential' happening, that it is from first to last I-faith, which can and should be sung in I-hymns. But there will take place the necessary 'de-mythologization' of the 'I' which Paul carried through in *Gal.* 2: 20: 'It is no longer I who live, but Christ lives in me.' "[13] The Holy Spirit does foster a "I-faith" in the believer, a personal experience of being transferred from the state of sin to the state of grace, but the Spirit does so by effecting a christological alteration of the believer's being and not merely a change of consciousness which has nothing to do with ontology. Barth strives to fashion his pneumatology, or theology of personal sanctification, in line with his christology, or theology of objective justification. Only in this way can he avoid the theologically vacuous position which defines the power of grace as an innate drive inducing a person to acknowledge redemption without transforming him in the process.[14] By designating the Holy Spirit the divine power who alters man's being from within by uniting him to the actual being of Jesus Christ, Barth intends to offset excessive christianocentrism with christology and to counteract all too immanent understandings of grace with pneumatology. The Spirit of Jesus Christ is the power of the divine alteration of man which comes to him and transmutes his being. Within the "I" experience of the Christian the Holy Spirit makes man's being "christological" so that he enjoys real participation in the live reality of Jesus Christ. In granting the Christian forgiveness and peace, Christ's Spirit not only renders grace accessible and applicable to him, but also alters his being.

What is of prime importance to Barth, however, is that the Holy Spirit does all this in a visible way, since His action invariably creates an event in space and time. The Holy Spirit is the life-giving power of Jesus Christ taking on historical form in the Christian community. The Spirit communicates the being of Jesus Christ through discernible events: "For the work of the Holy Spirit as the awakening power of Jesus Christ would not take place at all if the invisible did not become visible, if the Christian community did not take on and have an earthly-historical form"[15] This insight leads Barth to develop his unique concept of Christian baptism in *Church Dogmatics* (IV/4). In the rite of baptism Barth locates the visible response of the Christian to the invisible divine alteration of his being brought about by the power of the Holy Spirit. Thus the reconciliation of man takes on and maintains earthly-historical form through water baptism, the symbolic response to the awakening power of Christ who is received through Spirit baptism. It is pertinent to this entire study that Barth's teaching on Spirit baptism corroborates and concretizes his claim that the Holy Spirit has become central in his theology of reconciliation. In pneumatology Barth discovers the totality in which revelation's *extra nos* in Jesus Christ is perfectly mirrored by the *in nobis*, that same revelation's goal in the baptized Christian. God's Spirit is at work when this happens. The Holy Spirit achieves in baptism a visible sign of the totality of Christian truth: God acts outside and inside man so as to transform him ontologically.

To underline that baptism is God's altering of man's being, Barth insists that the real sacramental power of this event which marks the beginning of Christian life does not lie in the human action of water baptism, but in the divine action of Spirit baptism: "Baptism with the Spirit is *effective*, *causative*, even creative action on man and in man. It is, indeed, *divinely* effective, *divinely* causative, *divinely* creative. Here, if anywhere, one might speak of a sacramental happening in the current sense of the term."[16] Barth views baptism with the Holy Spirit as a direct encounter with Jesus Christ who shares with the Christian His own divine life. Water baptism, however, does not repeat the death and resurrection of Christ or independently create in the believer a share in Christ's life. The symbolic activity of the believing community serves both as a grateful apprehension of what the power of Jesus Christ has wrought and as a visible reflection of the divine activity in the world. By differentiating two distinct aspects of baptism, Barth rejects any notion of sacrament which could be interpreted as producing in the Christian a competitive duplication of the history of Jesus Christ. Water baptism is itself not a sacrament, but a reflection of the one sacrament, which is Jesus Christ's own history, bestowed on the Christian by the Holy Spirit: "Baptism as water baptism takes place in the light of the baptism of the Spirit, and with a view to it. As such, however, it is not itself baptism of the Spirit: it is always water baptism. Baptism takes place in active recognition of the grace of God which justifies, sanctifies and calls. It is not itself, however, the bearer, means or instrument of grace. Baptism responds to a mystery, the sacrament of the history of Jesus Christ, of His resurrection, of the outpouring of the Holy Spirit. It is itself, however, not a mystery or a sacrament."[17] The only sacrament which Barth acknowledges is the history of Jesus Christ which remains alive and operative in the Church through the activity of Christ's Spirit. The decidedly central place which

Barth attributes to the function of the Spirit in communicating Christ's life
to men at Spirit baptism enhances the pertinence of his pneumatology within
the christocentric structure of the *Church Dogmatics*.

Yet the apparent importance of the Holy Spirit in Barth's theology of
baptism is somewhat deceptive. The main point of his treatise is to defend
once more the independence of Christ in Christian theology. Barth will not
compromise with any attempt—whether Roman Catholic, Reformational,
Neo-Protestant or Existential—to confuse Christ and the Christian. There
can be no representation or re-enactment of Christ's life in that of the
Christian. There can only be a pneumatological synthesis of the two independent realities once the Holy Spirit has created a reflection of Christ's
being in the being of the community. Pneumatology must bolster genuine
christology. For this reason, Barth is against both Bultmann and Urs von
Balthasar, against both "the theology of the younger Luther" and "any
existentialist translation of the sacramental teaching of the Roman Church,"
since all of them are only "attempts to make the history of Jesus Christ
coincident with that of the believer and *vice versa*."[18] Barth is convinced
that Christian life in the Spirit is purely recognition of the life of Jesus
Christ, not its repetition. If Hans Urs von Balthasar brands this a "christological restriction" of Christian theology, Barth's unflinching reply is that
the "christological renaissance" in the Catholic Church, which for him
comprises the most positive element in Urs von Balthasar's thought, is
again falling into the danger of confusing justification and sanctification. In
doing this it can only link itself to the persistent tendency of Existential
Protestantism: "If only we were agreed—and this applies to my neighbors
on the left (Existential Protestantism) as well as on the right (Roman Catholicism)—that the ultimate and the penultimate things, the redemptive act
of God and that which passes for our response to it are not the same.
Everything is jeopardized if there is confusion in this respect."[19]

How to avoid this confusion and to reconcile these differences? Only a
proper theology of the Holy Spirit can do so, because the Spirit alone is
the mediator between the justification of the believer and his sanctification,
between the redemptive act of God and man's free response to it, between
the ultimate and penultimate things. Because the divine being and work of
the Holy Spirit mediate between Christ and the Christian, His presence and
activity are operative at both poles. He is the Spirit of the atonement's *extra
nos* in Jesus Christ and also the Spirit of the atonement's "existential reach"
in nobis. The Spirit's sanctifying work in the Church can neither be fused
with nor severed from his prior justifying work as the one who poured
Himself out on Jesus Christ and made Him the life-giving Spirit for all men.
The Spirit conjoins but does not confuse. The Holy Spirit can perform such
mediation precisely because, as God's historicity and reciprocity, He is
God's own mediating principle within and outside Himself. The desire for
such a balanced pneumatology stands behind Barth's question to Bultmann
and to Roman Catholicism: "Is it not better to make justification, even in
its significance for sanctification, genuinely *justification*, instead of trying
to understand it from the very outset as merely the beginning of sanctification?" The search for a proper pneumatology stands as well behind Barth's

query to Luther, Zinzendorf and Kohlbrügge: "Is it not advisable to make sanctification, even in its connection with justification, genuinely *sanctification*, instead of trying to understand it from the very outset merely as a paraphrase of justification?"[20] The leitmotif pervading the ecclesiological dimensions of Barth's pneumatology, which explains his controversial teaching on baptism, is that the being of the community is not determinative of, but depends on the being of Jesus Christ: "Nor does Jesus Christ exist for His part only as the *community* exists. No, the community exists as *He* exists . . . by the enlightening power of His Holy Spirit."[21] Barth intends to quell the controversy between the extreme "justificationists" and the extreme "sanctificationists" with his pneumatological ecclesiology. The Holy Spirit at work in the Church is the divine mediator between the source of justification in Jesus Christ and the human experience of sanctification in the believer. In allowing the community of redeemed men to exist as their Reconciler exists, and thus to share in His being, the Spirit neither blurs the distinction between Christ and Christians nor exaggerates it.

2. Church as Parousia: Christ and History in Transition

Barth's understanding of the Spirit's role in the Church is not exhausted once he establishes that the Spirit is the source of the community's altered being, namely, its being in Jesus Christ. This first description is developed and broadened when Barth proceeds to consider the Spirit as the source of the community's being in transition, or eschatological being. Soteriological and eschatological dimensions coalesce in Barth's pneumatological thought as he probes the significance of the Spirit's presence in the Christian community. The goal of the Father's redemptive turning towards man is achieved when Jesus Christ's alteration of mankind's status is not only acknowledged but also accepted. If it is through the power of the Holy Spirit that this goal is assured in the Christian community, then the Holy Spirit is God orchestrating the spatio-temporal movement from Jesus Christ to man, overseeing the transition from His sphere to man's sphere. The dynamism of this divine movement is, in Barth's eyes, the essence of biblical eschatology. For this reason, the parousia is to be understood as one divine event which enfolds in three progressive stages: the resurrection of Jesus Christ, the promise and impartation of the Holy Spirit and the final coming of Jesus Christ in glory. In each of its forms the parousia of Jesus Christ is an eschatological event; it is a turning from God to man which has already begun, is now in transition, and will one day reach completion. The middle or penultimate form of the parousia is the time of the Spirit's activity in the Christian community. The Spirit makes the community aware that its existence is of a provisional nature; the being of the Church is in transition to ultimate being; in short, it is eschatological being.

The community in which the Spirit is Lord constitutes the middle form of the parousia of Jesus Christ. It is through the presence of the Spirit that Jesus Christ's coming is as real for the community "between the times" as it was for the first community at the resurrection and as it will be at the community's goal, the final coming of the Lord. The central position of pneumatology in Barth's ecclesiology rests on this insight: "The Easter event is the original because the *first* eschatological event. The impartation of the Holy Spirit is the coming of Jesus in the last time which still remains. As we shall see, it is the promise, given with and through the Holy Spirit, by which the community, and with it the world in which it exists and has its mission, may live in this time which moves towards its end. Hence the new coming of Jesus Christ has an eschatological character in this *second* form too."[22] The Holy Spirit grants the community a teleological character: He enables its being to be caught up in the dynamic event of the parousia. The community exists as its Lord does, since the risen Jesus is in its midst as He makes His way to the ultimate form of His self-manifestation as Lord of the cosmos. The Spirit's very presence in the Church is the penultimate coming of Jesus Christ.

Key to Barth's entire ecclesiology, therefore, is the event of the outpouring of the Holy Spirit on the community at Pentecost. This event signifies the divine pledge that the community is already underway with its glorious Lord towards the final goal of world-occurrence. The Holy Spirit makes accessible to the community the presence not only of the risen Christ, but also of the cosmic Lord who, though not yet fully manifest, is in transition towards His final appearing. As the penultimate pledge of the parousia, the Holy Spirit assures that the community is already enclosed by the ultimate pledge that it will be present at the return of Christ and participate in the new creation. Through the power and work of the Holy Spirit the community is at each moment the recipient of the promise of the eternal kingdom. The hope of Christians is well founded since the penultimate parousia is not to be separated from the ultimate; rather the ultimate parousia is contained within the penultimate.[23] For this reason, Barth understands the Holy Spirit as none other than God Himself granting men an ultimate pledge in a penultimate form. The Christian community is the parousia, and, though it is in transition, the community is thoroughly eschatological.

By designating both the resurrection and the Church as forms of the parousia, Barth admits basic agreement on this matter with Neo-Liberal theology in general and Rudolf Bultmann in particular. But, since Barth understands Easter as the first and Pentecost as the second form of the parousia of Jesus Christ, and insists that these events are inextricably connected to their ultimate unrealized form, Barth radically qualifies his agreement with Bultmann. Though Barth does so only implicitly, he indicates that his need to make a correction of Bultmann's thought is pneumatologically motivated. This is in line with Barth's general contention that Bultmann's Existentialism could be interpreted as a theology of the Holy Spirit if his anthropological reading of revelation were augmented by an objective christology. Again Barth holds his pneumatological reinterpretation of Bultmann in abeyance, because he is convinced that a sound christology is lacking: "We are then forced to accept the statement of Rudolf Bultmann (with particular reference to John's Gospel): 'The parousia *has* already *taken place*,' although we must be careful to make the proviso that this statement is not to be taken exclusively, but needs to be amplified by the recollection that this is not the whole story. The outpouring of the Holy Spirit *is* also the parousia. In this it has not only taken place but is still taking place today. And as it has taken place in the resurrection and is taking place today in the outpouring of the Holy Spirit, it is also true that it *will take place* at the end of the days in the conclusion of the self-revelation of Jesus Christ."[24] Barth thus implies that Bultmann's statement could be a valid pneumatological assertion if it were to include genuine christological content as well; instead it remains in Barth's eyes an anthropological reduction of biblical revelation's christological content.

How is pneumatology to maintain its roots in the Christ-event? The work of the Spirit will without exception have to be welded to the ongoing movement of Christ in history. Otherwise the present will become unmoored from the past and the future. This reasoning leads to the key insight concerning the Holy Spirit in the *Church Dogmatics* (IV/2): the exigencies of the doctrine of reconciliation compel Barth to explain the very "holiness" of the Spirit by defining Him as the eschatological power of the risen Christ: "The Spirit is no other than the presence of Jesus Christ Himself: Christ's stretched out arm; Christ Himself in the power of His resurrection, i.e., in the power of His revelation as it begins in and with the power of His resurrection and continues its work from this point. It is by the Spirit's power that Christ enables men to see and hear and accept and recognize Him as the Son of Man who in obedience to God went to death for the reconciliation of the world and was exalted in His humiliation as the Son of God, and in Him their own exaltation to be children of God."[25] With this identification of the Holy Spirit with the power of the risen Christ, Barth clarifies ecclesial existence as man's direct share in the eschatological event of Jesus' resurrection. Only this indispensable link of the Spirit's work in the Christian community with the resurrection of the God-Man preserves revelation's witness that the Church takes part in the eschatological glory which objectively commenced in one man's history.

To make this link even clearer, Barth forcefully argues that the Holy Spirit is neither some amorphous entity, nor, as Schleiermacher held, a spiritual determination of human consciousness, but the Spirit of a unique man. Although in dealing with the Holy Spirit one deals with God, one does not deal with God in an unmediated way, "but with God (directly) in the form of the power and lordship of the man Jesus."[26] An encounter with the Spirit, therefore, does not have obscure but definite features. It is an encounter between man and man, between the man Jesus Christ in the power of His lordship and another man. The Holy Spirit is thus the Spirit of a man, of the God-Man Jesus Christ. The actions of the Holy Spirit among Christians are interpersonal, since through His activity the person of the exalted Son of God encounters other persons. In so doing the Spirit allows the eschatological being of the risen Lord personally to alter the ontic status of Christians. Interpersonal contact with the exalted Lord on His way to ultimate victory is the privilege of those who live in the eschatological time of the community. To deny this is to claim that the work of the Holy Spirit in the Church can be understood apart from the past and the future coming of the man Jesus Christ. With this exclusive christological understanding of the Holy Spirit Barth intends once more to de-philosophize and to de-psychologize pneumatology. The very meaning of the Church as an eschatological community would be jeopardized if the Holy Spirit were not the self-revelation of the man Jesus who is the sole source of mankind's salvation.

What then does the Holy Spirit add to the salvific work of Christ? Is the Spirit so fused to Christ that Barth can find no distinctive role for the third mode of God's existence? Barth's answer is that the Holy Spirit in fact belongs at the center of his dogmatics.[27] For, the solution to the central theological problem of rendering the transition, the mediation, the union between Jesus Christ's history and man's history must be a spiritual one. Only God who is Himself Spirit can solve a problem of such great magnitude. God, as He does this, is the third mode of divine existence, the Holy Spirit, the spiritual center and principle of God's own being as Father and Son. Barth comes to this conclusion first by considering the solution to the historical problem of the connection between Jesus Christ and His community: "We have been considering the *history* which takes place between the existence of the man Jesus and that of other men . . . when as a result of this communication we have to reckon with the reality of His community, of Christians, as well as with that of Jesus Christ Himself. . . . The outpouring of the Spirit as the effect of *His* resurrection, of *His* life in His death and in the conquest of His death, and therefore the occurrence of *His* self-impartation ('Because I live, you will also live,' *Jn.* 14: 19) is the answer that we have given to this historical problem under the guidance of the New Testament."[28] The 'christocentric' theologian of the century openly admits that the solution to God's problem concerning man, His problem *ad extra*, is the Holy Spirit.

Barth does not stop here. This pneumatological solution only answers God's problem with relation to His creation. If the Spirit were only God's solution to the problem of relating man's earthly history to that of Jesus Christ, the Holy Spirit would be alien to God, some kind of magical third between Jesus and the Church. Barth thus concludes that the Holy Spirit is, previous to creation itself, the divine solution to God's own interior problem, that is, His eternal existence in tension and conflict as Father and Son. In God Himself there is a distance which must be freely narrowed, a confrontation which must be mediated, an encounter which must lead to communion and a history which must be worked out in partnership. The tensions and antitheses which men experience between themselves and God are not foreign to God's eternal being as Father and Son. These intradivine antitheses remain, but are overcome continually by the solution and answer to His own problem, the Holy Spirit. God's problem with man is similar to God's own problem with Himself; God's solution of the historical problem is the very solution of His internal conflict: "This is the problem which with its answer and solution is primarily *His own*, so that we are not alien to Him, nor He to us, when in the Holy Spirit He intervenes with the solution and answer for the problem of these antitheses before and in which we also stand. He knows this problem long before we did, before we ever were and before the world was. For He knew Himself from all eternity, the Father the Son and the Son the Father. And we must not try to know it in any other way than as a spiritual problem, characterized by the problem of God Himself by its answering and solution in the presence and action of the Holy Spirit."²⁹ Because God is also Spirit, Barth finds a pneumatological resolution at the center of God's being which serves as the model for his own dogmatics.

Barth is thus led to see the relevance of the order of divine being for the order of grace. That the Holy Spirit is the transition between Christ and Christians and between Father and Son indicates that God has provided a correspondence between ecclesial existence and His own being. This correspondence is the Holy Spirit. As the one transition both from Father to Son and from Christ to the Christian, the Holy Spirit is Himself the co-incidence between God's being both inside and beyond Himself: "Only one of Christian history's three factors coincides with one of the three modes of being (or 'persons') of God, although in this case the coincidence is quite unequivocal, the *third* and middle factor, the divine power of the transition from Christ to Christendom, being identical with *God* in the mode of being of the *Holy Spirit*. It is from this center that we shall have to think if we are to recognize the light of the Christian thought of God, or let us say objectively, the light of the triune God which shines in and over this history."³⁰ This pattern of thought forces Barth to view the Holy Spirit as the mediating principle *(das Vermittlungsprinzip)* between Christ and the Church as well as between God the Father and God the Son. All antitheses are mediated by God the Holy Spirit as He spans time and eternity. For this reason, the Spirit's function as the middle form of the parousia of Jesus Christ affords Barth a legitimate theological center of his ecclesiology.

Yet Barth's reflections on the Holy Spirit as the mediating power of God influence his christology as well. On the one hand, insistence on the priority of Christ seems to overshadow the admittedly central function which Barth attributes to the Holy Spirit in the Church. On the other, the priority of Christ seems to be intelligible only because the Holy Spirit was and remains the central factor of Jesus' existence. The first trend is evident in the many passages in which Barth understands the Holy Spirit as the divine agent of transition between Christ and the Christian. Christ's existence is the primary pole; it is the objective *prius*, that which God *de jure* accomplished in one man for all men; the *illic et tunc* of Jesus Christ marks the ontic ascription of new being to mankind. In contrast, Christian existence is the secondary pole; it is the historically realized *posterius*, that which God accomplished *de facto* in many; the *hic et nunc* of the Christian community marks the noetic apprehension of the new being ontically rooted in Christ. It is the work of the Holy Spirit that these two poles, though they remain in tension, exist in such a way that the first is in constant transition towards the second, and is, in the case of Christians, united with it.³¹ Barth's reflections on the eschatological being-in-transition both of Christ and the Christian community compel him to regard the Holy Spirit as the divine source of this otherwise impossible symbiosis of God and man. This understandable desire to avoid ambiguity and thus to underline the Spirit's function of creating a reflection of Christ's existence in Christians necessarily lends Barth's pneumatology in its various forms an essentially christological character. Even in the ecclesiological aspects of his pneumatology Barth returns continually to the christological basis of the being and operation of the Holy Spirit.

The converse, however, is also evident especially in the *Church Dogmatics* (IV/2) where Barth counterweighs his christological pneumatology with a surprisingly well-developed pneumatological christology. As the Spirit becomes more central in his ecclesiology, his christology becomes more Spirit-centered at the same time. Though in earlier volumes Barth had sketched the outline of a pneumatological christology, within the doctrine of reconciliation these initial attempts are developed at length.[32] Just as the Christian is awakened, impelled and sent by the eschatological Spirit of the Reconciler, so the Reconciler Himself, whose reflection the Christians are, is seen as driven and guided by the same divine Spirit. How can Jesus Christ be both sent by and sender of the Spirit? Barth responds that as suffering servant and as risen Lord Jesus lives by the Spirit. The Reconciler is not only conceived by the Holy Spirit but is the unique bearer of the Spirit; His entire existence is Spirit-filled without measure. Jesus' humanity as that of the Son of God is determined by the fact that He is "fully and completely participant not only in the *good-pleasure of the Father* but also in the *presence and working of the Holy Spirit*—fully and completely because in virtue of His *origin*, because as the *Son of God* He is also the Son of Man."[33] Barth thus understands the human existence of Jesus Christ as completely initiated, sustained and directed by the Spirit of the Father and the Son. The incarnate Son thus bears the Spirit in a definitive way.

Moreover as risen Lord, Jesus Christ sends the Spirit. It is while he reflects on the ecclesiological aspects of his pneumatology that Barth describes the permanent metaphysical change effected in the man Jesus by the Holy Spirit at the resurrection. By the Spirit the risen Lord became "a spiritual man" so that "His being in flesh is directly as such His being as Spirit also." By the life-giving and death-destroying Spirit (1 *Pet.* 3: 18) "this man is the Lord who is Himself Spirit." Barth thus asserts that the man Jesus has become, is and remains Spirit; He now lives and is present to all men in the Spirit's eschatological power: "The Spirit is holy as the power in which the man Jesus is present and *alive* even after death as the One who was crucified for the world's salvation, and in which He continually acts as the man He became and was and is, as the One who was crucified in the flesh."[34] Through the Spirit Jesus Christ now carries out His salvific mission in the world, not only because He is filled and impelled by the Spirit (*Mk.* 1: 10, 12), but also because He exists in the activity of the Spirit, furthers the Spirit's work, "incorporating the Spirit in Himself as the capacity to receive the grace of God and its influence in the creaturely world. He is the *pneuma zoopoioun* as Paul calls Him (1 *Cor.* 15: 45; 2 *Cor.* 3: 17) and as such the 'man from heaven,' the second and definitive, the *eschatos Adam* (1 *Cor.* 15: 45-47), the Elect, the Beloved, on whom there rests the divine good-pleasure in defiance of the sin of man (*Mk.* 1: 11; 9: 7)."[35] Not only does the Spirit carry out the work of the risen Jesus in the ecclesial community, but according to Barth's pneumatological understanding of christology, the risen Jesus carries out the work of the life-giving

Spirit of God. Jesus can send the eschatological Spirit to the Church because He is alive by the power of the same Spirit whom He possesses in fullness. Barth's christological pneumatology rests in his pneumatological christology and *vice versa*.

The Spirit made Jesus come alive from the dead and gave Him eschatological life in fullness; now Jesus is able to be present to all men before His final exaltation as the sender of the Spirit whom He Himself received. To exist in the Church means to receive the Spirit from the risen Lord as the pledge that one is a participant here and now in Jesus' eschatological glory. The Spirit in turn directs the Christian backwards to the resurrection and forwards to the parousia and unites him to the origin and goal of his redeemed existence in the Spirit-filled Jesus who is Lord of the Church and the cosmos. How to understand this complexity? In answering Schleiermacher, the Existentialists and Roman Catholics, whose theologies are almost totally pneumatocentric or christianocentric, Barth stresses that pneumatology must be christological. In answering the early Luther, Zinzendorf and Kohlbrügge, whose theology is almost totally christocentric, Barth insists that christology must be pneumatological. In his own theology of the Church Barth attempts to bring both insights together: the eschatological being-in-transition which the Christian experiences through the Holy Spirit is a share in Jesus Christ's glory, the sole origin and goal of his new life; but the Christian equally experiences that Jesus Christ encounters and enlivens him only through the power and lordship of the Holy Spirit who first quickened Jesus and made His parousia the ground of his eschatological life in the Church. For this reason the Spirit stands at the center of Barth's theology as the divine transition between Jesus Christ and mankind.

3. *Metaphysics of Faith: God's Ontic Noetically Realized*

When Barth speaks of the "being" of the Christian community, He invariably employs descriptive adjectives such as: new, christological, eschatological. These qualifiers indicate that what is at work in the *Church Dogmatics* is not a philosophical, but a theological notion of ontology. Barth's unique concept of being gradually developed as a reaction to the philosophical presuppositions underlying the theology of his main opponents. Barth asks what determines a theologically valid notion of being: Jesus, the *analogans* or the believer, the *analogatum*? *Deus homo* or *homo christianus*? The *unio hypostatica* or the *unio mystica*? Does Christian existence have an ontological ground outside itself, or is it simply noetic, that is, enclosed in the process of its own intellectual apprehension?[36] Barth opts for the first term of each pair; Jesus Christ's existence determines that of the world and of man, since "everything is plainly topsy-turvy if we picture this relationship [of Jesus Christ and the Christian] in such a way that the being of Jesus Christ is deduced and interpreted from the being of man and the world instead of the other way round, if we derive the atonement from creation instead of creation from atonement, if we derive as the first and eternal Word of God that which we think we can recognize, i.e., postulate and maintain as the final word on the evolutionary process of finite being and development."[37] In order to say everything the other way round and thus to correct the central misapprehension of modern theology, Barth returns again and again in the *Church Dogmatics* (IV) to what he considers the distinctly theological ontology which emerges from the study both of revelation's content and its effect on the existence of the ecclesial community.

Barth approaches the ontological character of the Christian community by analyzing the faith which it confesses as the objective ground of its very existence. The kernel of this faith is that all men in general, and Christians in particular, are called by God the Father to find the ultimate realization of their existence in Jesus Christ, His Son. There is no other interpretation of their existence which assures them the ontological truth about themselves: "For this reason unbelief has become an objective, real and ontological impossibility and faith an objective, real and ontological necessity for *all* men and for *every* man."[38] Belief in Jesus Christ is an ontological necessity for all men since they are enclosed by the circle of His being. God the Father makes an "ontological declaration" concerning the objective status of mankind in the revelation of His Son. As a result, there exists an "*ontological* connection" *(ein ontologischer Zusammenhang)*, totally independent of man's noetic understanding of it, between Jesus Christ and humanity. This insight is the germ of Barth's ecclesiology, whose main purpose is to show how the objective reconciliation of all men in Jesus Christ takes on concrete form when Christians recognize and proclaim the real union between their existence and that of their Lord. The confession of this ontological connection with Jesus Christ also places the Church in a special relationship to all other men, for through faith Christians know that they are ontically bound to those to whom their Lord is bound, namely, all humanity: "It is this ontological connection between the man Jesus on the one side and all other men on the other, and between active Christians on the one side and merely virtual and prospective on the other, which is the basis of the fact that in the New Testament the gathering and upbuilding of the community, of those who know Him, is depicted as a *necessity* grounded in Himself, and that this community is sent out, again with a *necessity* grounded in Himself, and entrusted with the task of mission in the world."[39]

The existence of the Christian community is not grounded noetically, that is, in the personal apprehension of revelation, but ontically in revelation's transcendent Subject, Jesus Christ. For only by putting on Christ do Christians experience an "ontic renewing" *(eine seinsmässige Erneuerung)*. This distinction is particularly clear in Barth's teaching on baptism. Baptism with water is the free human act which corresponds to the prior divine turning of God to man in Jesus Christ and in His Holy Spirit. Yet water baptism cannot alter man's being. It is only through the reception of Spirit baptism that a person is transformed into a new state, one in which he accepts his "ontic belonging" *(die seinsmässige Zugehörigkeit)* to Jesus Christ: "It is thus more natural to assume that *Gal.* 3: 27 ('For as many of you as were baptized into Christ have put on Christ') is looking back to the divine change, to the putting on of Christ which in Jesus Christ Himself has been effected objectively, and subjectively for the recipients of the epistle by His Holy Spirit, and that baptism is recalled as *the* concrete moment in their own life in which they for their part *confirmed, recognized* and *accepted* their investing with Christ from above, their ontic relationship to Him, not only in gratitude and hope, but also in readiness and vigilance."[40] This passage offers a key to understanding Barth's entire pneumatology. The Holy Spirit brings it about that a man can freely corroborate the already extant ontological relationship between himself and Jesus Christ. What is objectively a new being for each and every man through Jesus Christ, the divine Ontic, is confirmed by individual men through the Holy Spirit, the divine Noetic. With the notion of a new being already virtually operative in every human person and consciously operative in the Christian, Barth elaborates on what he means by the "ontological connection" between Jesus Christ and all men. He does so by making a distinction between the new being for every man which has been brought about *in nobis* by Jesus Christ, and the realization of this new being for every man which has not yet been brought about in each individual man. And it is precisely this latter process which is temporally accomplished by baptism with the Holy Spirit.[41]

As the power of the risen Lord, the Holy Spirit makes the post-Easter community cognizant of its ontological relationship to Jesus Christ, and incites its members to proclaim to all the new state of existence won for them in the resurrection. The Spirit's task is to induce the hearts and lips of men to recognize and to confess what in Jesus Christ is a real change of humanity's condition. As the Lord of the Christian community, the Holy Spirit binds men together in faith, the noetic recognition of their ontic relationship to the risen Lord. This recognition is not automatic; a free decision is necessary to close the circle of refashioned and reoriented life with which Jesus Christ surrounds each person. The Holy Spirit is the divine liberating power effective in the Christian, and at work in every man, enabling his personal freedom to close the circle, and thus to assent to the ontological status assured for him by Jesus Christ. In other words, the Christian, in anticipation of each and every man, rejects as an ontological impossibility a life in disobedience, and accepts as the only ontological possibility a life in faith. Barth does not envision incorporation in the Church as a *fait accompli* for all men; an individual must freely incorporate himself into the Christian community by personally acknowledging in water baptism the power of Spirit baptism to make effective in him his ontic relationship to Jesus Christ.

The Holy Spirit is the Redeemer precisely because He performs this function of liberating man from the impossibility of severing himself from the very alteration of his being accomplished by the Reconciler, Jesus Christ. Positively, the Holy Spirit awakens man to a new freedom so that he can personally choose as the determining factor of his existence the ontologically real thing, faith, existence in the community of Jesus Christ: "And it is the awakening power of the Holy Spirit that this impossibility as such and this necessity as such so confront a man and illuminate him that he does the only objective, real and ontological thing which he can do, not omitting or supressing or withholding but necessarily *speaking* the Yes of the free act which corresponds to it, choosing that for which he is already chosen by the divine decision, and besides which he has no other choice, that is to say, faith."[42] The Holy Spirit is the dynamic power of God confronting man with the false reality of his independent existence, and freeing him to agree to his true status as an elected and redeemed son of the Father because of his ontological relationship to Jesus Christ. The Holy Spirit creates an analogy of faith between the being of the believer and that of Jesus Christ: as Jesus Christ is for me, I am for Him. In this way, man discovers the direction his freedom is to take. Barth thus alludes to the "ontology and dynamic" of the law of grace which the Holy Spirit indicates to the Christian.[43] The Holy Spirit puts a man in the position where he can realize subjectively and noetically that he is not alone, but that he is objectively and ontologically a new, true and exalted man with Jesus Christ. The Christian community, which already has accepted and acted on the correspondence of its being to that of Jesus Christ through His Holy Spirit, is therefore entrusted with the task of publicly witnessing its new status to those who have not yet come to the personal realization of their ontological condition.

Despite his long-standing aversion to use of an obscure and extraneous metaphysics as the starting point or interpretative tool of Christian dogmatics, Barth does admit at the end of his theology to what can be called the "metaphysics of faith." Constraint must be exercised here in accord with Barth's own caution in this matter of ontology. He constantly protests against viewing the being and activity of Jesus Christ or His Spirit as a thought system or "as an interesting disclosure of an ontological reality."[44] But revelation itself compels Barth to describe the real, ontological character first of the Christ-event and subsequently of Christian existence in the Spirit. Yet Barth makes every effort to explain man's knowledge of the metaphysics of faith not as an abstract product of human wisdom but as a real state revealed and realized by the Holy Spirit. Only the divine power both of Jesus' unique existence and of the corresponding existence of Christians can reveal the truth about God's and man's being in human concepts. The metaphysics of faith is derived from the noetic apprehension of the truth about God and man which the Holy Spirit makes possible by convincing man of the verdict of grace pronounced by God: "This verdict is therefore both the ontic and also the noetic—first the ontic and then the noetic—basis of our *being*—not outside but in Jesus Christ as the elected Head of the whole race—but of *our own* being and to that extent of our being with Him and side by side with Him . . . The hearing and receiving and understanding of this verdict, faith in the risen and living Jesus Christ, is the presupposition that *we make* this recognition of our being in Him. Over this presupposition we have no power. Being as it is a matter of the *Holy Spirit*, of the faith which leads into all truth in the power and enlightenment of the Holy Spirit, it is only given and *will be* continually given to us."[45]

When an individual personally recognizes that the Father's ontic verdict of grace in Jesus Christ applies to him, the very goal of this verdict is achieved. It is the work of the Holy Spirit, the power of the living and risen Jesus Christ, that man comes to a knowledge of his true being concomitantly as he experiences his transformation into such a state through faith. This knowledge only follows the fact of faith. Through a metaphysics "from" faith, Barth guarantees that the real presence of the living Lord Jesus Christ in and for man remains such, and is not reduced to a subjective apprehension of self-evident historical truths or processes. What man realizes has first been realized in him. Thus, the metaphysics of faith depends on the prior experience of being altered objectively so that one personally realizes the ontological relation between Jesus Christ and himself. The Holy Spirit makes possible through the grace of faith a knowledge of being which respects the *de jure* ground of reconciliation in Jesus Christ, while the Spirit *de facto* brings this reconciliation home to the believer. Barth's entire pneumatology could be described as a metaphysics of faith. For, the Holy Spirit is the "divine Noetic which has all the force of a divine Ontic" in that He makes the ontological connection between the being of Jesus Christ and that of all men an existential reality for the Christian community, and in an anticipatory way, for the whole world.[46] The Holy Spirit not only carries out the prophetic self-declaration of Jesus Christ but also is Himself this prophetic self-declaration, since He is the divine Noetic with the full power of the divine Ontic, namely, Jesus Christ. The Holy Spirit can create knowledge about the new being of all men in Jesus Christ as it was won for them by the resurrection, because the Holy Spirit is the power of Jesus' resurrection and the penultimate form of His parousia. As the divine Noetic, the Holy Spirit can only reveal the divine Ontic to Christians by first bringing them into an intimate relationship with Jesus Christ. Thus, apprehension of the metaphysics of faith comes about through contact with its ground, the metaphysics of God.

Although Barth stresses that the Father's self-revelation in Jesus Christ and the Holy Spirit reveals both the ontic and noetic basis of Christian existence in the intradivine life of the Trinity, he still distinguishes between this eternal basis of ecclesial life and its historical recognition by the Church. Jesus' life, death and resurrection objectively grounds such a recognition, and the Holy Spirit's activity assures that this recognition becomes personal. In this way, Barth means to conjoin being and knowledge without confusing them; *nosse* is as important as *esse* in Barth's metaphysics of faith; the work of the Holy Spirit is as important as that of Jesus Christ; yet, in order to guarantee that being (Jesus' objective reconciliation) does not disappear into knowledge of being (the Holy Spirit's impartation of reconciliation), Barth insists on "the distinction between the ontic and noetic, or objective and subjective elements in the intercourse between God and man inaugurated and ordered in Jesus Christ."[47] This distinction provides the framework on which the ecclesiological aspects of Barth's pneumatology rest. In the redeemed community, the Holy Spirit creates a correspondence between the ontic nature of Jesus Christ and the ontological existence of the Christian because He is Himself none other than the Spirit of the divine Ontic. Furthermore, the Spirit creates a correspondence between Himself, the divine Noetic, and the human experience of knowing God through faith. The Spirit is distinct from the Father and the Son, yet is their "communityness" and knowability; He is also the penultimate form of the Son's return to the Father. For these reasons, the Spirit is God Himself underway towards incorporating all men in His divine community and granting them in the process human knowledge which reflects His divine self-knowledge. Without the divine Noetic the very communion and belief of the Church would exist apart from their metaphysical ground.

As his final answer to Roman Catholicism, Neo-Protestantism and Christian Existentialism Barth proposes what can be called a metaphysics of faith. In Barth's eyes each of these theological systems is covertly pneumatological at its core; the prime concern of each is with *nosse*, the Christian community's personal apprehension of divine life. Barth recognizes this concern as laudable, and accepts the stress on the experience of the ecclesial community as the necessary pneumatic pole of Christian dogmatics. But the noetic work of the Spirit in and for man, as indispensable as it is for a Christian theology, has ultimate validity only because the personal knowledge of the believer has an objective ground outside himself, that is, only because the Spirit who gives him knowledge is the "knowability" of God Himself. The divine Spirit brings the believer to know the divine being. Faith is grounded in divine metaphysics. Barth thus emphasizes in his pneumatology that *nosse* must follow *esse*, that neither the ontic nor the noetic aspect of revelation is to be absorbed by the other. For Barth, however, the precedence must clearly be given to *esse* if the import of *nosse* is to be secured: "The ontic or objective element *implies* as its consequence the noetic or subjective established by it. Conversely, the noetic or subjective element *implies* as its presupposition the ontic or objective which establishes it. If the implication is different from the two sides, it is still implication, and if we ignore it we cannot see or grasp on either side what is to be seen and grasped."[48] A Christian theology that is worthy of its name must be neither christomonistic or anthropomonistic, nor must it be either totally objective or totally subjective; it must contain both a christology and a pneumatology, or, as the structure and content of the *Church Dogmatics* suggests, a pneumatology which is rooted in Jesus Christ and a christology which is fulfilled by the Holy Spirit. To know this structure and content is to grasp the metaphysics of faith.

The ecclesiological dimensions of Barth's pneumatology highlight the essentially elliptical or bipolar character of his thought. It is the pneumatological pole which guards the *Church Dogmatics* from exclusive christocentrism, just as the christological pole guards it from extreme anthropocentrism. Spirit theology, as the complement to his Word theology, marks Barth's attempt to engage in the type of theology which he prescribes for his opponents: a theology with two poles in tension, a theology as equally christianocentric as it is christocentric, a christology colored by its pneumatological goal and a pneumatology colored by its christological origin. When a person is encountered by the Holy Spirit in such a way that he freely acknowledges and accepts his new being as a personal share in the ontological connection between Jesus Christ and all mankind, Barth's bipolar theology locates the germinal experience which it means it describe. If at the close of the *Church Dogmatics* the Holy Spirit comes to the center of Barth's theology, this is because here in the doctrine of reconciliation it becomes patent that Christians in community enjoy provisionally and vicariously what all men are destined to possess: a new, eschatological way of being which corresponds to the ontology of God. Through the Spirit of the Father and the Son, the eternally free gift of divine love which the Spirit Himself is, finds a home in the reconciled man. The community of such men who proclaim their new being to the world is the goal of divine reconciliation and thus the goal of God's being as "Revealedness" or Spirit. What the Spirit does eternally in the intradivine life, He does in the midst of the Church: He destroys discord and creates peace. This is the crowning insight of Barth's pneumatological reflections on ecclesiology and ontology.

PART III

IMPROVISATIONS ON BARTH'S SPIRIT THEOLOGY

CHAPTER VII

NATURE AS THE WORK OF SPIRITUS CREATOR

Modern theology cannot bypass the achievement of Karl Barth. Given the sheer volume and thoroughness of his Spirit theology, which the four previous chapters of this study only inadequately synthesize, it can be said as well that modern pneumatology cannot overlook Barth's contribution to this field. Besides the expanse and depth of his Spirit theology is the fact that it consistently serves as the element of his thought which disassociates him from his chief rivals; where they allow the autonomy of man, his experience, his history, his freedom and his reason to act as filtering elements by which Christian revelation is rendered intelligible, Barth posits the divinity of the Holy Spirit and His activity in man. Anthropology is thus totally conceived as the work of the Spirit; man's entire existence as well as his relationship to the God who longs to encounter Him is the domain of the third mode of divine existence. The Spirit alone exercises an hermeneutical function in Christian faith and theology since He is the noetic bond between the Father and the Son, which bond provides the sole paradigm of Christian knowledge. In illumining man's mind, the Holy Spirit constitutes his true being. Hans Urs von Balthasar succinctly expresses the all-determining role of the Holy Spirit in Barth's theology: "The divine Spirit, as the one who calls, establishes the human person; in establishing the person, however, the Holy Spirit presupposes his existence so that he can be the one who is called."[1] In short, the Spirit guarantees that man can know, love and serve God, since He is the eternal creator of this reality; He is the transcendent possibility of man's contact with God. Barth thus allows pneumatology to replace the entire concept of human nature.

It is well known that Barth disliked "Barthians;" he expected that others would persist in accounting for the being of God and the existence of Christian truth as they deemed adequate. No doubt what is to follow in this and the subsequent chapter could be read as a repudiation of the very foundation of Barth's pneumatology and as a return precisely to the insights which his Spirit theology aimed at eradicating. This is not the case, however. Behind what is to be said lies a deep appreciation of Barth's theological vision; in fact, the following comments spring from a sympathetic desire to preserve the depth of Barth's pneumatology by offering correctives which, in this author's mind, Barth himself at least foresaw as tenable, even though he did not pursue them himself.[2] For this reason, this entire evaluation is entitled "improvisations" on Barth's pneumatology. This word, on the one hand, resembles the word improvements; it is apparent that Barth's Spirit theology, because of the many critical voices which have been raised against it, stands in need of serious emendation. This chapter will attempt to restore an interaction between the Spirit of the Creator and the nature of man; the next chapter a balance between the work of Christ and that of the Spirit. On the other hand, the word improvisation connotes an impromptu, extemporaneous variation on a melody. Barth himself acknowledges the possibility that all could be fashioned differently, that one could start theology from the third article, that the concept of *Spiritus Creator* and the notion of Spirit Christology could have been developed to a greater degree. What follows is an essay at embellishing a Barthian theme by composing a Spirit theology which allots a more prominent status to the place of man and, ironically, to the place of the Spirit in an exposition of the third credal article.

The impetus behind this present chapter is the frequent complaint that God is so dominant in Barth's theology that man is reduced to a passive bystander. Karl Rahner isolates the problem in terms of Protestantism's refusal to develop a philosophical antechamber to theology. If Rahner cannot agree with all aspects of demythologization, he can at least recognize in Bultmann's theology the "serious" and "genuine" intention of introducing a transcendental-anthropological approach into modern Protestant theology, which, in reaction to Barth's method, is gradually realizing the need for a fundamental and apologetical starting point to an acceptance of revelation's truth.[3] This critique, of course, goes to the very heart of the matter, and Barth would undoubtedly regard it with the same mistrust which he expressed concerning the theology of Wolfhart Pannenberg: "Was he not building his house on the 'quicksand of yesterday and on the historical reckonings of probability which are so common today?' Was not his Christ merely the 'symbol of the presupposition of a general anthropology, cosmology and ontology?'"[4] Indeed Pannenberg directs his attention to the rampant subjectivism of both Barth and Bultmann who insist, in different ways, that revelation is man's sole source of knowledge about God; they both advocate a science of faith which is not open to the demanding process of verification or falsification.[5] This echoes the critique of neo-positivists, such as Hans Albert, who observe that Barth's understanding of truth only evades the self-governing function of human knowledge by hiding behind the "immunization process of hermeneutics."[6] Since Spirit theology affords Barth the sole interpretative instrument which can expose the validity of Christian revelation, it is the dominance of Barth's pneumatology which causes him to neglect the role of human reason in coming to divine truth. In effect, these critical positions can be summed up in von Balthasar's central point that Barth's Spirit theology prevents him from developing a theology of creation or of human nature.[7]

There are three divisions of Barth's theology which touch directly on hermeneutics, freedom and nature, namely, the trinitarian, anthropological and ontological dimensions of his Spirit theology. Thus the subdivisions of this chapter consider the ways in which Barth assures that the Spirit replaces the independent role attributed to man by his theological adversaries. Since the Spirit is conceived as the eternal knowability of the triune God, Eberhard Jüngel is correct in stating that "the position of the doctrine of the Trinity is therefore an hermeneutical decision of extreme relevance precisely because in this doctrine on the one hand the whole *Church Dogmatics* finds its hermeneutical foundation, and on the other hermeneutics itself finds its own starting point."[8] The very locus of Barth's refusal to entertain the thought that man must in some way be able to judge the truth of revelation, so that he can freely accept its absolute claim on him, is the role which the Holy Spirit enjoys as God's own hermeneutics. Thus Jürgen Moltmann points out that Barth's dogmatics begin "not with an apologetic prolegomena or with basic hermeneutical rules, but with the doctrine of the Trinity, which is for him the hermeneutical canon for his understanding of the fundamental Christian conviction that 'Jesus Christ is Lord.' "[9] Though Barth's christology will be discussed in the final chapter of this study, it clearly lies at the core of his insistence that the Holy Spirit is the *Spiritus Redemptor* and only as such also the *Spiritus Creator*. These various stances cause Barth's pneumatology to fulfill a decidedly noetic function. The Holy Spirit is primarily the divine teacher who transmits the truth revealed by and embodied in Christ. What Barth fails to admit, according to Paul Tillich and Wolfhart Pannenberg, is the need for a Christian theology of the Spirit as the Lord of all created life. Man's freedom and man's reason are given scant attention by Barth since he declines to lend his pneumatology an empirical basis by viewing the Spirit "from below" as the omnipresent Giver of life.[10]

Can the role of the *Spiritus Creator* be underlined without completely renouncing Barth's stress on the soteriological function of the Spirit? Can man's ability to interpret God's Word, his freedom over against God and the autonomy of his nature be affirmed without destroying the substance of the third article of the creed? Can the *ex patre* be underlined in Spirit theology without denying the *filioque*? Can the first article of the creed be given some independence from the second and the third, so that it can be legitimately stated that the Father acts through His Spirit beyond the boundaries of the Christian Church? These queries obviously shake the foundations of Barthian pneumatology. They muddy the waters which Barth, since the time when he distanced himself from Gogarten and Brunner and their stress on the first article, attempted to make clear and pure once more. Raising these questions again here no doubt creates the mood of "déjà vu" since they seem to be repetitions of questions which have often been asked before. John Thompson's disagreement with Colm O'Grady provides a terse expression of the possible futility of the debate: "O'Grady writes that Barth's 'theology of response and reflection' must be broadened to include a theology of participation, of 'sub-operation' and 'mediation.' This, however, is precisely what Barth has all along fought against—man sharing in a semi-independent way in the saving act of God in Jesus Christ, and so contributing to some extent to his own salvation."[11] What will redeem the following reflections from being mere reiterations, and thus allow them to add some new insight to the Barth question? First is the significant fact that Barth's pneumatology as such and not his christology or theological method is the starting point of the following improvisations. Second is the indisputable evidence not only that Barth himself develops a theology of the *Spiritus Creator* and a pneumatological approach to christology, but also that he singles out this very aspect of his thought as the possible path to a final truce between himself and his opponents.[12] The following critical remarks are thus made in the spirit of Barth's own self-doubt.

1. A Forward-Pointing Emphasis on the End-time Trinity

Although Barth repeatedly asserts that the experience of the Spirit reveals His essence, and that the immanent Trinity is known only through the economy of salvation, there is little evidence that he is consistent in maintaining this stance throughout the *Church Dogmatics*. Rather, once the nature of the Trinity is arrived at by means of an existential argument resting on Christian experience, Barth's teaching on the Trinity takes on an abstract, extraneous character which prevents it from constantly being discovered afresh through concrete happenings in the course of time. As a result, Barth's concept of the Spirit seems so fixed in advance that he senses no need for a continual development of his pneumatology as he considers the Spirit's activity in the midst of man's salvific journey.[13] Instead, there is a certain formalism in Barth's Spirit theology; all is already worked out by the triune God; man appears to be a privileged observer of a remote divine communion. As Henri Bouillard points out, "The history of salvation, as Barth understands it, takes on the form of a divine drama which is played out over the heads of men. One can easily assert that this history concerns us and that we are included in it, but the language which recounts the drama often seems to float over our heads."[14] Heinrich Zahrnt asks if something significant can really happen in history if everything has happened in eternity in the form of a "monologue in heaven."[15] If revelation is seen as objective only on the part of God, "one runs the risk of a speculative metaphysics in which man contemplates an accomplishment which takes place outside himself," as André Dumas observes.[16] These critical voices substantiate the impression that Barth's trinitarian pneumatology is somewhat sterile, and that this is the root of Barth's neglect of man's experience as the very locus where God allows His dynamic being to be comprehended anew throughout history.

No doubt Barth would view such reflections as a denial of God's aseity, of His eternal self-sufficiency apart from creation. But is this necessarily true? Barth himself sets out by trying to conceive the eternal being of God in an actualistic way; afterwards he surprisingly settles on a decidedly formalistic concept. Barth wants the eternal Trinity to be discovered through the image of the triune God which is found in Christian communion, faith, freedom and love; soon, however, Barth tolerates a gap to exist between the image and the reality.[17] Barth intends to speak of the triune God's presence in salvation history as the parousia approaches; predominant, though, is a transcendent view of the Trinity which lacks reference to the ongoing search of God for man in the drama of human freedom. Barth himself insists that his theology emerges from his lived experience in the world; yet the actual content of his trinitarian theology seems remote from the occurrences in social and political life.[18] Barth recognizes the need to view the present existence of the Church as a dimension of God's end-time; his doctrine of the Trinity in the *Church Dogmatics* nevertheless stresses God's origin and not His future. Barth means to present the being of God as relevant for the entire scope of history; what results, however, is a conception of the Trinity as a closed triangle in a timeless realm, and not as an open circle in which man constantly participates through grace. Barth's predetermined understanding of the Trinity accordingly has ramifications for his Spirit theology. What is at issue here is not God's aseity but the way in which God's sovereignty is made known to man and comprehended by him as it really is. Not the divinity of the Holy Spirit is questioned but the manner in which this reality is appreciated and related to the daily realities of human life.

This critique of Barth's theology emerges from a serious reading of both Protestant, Catholic and Orthodox theologians who in different ways aim at re-introducing the categories of human experience and world history into dogmatic theology. Wolfhart Pannenberg insists, in contrast to Barth's abstract and fixed concept of the Spirit, on emphasizing the Spirit as the Lord of history and of freedom, who is not yet fully revealed until the end of time itself.[19] Jürgen Moltmann rejects Barth's Spirit theology precisely because it is too noetic and past-oriented, and thus not adequately attentive to the new and hitherto non-existent activity of the Spirit of the Father and of the Son in the process of human liberation.[20] Along the same lines, Walter Kasper, a Catholic theologian, views history itself as a dialogue between God and man; this is evident in the history of Jesus, where there is a creative mediation between the eternal divine election and the temporal human obedience of Jesus; Barth's description of the three divine Persons as modes of being *(Seinsweisen)*, however, obscures the connection between God's eternally free love as a community of Persons and God's overflow of love into history.[21] All these theologians compel one to ask to what extent Barth's notion of the Spirit as God's *Vermittlungsprinzip* is really pertinent to the struggles of human persons and not just a formal pneumatological assertion without applicable content. Barth certainly sets out to understand the Spirit as the unique transition between God's history and man's history, but in actually doing so, does he overemphasize the Spirit's role and thus neglect man's part in this process of mediation?

In his pneumatolology, Barth fully intends to respect the dynamic biblical notion of salvation history. Why then does the trinitarian theology in the *Church Dogmatics* fall short of the historical dynamism which one would expect from such an initial emphasis on the actualism of God's self-revelation? What accounts for Barth's understanding of the Trinity as a perfectly united divine community from the very start and not as the Father's progressive series of gracious, self-communicating actions outside Himself in the midst of history? In other words, what ultimately explains Barth's formalistic and speculative trinitarian doctrine? More specifically, why does Barth conceive the Holy Spirit as the divine mode who completes God's internal wholeness, rather than as the divine mode who inaugurates and fulfills God's external disclosure of His being to man in the act of historical revelation, as the term "historicity" *(Geschichtlichkeit)*, with which Barth chooses to designate the Spirit, would seem to imply? If, as Hans Urs von Balthasar suggests, Barth opts for "theological actualism," a stress on God's activity in history, as a corrective to idle philosophical inquiry about God, it is hard to fathom why such a speculative notion of the Trinity characterizes the prolegomena of Barth's *Church Dogmatics*. Why not a dynamic concept of God which would serve both as the presupposition of Barth's actualistic theology and as the basis for the eschatological thrust which his approach seeks to guarantee?[22] Behind all these probings is the desire to respect the addressee of God's self-revelation as the real beneficiary of divine grace, and in such a way that man's entire being is radically altered by the Trinity's ongoing gift of itself for human salvation. Why then does the Holy Spirit seem so remote from the anguish of world-occurrence in the *Church Dogmatics*?

The accusation of formalism in Barth's Spirit theology must be traced back to his very concept of the Trinity itself. One therefore has to ask why Barth's expressly trinitarian pneumatology is open to the suspicion that it does not fully respect man's cooperation with the Spirit's liberating activity. Faced with this question, one must search for a way to revive a more dynamic biblical model of the Trinity than Barth presents in the *Church Dogmatics*, despite his original design to include precisely these elements in his pneumatology. Such a trinitarian model, one more compatible with the Scriptural understanding of God's self-revelation in history, is found among the Greek Fathers, and can be sharply contrasted to the Latin model which became fixed in the West with Augustine.[23] The Greek model begins with the revealed acts of God's three Persons and gradually reasons to His one being, rather than presupposing God's one being and then arguing that three Persons constitute this oneness as the Latin or Scholastic model of the West does. This insight is the result of the pioneering work of Theodore de Régnon and Michael Schmaus, both of whom rediscovered in the Greek Fathers a concept of the Trinity which is more in accord with the biblical witness of the New Testament.[24] The Greek model clearly points out the unity between the immanent and the economic Trinity and thus overcomes the opposition which subsequent models create between God's being in Himself and God's revelation in history.

The problem inherent in the Western model is that it invariably remains formal and "psychological" since it is constrained to explain God's threeness in terms of the inner processions and relations which take place within the absolutely inscrutable divine life. Thus, God at the deepest level of His mystery is not conceived as open to a reality outside Himself. Moreover, whereas in the East the interior relations of the three divine Persons comprise only the formalistic side of a trinitarian theology which rests primarily on the economy of salvation, the West makes the secondary, formalistic aspects of Greek thought the whole doctrine of the Trinity, and thus separates this doctrine from its roots in salvation history. In the West the result is that teaching on salvation contains only the minimum of trinitarian theology that is unavoidable for dogmatics. One is therefore forced, in contrast to the Greeks, to fill out the almost mathematical and formalistic doctrine of the Trinity with some content, and to make it more clear through what Augustine developed as a "psychological" doctrine of the Trinity.[25] In place of the Augustinian or Scholastic method, Karl Rahner advocates a less philosophical and more biblical way of speaking about the God who acts in three distinct ways in His dealings with the addressees to whom He communicates Himself in revelation. Rahner proposes that, to be true to the Scriptures, the theologian should constantly tend to veer towards the three-ness of God and only come to His oneness at the conclusion of the process of formalizing the doctrine of the Trinity; needed is a return to the historical and biblical thinking of the Greek Fathers: "Their trinitarian theology starts with the three Persons (three Persons who are of a single divine nature) or better, with the Father, who is the source from which the Son, and through the Son the Spirit, proceed, so that the unity and integrity of the divine nature is conceptually a *consequence* of the fact that the Father communicates His whole nature"[26]

If one juxtaposes the rediscovered Greek insights to Barth's trinitarian theology, one would at first have to admit that there are striking resemblances. The most obvious of these is that Barth soundly rejects purely philosophical and speculative notions of God. The doctrine of the Trinity plays an incontestable role in Barth's entire theology, since he conceives God as constantly acting, both objectively in His Son and subjectively in His Spirit, on man's behalf in the course of salvation history. The economic Trinity is the very image of the immanent Trinity for Barth. The often reiterated assertion throughout the *Church Dogmatics* that God corresponds to Himself *(Gott entspricht sich)* somewhat mirrors Rahner's insistence, for example, that God relates Himself as He is.[27] Barth thus takes a radical step away from a purely abstract concept of the Trinity because the historical communication of the Father's total self in His Word and in His Spirit is for Barth not a speculative doctrine unmoored from the witness of Scripture and the experience of Christians. Rather, it forms the very fiber of the anti-philosophical approach of the *Church Dogmatics*, where God is seen as continually revealing Himself ontically as well as noetically, *illic et tunc* as well as *hic et nunc*, and *extra nos* as well as *in nobis*, precisely through His incarnate Word and His poured out Spirit. Most of the central elements of the Greek model are therefore thoroughly incorporated into the very fiber of Barth's trinitarian theology. Barth, like de Régnon and Schmaus, relies on the Eastern Fathers in developing his trinitarian theology, and the influence of Athanasius, Basil of Caesarea and the other Cappadocians is particularly evident in his soteriological concept of the Spirit.[28]

One key element of the Greek insight, however, is glaringly missing from Barth's trinitarian theology, and since it is so significant, its absence accounts for the formalistic remnants in the trinitarian pneumatology of the *Church Dogmatics*. This essential element is the role of human mediation which builds the core of the Greek trinitarian model.[29] For, despite all the laudatory aspects of Barth's trinitarian thought, he adheres in the end to the Latin, psychological model, which tends to isolate God from the drama which he initiates with man as His partner; the God whom Christians confess as triune is the God who respects their independence. The neglect of the mediating function of man's experience in history, which results from the Western model, lends Barth's otherwise dynamic concept of God an undeniably static character. What explains this fact? The answer seems to lie at the very core of Barth's theology, that is, in his exclusively christological starting point of the doctrine of the Trinity. Barth finds himself, even when this doctrine is concerned, perhaps somewhat unwillingly slipping into an exaggerated Logos theology, which pays little attention to the generating Father and to the mutual spiration of the Spirit by the Father and Son. Everything circles around the all-important generation of the Logos. Thus the Logos is the central point of interest in Barth's trinitarian theology.[30] This unabashed preference for the Word consequently forces Barth to develop a trinitarian theology which is primarily concerned with explaining the pre-existence of Jesus Christ and thus with explicating the eternal relationship of the Logos to the Father and to the Spirit. Relatively scarce concern is given to grounding the being of the creature in the Father and in rooting his autonomy in the Spirit. Thus a serious question arises. Is there an inherent contradiction between Barth's Logos-trinitarianism and his intended actualistic description of the Trinity's function in human history?[31]

Although Barth plans to fashion an experientially based trinitarian theology and in fact does commence with the Father's historical, self-revealing act in Jesus Christ, he soon becomes so fixated with the theological implications of this one act for the triune God's inner life, that the original role of the generating Father and the equal place of the mission of the Spirit in salvation history are eclipsed.[32] The result of this christological penchant in exposing the Trinity's inner being is that Barth is distracted from the desired biblical and eschatological thrust of his entire theology. Barth thus allows the primary creative act of the Father before the incarnation and His truly new self-revealing act in the outpouring of the Spirit after the resurrection to be overshadowed, even in the trinitarian section of the *Church Dogmatics,* by a dogged stress on the revelation of the Father in His Son and the Spirit's corroboration in this act. It is this predominant Logos theology, at the expense of a theology of *ho pater* or of *to pneuma* which ultimately is responsible for the formalistic, Augustinian-Scholastic bent in Barth's trinitarian theology. Suddenly the eternal history of God's grace to man in His Son takes precedence over the historical preparation for and consequences of this gracious act before and after the Christ-event.[33] The Creator is seen solely as the *Pater Redemptor;* the Creator's powerful breath solely as the *Spiritus Redemptor.*

Barth's pneumatology is so influenced by his Logos theology and by the Latin trinitarian model that the Spirit seems to be relegated primarily to the intradivine noetic function of assenting to what the Father and the Son eternally decide. Barth subsequently tries to ground the external actions of the Spirit on His prior divine role of creating between the Father and Son unity, knowability, freedom, peace and love. Yet, though the Spirit forms a correspondence first between the Father and the Son and then between the latter two and the believer, the entire notion that the Spirit is the generous outpouring of the love of the Father and the Son into the world is lost. Instead of being understood as the excess love bestowed by the Father and the Son on man, the Spirit in Barth's trinitarian theology serves chiefly to weld the mutual relationship of the Father to His eternally generated Son and then to assure that a parallel relationship exists between God and man.

If Barth were consistent with the actualistic and eschatological intentions of his Spirit theology, he would have presented the Spirit from the beginning as the total opening of the Father and Son towards human history.[34] The Spirit would thus be conceived as the creative love of the Father and Son given to man, grounding his freedom over against God and driving him towards his promised participation in the Father's Kingdom which was announced, realized and offered to man by the Son. Rather, to guarantee the supremacy of the Logos, Barth views the Spirit as continually realizing in the world a divinely predetermined history. The Spirit's activity in creation seems to supplant that of man. In this way the interplay between God's grace and man's nature disappears from Barth's theology precisely because of his pneumatology "from above". The Spirit does not act to awaken human nature to its full freedom, but dominates over man because of His intradivine mandate.

The interaction of God's Spirit and man's nature is missing in Barth's theology, since the Spirit's intradivine function becomes more important; the Spirit's economic role appears to be a divine production played out on an essentially insignificant human stage. There is no new, as yet unrealized future of human nature which man can develop with the aid of God's Spirit; there is only a repetition in the noetic order of what already is a reality in the ontological order eternally grounded in the Logos.[35] This failure to grant human history and human experience an independent role over against the God who comes to man as the Spirit of love and helps to direct his course towards completion, ultimately denies the role of human nature as the supremely necessary counterpart to divine grace in the act of mediation which takes place when God's Spirit cooperates with man. Barth allows the Spirit Himself, God's eternal mediating principle, to become the sole point of contact between God and man in time as well, so that autonomous human actions lose their right to play even a subordinate part in divine-human interaction. Salvation history is not seen to be the result of an essentially dialogical encounter between God's self-communicating acts and man's freely offered response.[36] Man's own actions which are accompanied by the power of the Spirit are deprived, especially because of the nature of Barth's trinitarian pneumatology, of any mediating role. The Spirit looms so large that man subsequently loses his historical significance in Barth's backward-pointing trinitarian theology. The Spirit's eternal role in the Trinity as God's own self-interpretation and historicity leaves little room for the Spirit's future work among men in Barth's pneumatology. Man is caught up in too passive a fashion into the Spirit's origin. The trinitarian aspects of Barth's pneumatology lack the insight that the free acts of the Spirit, as He brings God's own historical self-communication to completion, are sparked by the equally free acts of man.[37]

It is not un-Christian to maintain that God chooses to allow man's grace-filled being to induce Him to reveal Himself. If God so ordains, He can mediate Himself through man's self-understanding and through man's history, although He remains transcendent in His mediation. Barth does not entertain this possibility, since it would seem to relativize the genuine and absolute transcendence of God's Spirit. Thus, for the sake of the Spirit's sovereignty, man cannot be a free participant in the divine-human encounter which occurs in salvation history. This reason is itself legitimate, but one suspects that behind this valid insight are other options which preclude granting man his due part in cooperating with the divine Spirit. The latter is conceived by Barth totally in terms of the second article of the creed; the role of the *Spiritus Creator* is viewed exclusively in the light of the explicitly christological function of the Spirit. To insure that this soteriological mission of the Spirit is not lost sight of, His creative function is clearly subsumed under it. The Spirit points back to the Son and even further back to the origin of all things in the Father's Yes to the election of grace. The Spirit, however, does not point forward to the return of Christ and to the Father's coming Kingdom. In a real sense, man has little part to play in the Spirit's work since Barth prejudices the Spirit's very identity by stressing the "originative" Trinity and not the "eschatological" Trinity.[38] The movement Barth opts for is "Father←Son←Spirit" and not "Spirit→Son→Father". In other words, the Spirit directs man back in time and does not encourage him forward to the completion of the cosmos; the sending of the Trinity prevail over the glory of the Trinity at the end of time.

Though Barth expressly rejects talk about God's future, it seems that a forward-pointing or eschatological concept of the Trinity acts as a corrective and complement to his emphasis on the originative Trinity.[39] Once the eschatological Trinity, as a movement from the Spirit to the parousia of Christ and to the Father's glory, is envisioned, the Spirit acts as the starting point, since He makes man aware of God's threefold effort to reach him and to direct him towards the Kingdom. To use the imagery of Pierre Teilhard de Chardin, one could say that the Spirit infuses the world with divine love-energy, and steadily guides its graced freedom to the point where it is one with the Son and the Father.[40] This admixture of divine reconciling love in history enables the eschatological Trinity to work with man in realizing the fulfillment of the world. Here the Spirit enjoys an indispensable part; in the eschatological Trinity the Pauline understanding of the Pneuma as the pledge of future glory and as the first fruits of hope (*Rom.* 8:23) can be effectively joined to the Johannine conception of the Spirit as the Advocate (*Jn.* 16:7). It follows that the eschatological model of the Trinity has far-reaching implications for the efforts of the dispersed Christian community to reunite, to engage itself in dialogue with Judaism and with other religions and to take increased part in the struggle for peace and equality which so preoccupies mankind today. All these inter-Church, inter-faith and inter-national efforts of the Church can ultimately be grounded on the unswerving activity of the eschatological Trinity which is being spearheaded by the Spirit, the source of righteousness in the midst of mankind's injustice.[41] Not only is the Spirit reconciling fragmented factions of the human community to one another, but He is also at work in the ecological forces of the earth which are straining as they wait for the revelation of the sons of God. The eschatological Trinity is at the vanguard of matter's and mind's universal desire for unity.

But this action of the Spirit is not simply limited to some future moment. The Spirit is already actualizing the love-intention of the eschatological

Trinity in the course of time. An emphasis on the future rather than the origin of the Trinity should have the effect that the immanent life of God is not divorced from God's present saving activity, but identified with it. The doctrine of the Trinity should not be understood as a private monologue at the beginning of time which has very little reference to the activity of God in history. Rather, the Trinity should be seen as an open dialogue which in cone-like fashion zeroes in on the world, reaches an intense point at the glorification of Christ and at the outpouring of the Spirit and then opens up again, so that the whole cosmos is caught up in the spiritual, reconciling and hopeful love-intention of the Spirit who leads all forward to Christ and through Him to the Father.[42] The eschatological Trinity attempts to highlight the relevance of God Himself to the world. This relevance, however, is bound to God's triune identity. To separate God's ever-present significance from God's eternal being as a community of Persons is to deprive Him of a threefold openness to the world and particularly to man. This openness is due precisely to the fact that God is open in Himself; God is not a closed monad, but a community of loving interaction who chooses to energize creation with grace, and through that energy make all things ready—specifically through man—to cooperate with God's Spirit and thereby to reach their promised fulfillment. Barth might consider such an improvisation a return to his socialistic and eschatological thought of 1919, and thus a speculative and non-christological Spirit theology. It does offer, however, a forward-pointing emphasis on the economic Trinity present in human longing, and preserves all the key elements of Barth's own trinitarian theology while it situates them in a decidedly pneumatic and eschatological framework, which is not incompatible with christology though not exclusively christological.[43]

2. The Free Interaction of Created and Uncreated Spirit

No aspect of Barthian theology has divided the mind of modern theology more sharply than his concept of anthropology. Barth insists that man is not spirit by nature, but only has spirit as the result of his graced encounter with the Holy Spirit. If the previous critical remarks lament the passivity of man which results from Barth's stress on the Spirit's role in the originative Trinity, this problem becomes particularly acute in his theology of man. Both Protestant and Catholic criticism of Barth's theological anthropology centers around his denial of man's created nature as a free being. By rejecting the category of being for that of relation, Barth stands accused of representing an unbiblical application of *sola gratia* to the being of man itself and not simply to the act of faith. George Hendry expresses his misgivings concerning Barth's failure to grant man a perduring relationship to his Creator: "If there is no relation between the Creator and the creation subsisting all the time, but only the relation established by the act of grace, it becomes difficult to maintain the existence of the creation as a reality *over against* God. In his treatment of the doctrine of creation, Barth resolves the Berkeleian doubt as to the existence of the world by merging it in its salvation: *esse est salvari*. The sovereignty of grace has become totalitarianism.''[44] Since Barth situates the very being of man within the domain of the *Spiritus Redemptor*, the critique of this position by Arnold Come points out Barth's pneumatological restriction of man. In the end the human person possesses no real freedom or proper identity of his own over against God's Spirit: "And it follows in Barth's theology that man *is* not spirit, but only has the Spirit of God, because man is only a thou to the I of God, and so can have no unity of spirit in himself. Therefore, the apparent conclusion: *man is no subject or person*, because God is Subject or Person in His totality or unity as Holy Spirit, and man's only unity consists of his unity with God and with other men in the Spirit of God.''[45] For the sake of guaranteeing the Spirit's supremacy, Barth deprives man of any inherent subjectivity or spirituality; it is only the Spirit's gracious coming to man which makes the emptiness of human existence take on extrinsic meaning; intrinsically man remains a no-thing.

Clearly Barth does not assert that man's spirituality is rooted outside himself merely out of obstinate anti-philosophical motives. His lifelong reaction to the anthropological excesses of Neo-Protestantism, Existentialism and Catholicism force him to develop an expressly biblical notion of man as the one who becomes what he is as the result of an unexpected encounter with the loving action of God on his behalf in Jesus Christ. It is Barth's understanding of man as God's covenant partner in salvation history which leads him to link human existence inseparably to the covenant of grace, and thus to define being as graced being, as being-in-relation-to-God, or as christological being.[46] Ironically, however, this insight is carried to an extreme when Barth characterizes the human response to the Spirit's gift of grace as something which is not proper to man himself. Albert Ebneter expresses this problem very well: "Pneuma can never mean a natural something *(Etwas)* which would be given to man. Spirit is always only divine action, divine behavior. When Barth speaks of the spirit in man, then it can only be meant figuratively and can signify nothing else than the soul which lives through the Spirit, that is, through the divine action in him *(KD* III/2, 402; *CD*, 334).''[47] The Spirit thus not only freely bestows grace, but in doing so also constitutes the being of the receiver by lending his inherent nothingness or grace-less-ness the freedom necessary to become the recipient of a promise, namely that he is related by the Spirit to the one real being, Jesus Christ. Thus Barth's pneumatic ontology of man and of creation itself, because of its pure actualism and its relational character, seems to be "tendentiously docetic.''[48] Despite the good intentions which underlie Barth's decision to strip man of those spiritual capabilities which his opponents may have presented in too static or naturalistic terms, Barth in effect robs man of a genuine role in either accepting or rejecting God's gracious activity on his behalf. Barth often reiterates the fact that man believes and not the Holy Spirit in man, but the latter is so predominant that man's role is that simply of hearing and affirming an action which takes place beyond the realm of his proper freedom.

These observations do not imply a total rejection of a pneumatic anthropology which conceives man as an unsolved mystery in need of God's Spirit. Barth rightly points out the inadequacy of understanding the human person apart from the divine mystery which inaugurates, surrounds and orients his life, and which thus constitutes his being as an open question which seeks and is meant to find an answer in the person of Jesus Christ.[49] But Barth's ontology of grace or pneumatic anthropology represents a one-sided theological position which is dangerously tilted towards a monistic notion of the Spirit. Barth preserves the undeniable spirituality of the Holy Spirit at the expense of erasing man's spiritual nature altogether. Thus it is no exaggeration to say that there is a pneumatological limitation of man in the *Church Dogmatics* which legitimately opens Barth's theology to the charge that his concept of man's being and of man's freedom is fideistic. Something is radically wrong here which must be corrected, lest Barth's pneumatomonism eclipse the Scripture's pneumatic concept of man as the being open to the eschatological power of God's Spirit but at the same time endowed with a free spirit of his own which certainly originates from God's graced breathing on him, but which also is free to stand before God as a true partner in the drama of history.[50] How is one to sketch a contemporary theology which is fully appreciative of the Spirit's primacy and which is thus a truly pneumatic anthropology, though not one biased toward either an anthropomonism or a pneumatomonism? Just as man's spirit cannot be totally isolated from, it cannot be totally synonymous with God's spiritual presence. In other words, can the valid aspects of Barth's stress on the *Spiritus Redemptor* and those of the traditional stress on the *Spiritus Creator* be brought together, so that Barth's exaggerated pneumatocentrism can be corrected? To do so, two steps are necessary: first, the deepest roots of this disorder in the *Church Dogmatics* must be laid bare and then an outline must be provided of a Spirit-centered concept of human nature which is at the same time compatible with genuine freedom on man's part.

The reason behind Barth's emphasis on the *Spiritus Redemptor* can be traced back to his Anselm book of 1931. Ontic must precede noetic rationality and necessity in faith and in theology; this is interpreted to mean that the Spirit, God's Noetic, is bound to God's Ontic, the eternal Word become flesh. Thus, any correspondence between God and man consists in a relation which the Spirit noetically achieves in the human person, so as to conform his faith to the ontic reality of his true existence in Jesus Christ. Apart from this ontological connection to Jesus Christ man has no natural relationship to God. Should there exist an analogy of being between the Creator and the creature, then Jesus Christ could be bypassed and the whole of Christian dogma consequently reduced to a vague religious anthropology. It is for this reason that G. C. Berkouwer, a supporter of Barth's position, states that "the triumph of free grace is the true counterpart to the *analogia entis*."[51] To assure that the Spirit confessed in Christian theology is the Holy Spirit, that is, the Spirit of Jesus Christ who brings man the gift of unwarranted grace, Barth identifies the work of the *Spiritus Creator* with that of the *Spiritus Redemptor*. A separation of these two terms is precisely the error of his main antagonists who thereby award the order of creation an autonomy over against that of recreation. Barth's pneumatology, and the anthropology which is based on it, are chiefly meant to bolster the central Christian tenet that Jesus Christ is the one real man who possesses ontological significance for every man, so that the being of man exists outside himself in the eternal election of Jesus Christ.[52] Thus, the source of the disarray which induces Barth to present the human person as a passive bystander to the Spirit's work within him lies not so much in Barth's pneumatology as it does in his christology, which in the end determines his entire view of man. Behind the controversy over *analogia entis* and *analogia relationis* is more than a protracted interconfessional debate; it is a matter of whether the *ex patre* can to some extent be seen apart from the *filioque*. The very meaning of a theological pneumatology is at stake.

Though the plethora of literature on the analogy question rarely touches directly on Barth's pneumatology, underlying much of the discussion is the meaning of the *obedientia potentialis* which Barth does concede belongs to man, even if he regards it as a transcendent possibility, a being-able which the Holy Spirit brings about in the creature. Hans Urs von Balthasar tries to reconcile Erich Przywara's insistence on the *analogia entis* and Barth's use of the term *analogia relationis* by showing that Barth's stance, especially in the later volumes of the *Church Dogmatics*, implicitly contains the Catholic notion of man's inherent orientation to God. Von Balthasar observes that at many points in the *Church Dogmatics* Barth describes the relationship between God and His creature according to the classical formulation of the *analogia entis*. Since the meaning of *obedientia potentialis* is fully accepted by Barth, "this guarantees once again the concept of the *analogia entis* in his thought—admittedly as Barth uniquely understands this concept: a function of that which he characterizes as *analogia fidei*."[53] It is precisely because Barth interprets the covenant as the internal basis of creation and creation as the external basis of the covenant that von Balthasar finds Barth's anthropology to contain a tacit acknowledgement of the ontological interconnection of nature and grace in man's own being. Gottlieb Söhngen corroborates von Balthasar's view by stating that "even for Barth there is today no *analogia fidei* without the external basis of an *analogia entis*."[54] One seemingly valid interpretation of this compromise is that the work of the *Spiritus Redemptor* presupposes that of the *Spiritus Creator*. Though there is only one Spirit, indeed the Spirit of the Father and the Son, He is active in creation in various ways, or better, stages, leading man to the full expression of the freedom which is rightfully his from creation and which is searching for its fulfillment outside himself.[55]

Barth might accept this approach, if it were properly presented, since he comes close to embracing a similar position in the *Church Dogmatics* when he concedes that Jesus Christ is the man who possesses the Spirit of God in a definitive way. Barth's entire anthropology of the Christian is modeled on the Spirit-filled Jesus. Though Barth's christology generally descends vertically from above, and thus tends to ground the significance of the Christ-event in its eternal divine origin rather than in God's spiritual presence in the course of salvation history, he does consider the free cooperation of the man Jesus with the Holy Spirit at length. Could it be maintained that the *Spiritus Creator* is at work in the human freedom of Jesus so that the former may achieve in this one man's humanity the redemptive freedom to which all men are called? Is the human spirit of Jesus the paradigm of the ontological freedom inherent in all men which the *Spiritus Redemptor* totally opened in Jesus' unique case to the freedom of God's Word? If so, christology itself may offer a pattern for describing the complementarity of nature and grace, of man's created spirit and the Holy Spirit. This could be held without making Jesus' freedom simply a special case of man's general gift of freedom. It could be affirmed that no human spirit is as open to the Spirit's total gift of Himself as Jesus' spirit was.[56] But the uniqueness of Jesus would not have to mean that the ontological principle which is discovered in His being is not an ontological principle which is given to every man, though it reached a fullness in Jesus which can only be accounted for by the total possession of the Spirit which He alone enjoyed.

The point of this discussion of the Spirit's role in christology is that the uniqueness of Jesus Christ as the bearer of God's eschatological Spirit in total fullness leads to the discovery of a general ontological principle in all men. In this way, christology plays a central role in anthropology without, however, denying a free ontological relevance to all men as such. Suggesting that christology has extreme importance for a pneumatological anthropology, which takes man's own freedom over against God's Spirit seriously, means that it is possible to develop an "anthropology from the Spirit" which grants both the vertical perspective of the Spirit's primacy and the horizontal perspective of man's native spirituality their full worth and independence. Man would then be seen as ontologically oriented, from the very beginning of his existence, by the *Spiritus Creator* towards the full possession of the *Spiritus Redemptor* who brings him to the explicit confession of Jesus as the Christ, the definitively anointed One. Such an anthropology would be christologically-inspired, but not christomonistic. It would begin its reflection with the concrete historical life of Jesus, but then would move to a consideration of His life-giving Spirit who is gradually leading man's ontic spirituality, which can exercise a graced autonomy, towards that full openness to God's Word which became an historical reality in the one man Jesus of Nazareth.[57] Man's spirituality would thus be able to possess the relatively independent ontological function of probing towards an encounter with God's Spirit on his own and of saying a free yes to God's Spirit when this privileged encounter takes place.

Such an anthropology from the Spirit would do justice to Barth's concept of the humanity of God; it would respect God's absolute transcendence over man, but also God's gracious accommodation to him, both of which elements are essentially present in the Christ-event. The Spirit of Jesus Christ, the Redeemer Spirit, can thus be seen as God's sovereign grace, while the Creator Spirit can be seen as His condescending grace, which respects man's freedom and adjusts itself to man's ontic spiritual yearning. What results is mutual freedom: "The grace of the Lord Jesus Christ does not override man's freedom; it respects it, it engages it to the full extent, it bows before it, because that is the very way in which a real relation, i.e., a personal relation between God and man can be realized . . . it does not only descend upon man vertically from above, reducing him to the condition of a helpless target, but comes to meet him at his own level and engages him at the point of his freedom which is his spirit."[58] Such an understanding of the Spirit's encounter with man's freedom would allow room for the notion of the Spirit as God's overflow of love before, in and beyond the Christ-event; it would subsume anthropology under pneumatology, but at the same time call for a theology of man based on an ontological determination which is proper to him and which enables him to be a free recipient of God's love. This idea is expressed well by John Haughey who speaks of the Holy Spirit's work in two ways; He conspires with man's freedom by working subtly within his nature so that man is directed towards God from behind; He also works by calling man outside himself so that he is brought to an eager acceptance of the uniquely Spirit-filled Jesus. The first function of the Spirit, the transparent stage as it were, is the work of the *Spiritus Creator*; the second function, the explicitly soteriological binding to Christ, that of the *Spiritus Redemptor*.[59]

This sketch of created spirit encountering uncreated Spirit departs substantially but not totally from Barth's christological concept of man. It is inspired by Barth, but leans more towards a Catholic position as represented by Rahner, von Balthasar, Kasper and Dulles.[60] It also resembles to a certain degree Paul Tillich's "correlation-theology" and G. W. H. Lampe's pneumatology, both of which depend on the central notion of the Spirit as God's spiritual presence in creation.[61] Of course, this sketch also comes a step closer to Schleiermacher and Bultmann than Barth would ever go, in that an understanding of the Spirit's activity in the cosmos precedes and prepares the way for an understanding of Christ. The main direction of the present critique admits that Barth's reaction to Roman Catholicism, to Neo-Protestantism and to Existentialism was indeed too strong. His pneumatological correction of their often exaggerated anthropological approach leads to a virtual suppression of man's freedom and spirituality. Yet, this outline of a possible pneumatic anthropology is one which is certainly a recognizable variation on Barth, which, because of its insistence that the notion of analogy must deal with being and participation and not just with relation and encounter, creates space for man's own ontological independence in the presence of God's Spirit.[62] An attempt has been made to preserve what Barth seeks to safeguard in his own Spirit theology, without embracing his pneumatological restriction of man. This improvisation starts, as Barth's Spirit theology does, soteriologically and ecclesiologically; it also adheres to the christological determination and goal of creation; in respecting the supremacy of God's Spirit, it is ready to relativize and set limits to man's own freedom and spirituality; it even respects the notion that man's "being-able" is a graced or transcendent possibility which is only discoverable from the actual experience of being encountered by the *Spiritus Redemptor*.

The substantial departure from Barth is clearly the attempt to separate, for the sake of theological clarity, the Spirit who proceeds *ex patre* and the Spirit who proceeds *ex filio*. The one Spirit's actions are aimed at the same destination, but arrive at it in fundamentally different ways. Under the aegis of the *Spiritus Creator* the entire work of God beyond the Church and at least explicitly apart from Christ can find a genuine place in a Christian theology. Barth concerns himself throughout his writings primarily with redeemed man. What Barth discovers there, however, should be applied in an implicit way to the one who does not yet confess Jesus as the Christ. Thus the improvisation presented here also respects the steps or grades of awareness by which man perceives the christological and pneumatological orientation of his being.[63] It sees the graced dynamism of man's nature as open to God's free gift of His Spirit; man's ontic freedom is essentially related to God and objectively meant for Him, but man can also reject this orientation and find it necessary to pray in trembling for a new freedom from the Spirit who can encounter, transform and free him for Himself. Thus this sketch aims at incorporating both the graced but autonomous nature of man's freedom and the sovereign but humble transcendence of the Spirit's freedom in a truly dialogical theology of man which can be more properly called an anthropology from the Spirit. Does man then cooperate in his redemption? Yes, but only because the *Spiritus Creator* graces him with an obediential capacity from creation so that his nature longs for and finds rest in the saving work of the same Spirit who meets him as Redeemer and Lord.

Barth's pneumatology looms so excessively large since he does not accept such a graduated understanding of the means by which grace reaches man. Any mention of human freedom which is given by God at creation as the very condition of possibility that men exist who can be endowed with the fullness of grace in Christ strikes Barth as heretical. To assert that the *Spiritus Creator* bestows on all men the permanent gift of graced human nature does not automatically involve an idolatrous autonomy and indifference to the christological origin and goal of every manifestation of grace. Rather, as the experience of converts attests, there is invariably clear recollection that, while the future believer was searching for meaning, initial seedlings of the grace that was to bloom into acceptance of Christ were present both within his being and in the persons and places surrounding him. Thomas Merton would be the first to admit that grace is always christically and pneumatically determined, but that it is mediated to the human person through the dynamism of his free, spiritual nature: "Yet, strangely enough, it was on this big factory of Columbia's campus that the Holy Spirit was waiting to show me the light, in His own light. And one of the chief means He used, and through which He operated, was human friendship . . . So now is the time to tell a thing that I could not realize then, but which has become very clear to me: that God brought me and a half a dozen others together at Columbia and made us friends, in such a way that our friendship would work powerfully to rescue us from the confusion and the misery in which we had come to find ourselves."[64] This and similar passages indicate that pneumatology cannot be concerned only with the explicitly ecclesial expressions of grace; indeed the Spirit of the Lord is free to move beyond the bounds which Christians are obliged to adhere to. Rather than seeing itself as the paradigm of what occurs in the wider world, the Church must also look beyond itself to find the direction in which the Spirit is calling it: "This is a truth too easily forgotten and ignored by those who would restrict the Spirit's working to the sphere of the Church. Nor is it enough to say that the study of His working within the Church is the only safe clue to the discovery of His working in human life as a whole. Indeed the reverse may be true."[65] Thus genuine Christian pneumatology has to include, to fulfill its theological responsibility, an investigation of the graced dimension of human freedom.

Once this has been said, it must immediately be added that the knowledge of the Spirit's activity beyond the sphere of explicit grace is known only through the latter. This does not mean that the power of grace in any of its non-Christian manifestations is therefore less valid or less salutary, since once again all grace is christic and pneumatic. The Christ-event and the Pentecost-occurrence now determine all human experience, but at the same time do not do violence to the autonomy of human freedom. Hendrikus Berkhof makes this point forcefully: "From now on the world has the center of God's activity in its midst. Jesus Christ is the acting God present in our world. God's Spirit from now on is Christ's Spirit, without ceasing to be present in a more general way in the created world. God's action in Christ is His more specific operation, in the light of which His general operation is revealed in its ultimate meaning."[66] Barth's concept of human freedom, which is dominated by his desire to preserve the totally self-sufficient freedom of God, does not incorporate the more general operation of the Holy Spirit in the *Church Dogmatics*. The result is that the narrower circumference of the Spirit's power in the Church keeps him from examining the wider circumference of the Spirit's forceful proddings in creation, history and culture which are also aimed at the consummation of all things in Christ. The Spirit is seen exclusively as the one sent from Christ, but not inclusively as the one leading all things to the glory of the end-time through the mediation of mankind's secular experiments. Though Barth urges one to read the news of the day in the light of the Gospel, he does not see the events of the times as revelatory. Langdon Gilkey calls both major Christian confessions in the West to a new apologetical task which is at the heart of this improvisation on Barth's Spirit theology: "If Catholicism or Protestantism is to achieve the task of mediating the divine grounding, judgment and possibility to our secular experience, it must widen the scope of both word and sacrament far beyond their present religious, ecclesiastical, dogmatic and 'merely redemptive' limits."[67] Barth would no doubt suspect such desires as anthropologizing tendencies; the failure to attribute any God-given salutary power to human nature in his theology of the Christian, however, causes Barth's pneumatology to stifle graced human potential in an equally dangerous way.

3. Natural Theology as an Inherent Facet of Pneumatology

Just as the trinitarian aspects of Barth's Spirit theology overshadow man's role in history, and the anthropological aspects his God-given autonomy, so the ontological aspects overshadow his reason. As the study of God's own Noetic, pneumatology replaces the entire function which natural theology plays in the thought systems of Barth's theological opponents. Man's mind does not possess a native ability to reflect divine truth, since man is only made into the Creator's likeness by a continual encounter with the Holy Spirit; man pre-exists as the image of God in the Holy Spirit, but does not enjoy this privilege as a divinely ordained yet independent human right. Furthermore, since the christological mode of God's being alone embodies the divine Ontic, the pneumatological mode can only follow and not precede the Word of God. Consequently, the Spirit is deprived of any ontological significance other than that of the Word. Man's share in truth similarly depends on the ontological determination of his being and his reason which is located outside himself in another man, Jesus of Nazareth.[68] The Spirit exercises only the function of creating a correspondence between the being of Jesus Christ and that of man. This correspondence is already ontically grounded in Jesus Christ; it is, however, not yet noetically appropriated except in the case of the Christian whose being has been altered by Christ's Spirit. Again one comes face to face with the problem that the Redeemer Spirit so monopolizes Barth's attention that the Creator Spirit has no power to lead man to truth which is not explicitly christological. Thus, man cannot attain ontic certainty apart from the historical appearance of divine reality in the person and work of Jesus Christ. The pneumatic mediation of truth which dominates the *Church Dogmatics* makes the free search of human reason irrelevant, because the latter is ontically vapid. Barth's exclusively theological interpretation of analogy and ontology thus leaves no room for natural theology. In the end, his metaphysics from the Spirit, or ontology springing from faith, obviates the Spirit's influence on man's reason in a way which prescinds initially from the reality of Christ.[69]

If man's intellectual faculties are seen as completely darkened except for the light which the Holy Spirit brings with revelation, a denial of revelation's very possibility is involved, since the ability of man to consent to the claims on truth made by the person of Jesus, by the Scriptures and by Christian preaching depends on whether he is able to judge the validity of these claims against the background of his prior comprehension of God. Barth's pneumatology is positivistic precisely because he does not openly admit revelation's presupposition of an ability in man to discern that the truth of the Christ-event is identical with the truth about God which he seeks naturally. Thus, natural theology is not only known through revelation, but is also valid apart from its source. Karl Rahner continually makes this point when he considers the danger of resting theological method on too narrow a concept of revelation: "Revealed theology has the human spirit's transcendental and limitless horizon as its inner motive and as the precondition of its existence. It is only because of this transcendental horizon that something like 'God' can be understood at all. 'Natural,' 'philosophical' theology is first and last not one sphere of study side by side with revealed theology, as if both could be pursued quite independently of each other, but an internal factor of revealed theology itself."[70] For this reason, the suggestion that the Holy Spirit can operate within man's reason independently of Christian faith does not deny revelation's uniqueness, but does protest against its distortion due to a misunderstanding of its content. Behind the account of mankind's salvation in the Scriptures is the active presence of the *Spiritus Creator* who predisposes man's intellect to accept the truth which the Father reveals in Israel and in Jesus Christ. In other words, the explicit work of the *Spiritus Redemptor* presumes the same Spirit's hidden work in human intelligibility, so that the truth of Christ can be cogent to minds prepared to receive it. As Heinrich Fries asserts, natural theology has its foundation in the particular knowledge that Jesus Christ and His Spirit reveal God's being in act, and on this basis can then argue to a general philosophical notion of God. Thus, natural theology originates from the living faith which is dependent on God's historical self-manifestation, but then proceeds to speak of faith in terms intelligible to every man.[71]

The intelligibility of faith to every man is, of course, what Barth will not concede. As a result, the Holy Spirit is seen as the sole reality and possibility of personal faith in God's self-revelation. The sharpest critic of Barth's stance is Wolfhart Pannenberg who insists on the independent ability of man's reason to acknowledge the truth-claim of the Scriptures. By substituting the Holy Spirit for man's own reasoning ability, Barth misuses the biblical concept of the Spirit: "A message which is not convincing in another way cannot gain the power to convince by calling upon the Holy Spirit. When one who is convinced of the message of Christ confesses that his knowledge is the work of the Holy Spirit, this ought not to be understood to mean that the Holy Spirit is the criterion of the message of truth. Rather the reverse is true: the assurance that one speaks in the power of the Holy Spirit needs a criterion for its own validity (1 *Cor.* 12:1f.) and this criterion is the confession that Jesus Christ is the Lord (*ibid.*, v. 3), that is, the content of the message. The convincing power of the message of Christ cannot be seen apart from its content."[72] Put differently, it can be said that Barth attributes to the *Spiritus Redemptor* a function which is really that of the *Spiritus Creator*, the Lord and Giver of life who is present in every dimension of human existence and particularly in the quintessential dimension of reason. The Spirit of the crucified and risen Christ cannot be stressed at the expense of His concomitant identity as the Spirit of the all-powerful Father. Barth persists, however, in absorbing the more general anthropological working of the Spirit into His more specific soteriological mission. Reason is engulfed in faith; the Gospel alone grants intellect meaning. Man's mind on its own cannot yearn for the Spirit of Christ whom it judges to be the fulfillment of its graced potentiality from creation.

Natural reason is neglected for the sake of Barth's exclusively pneumatic insight into the nature of Christian knowledge of God. For all its claims to objectivity, the *Church Dogmatics* slips into a subjectivism which only furthers that of Liberal Protestantism rather than counters it: "The Christian religion could not have expected any other fate than the divorce of piety from reason, if it were to engage in such a separation of itself from reason and in a corresponding retreat into the purely religious, as Schleiermacher advocated and as it is proposed to a certain extent and rather paradoxically by Schleiermacher's great critic and antagonist, Karl Barth."[73] The ultimate failure to counteract Schleiermacher lies in Barth's pneumatological restriction of reason which dispossesses man of a relatively independent access to the truth. Such an allowance would create space for the Spirit's free encounter with man's inherently graced reason. Instead of developing the latent pneumatological character of Schleiermacher's theology along the lines of a dialogic meeting of man's rational spirit and God's Holy Spirit, Barth appeals to a rigid theology of revelation which pivots on a totally transcendent pneumatology. In effect this choice limits mankind's share in ontic truth to the one Spirit-filled person, Jesus Christ. Thus Barth loses the opportunity to conceive ontology more universally; if he had done so, he could have admitted that truth always emerges from an encounter of the Spirit's activity and man's reason in every instance, and thus before and after as well as in the Christ-event.[74] As it is, man's free avenue to truth, with which he is gifted by the *Spiritus Creator* is overseen in Barth's pneumatic ontology. It is invariably the *Spiritus Redemptor* who leads man back to a christologically-founded notion of truth. The *Church Dogmatics* indeed speaks of the Holy Spirit's contact with man as a rational encounter, but restricts the ontological basis of this rationality to one instance. Jesus Christ's total possession of the Spirit is understood to ground itself and not to rest on a general ontological principle which is rooted in man's created nature.

There is no disagreement with Barth's attempt at an ontology from faith which closely links knowledge of God's being with His actions in history, and which does not divorce the metaphysical from the actual.[75] This is the great achievement of Barth's study of Anselm, which enables him to comprehend the inherent rationality of revelation and at the same time impels him to stress the primacy of the concrete in the metaphysics derived from faith. The problem is that the Spirit's role in awakening man's powerless reason to truth is so perfectly achieved in the ontically unique Jesus that the Spirit's subsequent role among men, though it is made much of in the *Church Dogmatics*, seems anticlimactic. There Barth centers all truth in Christ and in His Spirit, and relegates man to the passive role first of hearing a foreign message and then of saying yes to an ontological reality which is, as it were, completely incomprehensible to him. Since the Spirit has already accomplished in the man Jesus the "sacramental" expression of the divine Ontic, the Spirit's noetic mission in the world appears hallow and man's cooperation in it superfluous. In other words, Barth's theology does not allow man's rational acceptance of the Gospel to add something new and in this sense to surpass the Spirit's activity in the person and work of Jesus Christ without denying the latter's absolute uniqueness. Missing in Barth's theological ontology is a cautious but necessary "renunciation" of the Word for the sake of allowing the Spirit to be immanently at work in man's rational being before and after the Christ-event in a way which is free from the Word and yet endowed with equal ontological validity. The Spirit would then be free to create new ontic expressions of divine grace which would not deny but affirm the second article and universalize it.[76] The deceptive importance of the pneumatic moment in Barth's metaphysics from faith underlines the need for a theological ontology which, while remaining pneumatic, would grant man's reason the relatively autonomous ability to recognize divine truth and to give glory to God. Such an ability on man's part would intensify but not minimize the truth revealed in Jesus Christ. In order to make the Spirit's dominance over man less rigid, the Father's self-revelation in Christ should be viewed as the measure and criterion rather than as the total manifestation of truth. In this way, the Spirit of the Redeemer can create in and through the spirit of man ontic participants in grace who certainly reflect and are conjoined to the reality of the Word made flesh, but whose suffering and joy, praise and service enhance the glory of the Creator.[77]

The phrases used above, such as "renunciation of the Word," "surpassing the Spirit's activity in the person and work of Jesus Christ," "intensifying the truth revealed in Jesus Christ" and "Jesus as measure and criterion rather than total manifestation of truth" are not meant to shock but to answer two legitimate questions. Why the first and third articles of the creed at all if the Spirit is not in some sense the forerunner and developer and not merely the repeater of what God achieved in and through Jesus Christ? How is the totalitarian dominance of the Spirit over man's mind to be mitigated unless the Spirit is conceptually freed from His teaching function and given once more the prophetic task of fostering new realizations of divine truth among men which complement but do not obliterate, bring to fulfillment but do not jeopardize the unique revelation of truth in the incarnation? Barth's intellectual adversaries fascinate him since they take up precisely these questions, but they disturb him, just as would the direction taken in this improvisation, since they seem willing to jettison the "ballast of christology." It is not a question of rejecting Christ, but of pointing to God's plan that Christ must be recognized as universal Lord through another totally different yet equally revelatory act of God, the creative and recreative sending of His Spirit. Barth concedes that Revealedness is as important as the Revealer and the Revelation, but treats Revealedness in such a way that man's reason is severely restricted in order that God the Spirit can act out His eternal noetic function. Man's mind is circumvented as the divine Noetic performs His revelatory mission. It does not seem that the Word and the Spirit are understood "incarnationally."[78] What is called for is a pneumatology which respects God's desire to make the Christ-event known to all men through the Holy Spirit, but which also respects man's free intellectual power as the means which the Holy Spirit wisely uses to create the full manifestation of divine truth which is most intense in Jesus Christ, while it still seeks for ontic reinforcement until Christ returns.

The task of making prudent use of man's mental faculties in His revelatory mission is not new to the Redeemer Spirit. He has been involved in such mediated forms of persuasion from the beginning of history by working immanently within man's mind and heart as the Creator Spirit. Not by abdicating His transcendence but by expressing it in and through His immanence, the Holy Spirit is God's hidden Revealedness acting within man's search for the God whom he of all creatures can come to know. This search is possible since man bears God's image due to his Creator's mysteriously generous yet fully earnest bestowal of grace from the moment when human nature emerged in space and time. In the light of these reflections, it can be said that Barth responds to Schleiermacher's extreme stress on the Spirit's immanence with an exaggerated stress on the Spirit's transcendence. It is necessary, therefore, to propose a Spirit theology which begins with man's experience of being led through the Spirit to the fullness of divine truth as one is surrounded by the overflow of God's love poured into his very nature. This would entail an understanding of God's pneumatic activity wherever there are human beings who express creation's dynamic restlessness in their quest for transcendence.[79] Such a pneumatology would affirm that the Spirit is the *Vermittlungsprinzip* of theology as well as of God's own truth; but it would also emphasize that the Spirit communicates divine truth by means of man's own acts of mediation. Such a theological construct would open the way for a metaphysics from faith in which man is brought to an inchoate knowledge of divine truth through his encounter with God's immanent Spirit, who accommodates Himself to man's own ontological structure and who works so that this independent structure becomes capable of participating in His own transcendence.

To allay any fears that such a pneumatology is not expressly Christian, one could argue that it can be arrived at precisely through a reflection on Christian experience and then generalized in a legitimate fashion to include as its presupposition a divine ordinance of the universe which far outreaches the domain of the Church. Such a Christian pneumatology would necessarily conceive the Spirit both as the *Spiritus Redemptor* and as the *Spiritus Creator*. On a first level of reflection the Spirit can be described as making the unique eschatological reality of Christ's Spirit-filled being a reality for all men. On a second level it must be asked how the Spirit is able to accomplish His soteriological function; here the Spirit must be described as God's life-giving power who allows man to possess from the beginning a rational human nature so that he can be receptive to God's eschatological activity and freely respond to it.[80] Barth's pneumatology can be criticized because the second level of reflection is deficient. He does not admit a correlation of God's Spirit and man's spirit, of God's Noetic and man's rationality. At least Barth will not attribute permanence to man's spirit and mind. He will not concede that man is created by God with a nature which is open to the Spirit's proddings, but which is at the same time free to accept or reject God's immanent spiritual activity on both a soteriological and an anthropological level. Barth must be commended, however, for highlighting the interconnection between the soteriological and the anthropological dimensions of the Spirit's activity. Obviously, the work of the *Spiritus Creator* cannot be totally separated from the same Spirit's work as *Spiritus Redemptor*; the two functions have to be kept in dialectical tension. The knowledge of one dimension must enhance the knowledge of the other. Thus Barth is in theory not opposed to reflection on the anthropological work of the Spirit. He too acknowledges that it could be understood to follow logically from the Spirit's soteriological activity.

However, the lacuna in Barth's pneumatology is that, once the ultimate union of the dual facets of the Spirit's mission is pointed out, he proceeds to stress the soteriological to the exclusion, for all practical purposes, of the anthropological. Walter Kasper has delineated the difficulty in distinguishing and yet conjoining the two aspects: "One finally stands face to face with the same problem of mediation. On the one hand we had to consider the universal activity of the Spirit in the whole of creation, in nature and history; pneumatology was therefore a help to express the universality of the salvation that has come in Jesus Christ. On the other hand we had to hold strictly to the uniqueness of Jesus Christ, and define the Spirit as the Spirit of Jesus Christ."[81] Though Barth knows this dilemma all to well because of his continual disagreement with his rivals over pneumatology, he never adequately acknowledges the salvific validity of the universal work of the Spirit in human nature and particularly in human reason. Barth does not entertain the possibility that what he brands a natural theology may in effect be a pneumatology of creation, history, culture and reason. This is not a farfetched theory since Barth himself continually is ready to interpret the anthropological tenets of his opponents as covert theologies of the Holy Spirit. Instead of accepting the validity of a theology of the Creator Spirit and linking it forcefully to reflection on the Redeemer Spirit, Barth rejects the former altogether, does not meet the objections of his opponents and likewise falls into an unmediated and subjective theology of revelation.

What holds true of Barth's rejection of natural theology also applies to his repudiation of a universal concept of being in which to situate the truth of revelation. In short, Barth will not ascribe to man an independent nature capable of knowing and embracing the truth about God which it perceives. All truth derives from the work of the Redeemer Spirit; the Christian theologian is thus confined to a metaphysics from faith.[82] Granting an independent ontological function to man's rationality, however, does not necessarily mean depriving God's Spirit of His sovereignty. A Christian natural theology springs from faith and leads to fuller faith. But faith is itself the result of an encounter of the Spirit with man's spirit. The analogy derived from faith thus rests on a prior analogy rooted in being, which aims at demonstrating that the Holy Spirit respects man's created, and therefore relatively free search for truth in the process of coming to faith. A pneumatic ontology, contrary to Barth's understanding, must allow man's natural spirit (the work of the *Spiritus Creator*) a true role in cooperating with the ontological and eschatological power of God in Christ and in the Church (the work of the *Spiritus Redemptor*). The ontological function which the Holy Spirit freely gives to man to use freely must be honored in a metaphysics from the Spirit.[83] Instead, Barth deprives man of his ontological ability to respond to God and places this ability totally in the Spirit Himself. A correlation of the divine and the human *Können* is impossible in Barth's theology since man's *transzendente Ermöglichung* can only mean a possibility which comes from God's side at every moment, and which necessarily denies an autonomous ontological structure to man himself. A balanced Christian anthropology should hold that this structure naturally corresponds to God's own being and not that this structure enjoys a relationship to divine being only through faith. God's Spirit permits man's being to be analogous to His own by making it free for the truth from creation.

Since Barth never allows this concession to man's own being, his Spirit theology maintains the character of transcendence which belongs to the divine *Pneuma*, but fails to restore to Him the immanence by which He is graciously present to man's spiritual nature as a free and rational being. The Redeemer-Spirit is never quite fully acknowledged as the Creator-Spirit of man's corporeal being and rational dynamism. It is unfortunate that the ecumenical possibilities, which Barth could have opened up for theology through a more balanced Spirit theology did not fully materialize. Such a pneumatology would have allowed more room in his anthropological reflections for man's created spirit as a true partner in an encounter with the Holy Spirit. This failure isolated Barth from such thinkers as Karl Rahner and Paul Tillich. Rahner's concept of man as spirit in the world and Tillich's attempt to speak about the ambiguities of man's spiritual life could have helped Barth to find a correlation and counterpole to his purely transcendent Spirit theology, which lacks precisely a consideration of man's nature as the work of the *Spiritus Creator*. Tillich points out this possibility of a reconciliation between himself and Barth which centers on the theology of the Spirit: "If for a moment I may be allowed to be personal, you see this same conflict going on between my own theology and Karl Barth's; the one approaching man by coming from the outside and the other starting with man. Now I believe that there is one concept which can reconcile these two ways. This is the concept of the divine Spirit. It was there in the apostle Paul. Paul was the first great theologian of the divine Spirit. It formed the center of his theology."[84] The anthropological aspects of Barth's pneumatology are in the end too reactionary and not open to needed ecumenical dialogue, because they so blatantly neglect the role of man in salvation history. But, as Tillich has seen, the possibility for an opening to other thought patterns in theology and outside of it can be found in Barth's Spirit theology more than in any other aspect of his thought.

CHAPTER VIII

CHRISTOLOGY IN A PNEUMATIC FRAMEWORK

The previous improvision envisions a pneumatology in which the Holy Spirit would not preempt man's role in the drama of salvation but would conspire with him by permeating and orienting his history, his freedom and his reason. Such a corrective to Barth's pneumatological restriction of man seems necessary, since the Spirit dominates human nature to the degree that creation is swallowed up in recreation. Now another improvisation is called for which does not center on the trinitarian, anthropological or ontological aspects of Barth's pneumatology, but on its christological and ecclesiological dimensions. In the latter, not only man suffers neglect in the *Church Dogmatics*, but the Spirit of God as well. This rather drastic statement may appear paradoxical; whereas it was stated above that the Spirit lords over man, now it is claimed that the Spirit does not prevail enough. Can Barth's pneumatology be both excessive and insufficient at the same time? The thesis here is that the Holy Spirit plays an inordinate part in Barth's theology of man but an inadequate one in his theology of Christ and of the Church. The germ of this paradox is the historical irrelevance which marks Barth's theology of the Spirit and of the Christian community because of his pronounced conviction that everything significant has been achieved by Jesus Christ. Barth is hindered from allowing the Holy Spirit's activity in human history to have its own salutary and innovative character, precisely because these general attributes of all God's self-revealing actions are confined by Barth to christology.[1] They are blatantly missing, however, from his pneumatology, that division of theology which is normally supposed to guarantee the spontaneous salvific power of God in a heightened way.

How can this central failure of Barth's Spirit theology be brought to light? On the one hand, the following series of questions can be posed: Is the role of Jesus Christ so exaggerated in Barth's account of salvation history that the work of the Spirit, as a distinct salvific self-communication of the Father, is relegated to a decidedly second place in the whole sweep of the *Church Dogmatics*? Does the activity of the Spirit add anything new to God's self-revelation in Jesus Christ?[2] Is the "objective-subjective" dichotomy really appropriate to describe the difference between Christ's mission on behalf of man's salvation and the Spirit's mission to this same end? On the other hand, an additional set of questions comes to mind: Does the ongoing history of the Christian community have genuine theological significance for Barth, or does he view the Holy Spirit so exclusively in the light of Jesus Christ that the history of the God-Man all but overshadows the earthly struggles of those who are joined to Him by the Spirit? Is mankind's future, even beyond the Church, important for Barth, or does the constant stress on the intrinsic perfection of Christ and on the notion of already realized eschatology undermine man's graced yet free participation in the world's liberation?[3] In other words, are present human endeavors towards God's coming Kingdom given more than superficial attention in Barth's Spirit theology? In the light of these questions, two flaws become evident in the christic and ecclesial dimensions of Barth's pneumatology: the Spirit is deprived of an independent contribution to the process of salvation and to the arrival of the *eschaton* in the *Church Dogmatics*.

The difficulty indicated here is closely related to what was pointed out in the foregoing chapter, namely, Barth's failure to develop a theology of the *Spiritus Creator*. There the dominance of christology was alluded to, but not focused on; the *Spiritus Redemptor* overtakes the role of the Father's life-giving Spirit at work in all of creation, because Barth understands pneumatology in an exclusively christic sense. Here the problem is that the *Spiritus Redemptor* in effect has no proper role in the Christ-event and in the Church, since the reconciliation of God and man is seen as having been totally accomplished by the incarnate Son. From two distinct angles, therefore, it can be said that the Spirit is neglected in the *Church Dogmatics*. Furthermore, this fact is clearly due to Barth's tendency to absorb the first and third articles of the creed into the *"et homo factus est."* Thus, the immediate task with which one is confronted here is that of taking a position on the christomonism, as Paul Althaus calls it, or christological restriction, as Hans Urs van Balthasar prefers to designate the indisputably central place of Christ in the *Church Dogmatics*.[4] The findings which emerge from this study's exposition of Barth's Spirit theology make it clear that he at least intends his dogmatics to be as anthropocentric in its expressly pneumatological sections as it is christocentric in its explicitly christological ones. The image of the ellipse, which he found missing in Schleiermacher's unipolar theology, seems to convince Barth of the need to lend a bifocal character to his own thought. The problem, however, is that Barth does not execute in his pneumatology the balanced view which he intellectually strives for. Thus, the overemphasis on the objective (christic) and the subsequent neglect of the subjective (pneumatic) element, though it pervades the entire *Church Dogmatics*, should not be considered more than a dangerous tendency or persistent bias in Barth's theology. For, as Walter Kasper observes, Barth gradually moves beyond his initial christological restriction of the human by granting a relative independence and value to man's history.[5] It is because of this ever-present christological bias, however, that the Spirit's creative and redemptive functions are considerably eclipsed.

Thus, even a firm stance on the side of moderation with regard to the predominace of christology in the *Church Dogmatics* should not prevent one from critically examining the distortions which this evident bias on Barth's part introduces into his pneumatology. Yet one no doubt tampers with the very underpinning of Barth's thought when one voices questions concerning the christology which clearly provides the substructure of his Spirit theology. By claiming that this aspect of Barth's dogmatics is needlessly restricted because of his christology and by suggesting that christology itself should rather be considered a function of pneumatology, one is urging a reversal of Barth's conscious decision to conceive the Spirit totally in terms of Christ.[6] A similar reversal is called for by implying that the Spirit's work in the Church is too narrowly associated with the Christ-event and by advocating that ecclesiology be understood as a function of a more independent pneumatology. Barth surely sets out to place the community under the sign of the Spirit, but in fact so invariably presents the Christian's life in the Spirit as a reflection of the life of Jesus, that the poignancy of the Church's ongoing "now" is severely relativized by the uniqueness of Jesus' "then." Balance is thus jeopardized, and Barth cannot concede that the ecclesial activity of the Spirit not only mirrors the promise fulfilled in the crucified and risen Jesus, but also reaches out beyond Him towards the not yet realized future completion of the Christ-event which the Church is called to prefigure.[7] By attempting to interpret both christology and ecclesiology as functions of pneumatology, the present improvisation is pursuing a direction which Barth judges to be possible but dangerous; such an approach runs the risk of making christology dependent on a rootless pneumatology which is a disguised anthropology, even if it appears to be based on a biblical concept of the Spirit. Because of this risk Barth stood to the end by his Logos theology and its backward-pointing concept of the Spirit and of man, although he sensed that doing so necessarily reduced a pneumatically oriented christology and a forward-pointing ecclesiology to the level of interesting corollaries on the primary christological theorems of the *Church Dogmatics*.

This improvisation is aimed at allowing the corollaries to come more to the fore, not by minimizing the importance of christology and ecclesiology, but by stressing the crucial importance of an overarching pneumatology for a genuine Christian theology. In what follows, christology as well as ecclesiology are conceptualized in expressly pneumatological terms.[8] A major corrective of Barth's theology is intended here. Had Barth left more room for the work of the divine Pneuma within his christology, he would have allotted the man Jesus a more substantial role in the unique salvific encounter which took place in Him between God and man. And had Barth likewise permitted the Spirit a more independent role in his presentation of ecclesiology and of eschatology, he would have regarded man's own search for a just future as indicative of the manifold salvific encounters of God and man which occur in the Church and beyond it. The difficulty, however, is that Barth's Logos Christology, because of its dominant transcendental overtones, is basically imcompatible with such a pneumatic understanding of salvation and eschatology.[9] By choosing the former, Barth necessarily has to downplay the latter. Thus only an expressly pneumatic understanding of Jesus Christ and of human salvation would have enabled the relative independence of man and his history to be given more credence in the *Church Dogmatics*. The ensuing reflections propose placing christology and ecclesiology within a decidedly pneumatic framework. They envision a pneumatology in which Christ and His community would not abrogate the Holy Spirit's unique role as the Father's eschatological power at work in the entire cosmos. In the strivings of the Christian Church towards the Kingdom and in the efforts of all just men towards peace the Spirit is present in myriad ways until the completion of the divine saving mission inaugurated in the incarnation and made universal in the resurrection of Jesus Christ.

1. A Case for the Ontic Validity of the Spirit's Mission

If one were to diagram the role of God's Spirit in the *Church Dogmatics* upon the biblical spectrum of salvation history, one would soon discover that His activity is almost totally confined to the part of the spectrum which begins with the resurrection of Jesus and goes on from there. The Spirit is restricted to the domain of the Church since He is the outreaching power of Jesus Christ's resurrection and the penultimate form of His parousia. This fact does not deny that Barth argues retrospectively from the soteriological function of the Spirit in the Christian community to His anthropological function within each human person from creation, so that man is what he is by reason of the promise of the convenant from the very beginning of his existence. But the fact remains that the work of the Spirit is conceived by Barth primarily in terms of the ongoing action of the risen Christ. This preference for understanding the Spirit in connection with the post-Easter community is certainly justifiable, since the New Testament repeatedly refers to the Holy Spirit as the Spirit of Christ. Barth is one-sided, however, since his preference represents only one strain of biblical language about the Spirit. The other understands the Pneuma as the life-giving power of the Father which begins to permeate the cosmos at creation and continues to energize history until the very goal of time itself.[10] Wherever God acts on behalf of man's salvation, man encounters Him as the vivifying divine power, so that God Himself can be defined as Spirit. Though Barth certainly is well aware of this latter strain of biblical pneumatology, he clearly chooses to emphasize the former throughout most of the *Church Dogmatics*.

The result of this one-sidedness is that the person and activity of Jesus Christ so dominates Barth's dogmatics that pneumatology virtually becomes a subordinate function of christology. Barth is certainly right in refusing to divorce the Spirit from Christ, and thus in not permitting Spirit theology to be so preoccupied with man's universal search for salvation that it circumvents the unique salvific import of Christ for all men. But, correct as Barth is in insisting on an essentially christological pneumatology, one still can lament the fact that the Spirit is thus undoubtedly divested of His unique role in God's salvific encounter with man throughout history—and even in the case of the man Jesus.[11] Why does Barth consciously take the risk of foreshortening the Spirit's person and work in the *Church Dogmatics*? Put differently, what causes Barth to view everything necessary for man's salvation as already ontologically determined even from eternity by the salvific Yes on man's behalf by the Word of God? Why is the Spirit limited merely to the noetic task of illumining for the Christian his fully attained salvation? The answer is rooted in the historical genesis of Barth's pneumatology.

Since his chief intellectual rivals espoused pneumatology at the perhaps unwitting expense of christology, Barth is bent on rectifying such an apparently orthodox, but in the end vitiating theological stance. To assure that no confusion about the unequaled sovereignty of Jesus Christ can be distilled from his own theology, Barth identified ontic truth with the incarnate Word, and insists that a Christian Spirit theology which does not preserve the ontological uniqueness of the second credal article is no Spirit theology at all. For Barth, the Spirit does not surpass the work of Jesus Christ but is fully bound to its primacy and unfailingly committed to its noetic apprehension. As a result, the Spirit is purposely conceptualized as possessing from eternity a purely noetic function. For this reason, it can be said that even Barth's pneumatology is wholly or comprehensively christological.[12]

This restriction of the Spirit to a secondary function necessarily leads Barth's theology to a curtailment of man's role in salvation history. Instead of conceiving the Spirit as God's power to raise man up, to correct him, to judge him, to move him to conversion and to acceptance of God's new salvific acts of love on his behalf aimed at the fulfillment of history, the Spirit is seen rather formalistically as the divine Noetic whose function is to reaffirm on a universal scale the fully effective salvific work of the divine Ontic, Jesus Christ. The role of the Spirit and of man is reduced to that of noetic and subjective compliance with the ontic and objective reality of Jesus Christ. In the end the Spirit and man are not, as Barth feared they might be, divorced from Christ; rather they are so linked to Him that an adequate distinction between them seems nebulous in the *Church Dogmatics*. Man's own successes and failures on the road to salvation through union with the transcendent are not seen as the media through which God's life-giving Spirit encounters him. Again one faces the dilemma that has become the leitmotif of these improvisations: Barth's christological coloring of pneumatology leaves doubt as to whether there is any real gap between the man Jesus and other men, and also as to whether man's free quest for liberation is seen as a necessary counterpole to God's universal spiritual activity in and for the world which stands over against Him.[13] Granting ontic validity only to Jesus Christ and according the Spirit and man only noetic significance seem to debilitate against keeping a balanced tension between human and divine freedom. It also curbs the power of God to act in the world before and after the Christ-event in a way which enhances both the first and the last comings of Jesus Christ. The Spirit and man do not have the privilege of developing or furthering the work of Christ in any ontic sense.

Furthermore, this ontic-noetic dichotomy appears to contain an inner contradiction, as David Mueller insightfully remarks: "In this connection, something of a puzzle remains with respect to the objective reconciliation effected by God for all men in Jesus Christ and the subjective appropriation thereof by man. On the one hand, Barth speaks as though everything necessary for man's reconciliation with God has been accomplished by Jesus Christ. On the other hand, he depicts the work of the Holy Spirit as the completion or fulfillment of God's reconciling work. Is it possible to speak of reconciliation being accomplished through Jesus Christ without talking of man's appropriation?"[14] The solution to this puzzle can only be to award the Spirit acting among men more than the task of merely confirming on the intellectual level what has been fully attained outside man on the real level. In other words, the Spirit's universal presence before, during and beyond the Christ-event has to be attributed an ontic validity which equals and illumines the ontic validity of Jesus Christ, but which is not absorbed by the latter. It is necessary, therefore, to disagree with Barth's clear but prejudiced ontic-noetic distinction. Instead, the Spirit and the Son must each be given both ontic and noetic functions. To preserve the unity of the Trinity, it must be said immediately that christic and pneumatic activity is one; thus what the Christ and the Spirit gain for man on the ontic and noetic levels is aimed at the very same goal: the glory of the Father. Yet the distinction between Christ and Spirit must also be respected; thus the sending of the Son and that of the Spirit manifest inherent differences, the most obvious being that the Son acts in a concrete series of instances and that the Spirit works more universally beyond those instances but with an aim towards their occurrence and completion and not simply towards their recognition.[15] It can even be maintained that the Spirit has the overarching ontic and noetic role into which alone the Son's parallel ontic and noetic mission can be situated. In fact, such a reversal is more in keeping with the biblical notion of the Spirit who is active before and at the incarnation as well as during and after the death and resurrection of Christ.[16] This activity of the Spirit is ontically valid for salvation; to claim otherwise is to detract from the glory and the graciousness of the triune God.

What is proposed here is the possibility of placing christology and ecclesiology within the ontic and noetic framework of a biblical pneumatology. Barth does the opposite; he positions pneumatology and ecclesiology under the umbrella of christology. In doing so, he adheres to the general tendency of Western theologians to assign the Holy Spirit primarily an instrumental function in faith and in ecclesial existence, and thereby inevitably to confine the Spirit to a fundamentally domestic rather than cosmic role. At this point one can recognize the connection between trinitarian formalism and christological bias in Barth's pneumatology. The choice of the Latin model of the Trinity, in which the Spirit confirms God's inner community, instead of the Greek model, in which the Spirit communicates God's love to man, forces Barth to attribute to the Son the function which the Greeks appropriated to the Spirit. Without denying the theological importance of the *filioque*, one can also be justifiably critical of its oversystematization in the *Church Dogmatics*. The equally valid *ex patre* is neglected, and a pervasive narrowness results in Barth's pneumatology. The Eastern tradition, even as it is represented today by the Orthodox Churches, preserves the original pneumatic understanding of the Trinity and of christology as well. Many major Orthodox theologians regard christology primarily as a function of pneumatology, and thus provide a compelling counterbalance to Barth's decided choice of the opposite.[17] Recently Nikos Nissiotis has underlined the pneumatological dimensions of christology which result from the Orthodox tendency to formulate dogma in terms of salvation history: "The personal revelation of God in Christ cannot be realized or fulfilled without the work of the Spirit . . . In Him and in His power God's salvific plan is continually being actualized and continually becomes an historical reality."[18] There is no doubt that such a pneumatological understanding of christology and ecclesiology grants man's history and the Spirit's creative power a more independent ontic role than Barth is willing to do in the *Church Dogmatics*.

By suggesting that the Holy Spirit be understood to possess an ontic as well as a noetic office and by arguing that this stance can aid Western theology in allowing more than an instrumental role to the Spirit, one is respecting the central intention of Orthodox thinkers. They insist that the mystery of salvation is christological but non pan-christological, and that the Trinity's complexity must be operative in more than a formal way in Christian dogma.[19] If the doctrine of God's three-in-oneness is to deepen theological reflection, then the work of the Spirit cannot be subordinated to that of the Son; the former must be awarded equal validity. The penchant of Barth to assign ontic characteristics to the Word and noetic to the Spirit, and thereby to assure that the Spirit is not severed in any respect from the efficacy of the Word, in effect welds pneumatology too solidly to christology. V. Lossky advocates that the economy of the Spirit be viewed as God's new action which is not rigidly subjected to the work of Christ: "The personal advent of the Holy Spirit does not have the character of a work which is subordinate, and in some sort function, in relation to that of the Son. Pentecost is not a 'continuation' of the incarnation."[20] In Barth's theology one cannot but notice a tendency to constrict the Spirit to a backward-pointing, reflective role. Locating christology in a pneumatic setting can act as a corrective to this constant inclination of Western theology. This does not mean to imply that now the Son is to be seen as subordinate to the Spirit. The opposite extreme is not the solution. But a reversal of the over-all framework of Western theology, so that the Spirit is appreciated as the divine means by which the Bible accounts for both the Son's uniqueness and universality, protects the ontic significance of Christmas and Pentecost as well as of the creation and the covenant.[21] There are decidedly different ways in which God's love reaches man in history; the unity of God respects such differentiation but never distorts it.

Barth is well aware of this problem. He protests throughout the *Church Dogmatics* that sanctification should not absorb justification, just as justification should not assimilate sanctification. Barth thus continually attempts to draw a parallel between the work of Christ and that of the Spirit. But the very ontic-noetic categories which he employs invariably preclude the Spirit from any initiating function. Either the Spirit prepares man's mind for Christ or conforms man's mind to Him. There is little attention paid to the possibility that the Holy Spirit could bring about new salvific events and that His definition as Revealedness and Historicity could be interpreted to mean that the Spirit supplements the revelation of the Word or that the Church, because of the Spirit's presence, can make up what is wanting in Christ. Missing is what Alexander Schmemann views as the main theological contribution of the Orthodox Church to the West; Eastern thought exposes Catholic and Protestant theologians to an essentially pneumatic notion of ecclesiology; the Church is understood as the sacrament of the Kingdom in which the Spirit inaugurates in this world the ontologically new life of the world which is to come.[22] Barth cannot envision the Spirit creating a revelatory event which is ontologically new; all ontic relevance has been rooted in the Word from eternity. The consequence of Barth's position is that his Spirit theology simply reiterates the content of the Christ-event. In a real sense, sanctification has been absorbed by justification, Pentecost by the Cross. One could possibly interpret Barth's uneasy relationship to his opponents as fascination with their various attempts to spell out a pneumatology which takes the spiritual and cultural experiences of man seriously as ongoing manifestations of the Spirit who is at work completing the Christ-event through proleptic realizations of the Kingdom's presence.

The lack of creativity in Barth's pneumatology, as it touches both on the Trinity and on the person of Christ, can be traced back to the restriction of the Spirit which results in the West due to an almost exclusively ecclesial understanding of pneumatology. This conviction that the Spirit chiefly fosters faith in Jesus Christ and allegiance to His community causes Barth to neglect man's universal search for salvation under the guidance of the Spirit apart from the Christ-event and the Christian Church. Avery Dulles points out that Barth's theology is not sufficiently open to the salvific presence of the Spirit in other religions and in man's quest for religious meaning in general.[23] The fact is that Christ Himself has in Barth's mind already redeemed mankind ontically; the Spirit can do no more than noetically realize this achievement. Thus the Spirit is incapable of adding any substantial gain to Christ's universal efficacy. Both uniqueness and universality, reconciliation and sanctification are in effect accorded by Barth to Christ; the Spirit must only make redemption known to those who are living an ontological impossibility and are choosing nothingness instead of grace. Thus the Spirit cannot be active in other religions and in secular movements so as to effect new salvific initiatives; He can only thwart man's independent search for God by convincing him of the futility of such efforts; all grace has been won by Christ and thus mankind's apparent quest for salvation is aimless. Barth restrains the Spirit within the bounds of Christ's mission; the third mode of God's existence is understood as the Spirit of Christ, as the Spirit of His community and hardly at all as the continuing presence of the Father's outreaching innovative love.[24] This becomes particularly clear when Barth speaks of all men as ontologically or *de jure* in Christ on the one hand, and as on the way to a noetical, *de facto* relationship with Christ through the power of the Spirit on the other. Thus it seems that Barth swings between the extremes of universalism in his christology and ecclesiocentrism in his anthropology, without giving the Spirit a truly efficacious role in broadening the ontic sphere both of Christ and the Church through His presence in man's religion and in man's search for liberation.

A crucial dimension is missing, then, from Barth's christically-biased pneumatology. For, though the *Church Dogmatics* continually affirms the reality of Spirit as the divine mediator between Jesus Christ and His Church, the fundamental insight that the Spirit is at the same time the Father's communication of Himself to the eternal and incarnate Son—and, by extension, to all natural and human history—receives very little attention. In other words, Barth limits himself to developing his Spirit theology almost entirely in the confines of the second credal article, since the Spirit is conceived first in Barth's trinitarian teaching and then in his ecclesiology as Christ's own power to bind all men to Himself. The whole spectrum of the Spirit's activity from creation "in advance" of Christ and then after the resurrection but beyond the limits of the Christian community is handled cursorily in the *Church Dogmatics*.[25] It is true that Barth does entertain these insights as corollaries to his predominantly soteriological Spirit theology, but the Pneuma is so obscured by Christ even in Barth's explicitly anthropological pneumatology that He is deprived for all practical purposes of His proper ontic function as the Father's creative power outside of Himself and His Son and thus even beyond the incarnation and the Church. Such a statement is not an heretical attempt to deny that Christian pneumatology is a study of the Spirit of Christ, but it is an effort to underline the ontic and not merely noetic import of the Spirit's activity in the entire world. The Spirit can maintain His identity as the Spirit of Christ without working in every situation in an exclusively Christ-centered capacity.[26] A truly triadic notion of God in fact necessitates such freedom on the Spirit's part.

What are the consequences of the christological bias in Barth's pneumatology? Ironically it produces exactly what Barth wants to avoid by his insistence on the primarily noetic function of Christ's Spirit: it limits the universal power of the Father to bring all men to Himself through the Spirit, who indeed was and is and will be active in Christ, but who throughout time is also active wherever the Father's gracious love creates a new salvific encounter between Himself and man beyond the Word. In short, the effect of constricting pneumatology as Barth does is that christology itself suffers severe limitation; the absolute uniqueness of Christ's life, death and resurrection is preserved at the expense of His universality which is yet to be not simply acknowledged but accomplished. If one follows Hans Urs von Balthasar's suggestion of viewing the Spirit as "the Unknown beyond the Word," one can make the case that properly subsuming christology under pneumatology would not necessarily mean circumscribing the uniqueness of Christ; only Jesus is the totally Spirit-filled man raised to new life by the Father. But it would mean interpreting the definitiveness of Christ as a truly new eschatological breakthrough and universal opening of the Father to all men through the same power active in Christ, but also beyond Him, that is, through the Spirit.[27]

Barth's Spirit theology constantly leads back to the already fulfilled salvific event in Jesus Christ, instead of forwards to the as yet incomplete, but essentially open and available, Kingdom of the Christ who is still to come.[28] The Spirit works something truly novel not only in the one man Jesus, but in all men. This certainly happens through the Word who became flesh—but also, and this is the relevance of appending a third article to the creed—over and above the Word in an independent manner: "The new is at every moment the work of the Spirit; not so much the first creation is His work—laying the foundation of the cosmos is the work of the Father—but rather that transformation, which is similar to the new creation, which makes a living being out of a dead one, an eternal being out of a mortal one, a heavenly being out of an earthly one. In all of these transformations there is in each case a death and a resurrection, a leap beyond one's own limitations, which one can only make in the power of the Spirit. And yet this creative action does not happen without the cooperation of the one who is to be transformed. Christ has procured the new for us; the Spirit places it at our disposal as new open space."[29] This stress on the Spirit as the Father's transforming power everywhere in the universe is clearly derived from the Christian kerygma concerning what the Father has done in Jesus' resurrection through His life-giving Spirit. Yet the Spirit proceeds to transcend the explicit sphere of Christ by expanding the Father's power into the whole cosmos; such a pneumatology thus offers the setting, as it were, in which the light of Christ shines with greater brilliance, all the while it gives man hope that the same transforming power operative in Christ is at work wherever men are willing to move beyond their self-imposed boundaries into the open space promised by the Spirit. The most lamentable consequence of Barth's noetic model of pneumatology is that the singular knowledge which Christ brings to man about the being of the Father and the Spirit does not induce him to explain the very possibility of the Savior's person and work as the result of the *"conceptus de Spiritu Sancto."* Barth's christology does not broaden the ontic significance of his pneumatology but unnecessarily and unfortunately narrows it.

2. Ecclesial and Secular Completion of Christ's Victory

A further outcome of Barth's christological tendency is that his pneumatology is excessively preoccupied with the eternal foundation of the Christ-event and with its temporal inception. The participation of the Spirit in the past events of salvation looms so large that the Spirit's incessant responsibility for the future coming of Christ becomes a matter of minor importance. This problem has been hinted at sporadically up to this point; now the eschatological dimensions of Barth's pneumatology must be analyzed, for it seems that also in this regard the Holy Spirit is dispossessed of His own unique character as the harbinger of the Kingdom, just as the efforts of the Christian Church and of all men are dwarfed by Barth's all too ethereal concept of the *eschaton*.[30] Jürgen Moltmann's critique of Barth's theology centers exactly on the transcendental nature of Barth's eschatology; it is not enough that Barth reintroduced eschatological terminology into modern theology. A proper understanding of the end-time on Barth's part should have caused him to alter his triumphantly christological notion of human salvation, in order to allow the not yet completed future of Jesus Christ and of all men to gain significance in his theology. Barth's transcendental eschatology is anchored in the Word's eternal origin and revolves around the event of the resurrection through which Christ is present at each moment of history in the same degree. By stressing the beginning and middle of God's redemptive turning to man in His Son, Barth overlooks the promise given in the New Testament that history is open to the future of Jesus Christ and of all men through the work of the Spirit. For Moltmann, Barth's consistently christological and transcendental concept of time is at its core a denial of the pneumatic, social and political aspects of eschatology.[31]

It is precisely the eschatological motif of the third article of the creed which shatters the static notion that the *eschaton* is uniformly present at each moment. A pneumatically conceived eschatology makes it possible to conceive ecclesial and secular history as conducive to the cosmological fulfillment of the divine promise which derives its meaning not from the past but from the future self-revelation of God which has not yet been actualized. Although one discovers an openness to such a pneumatological presentation of eschatology in the later volumes of the *Church Dogmatics*, where Barth insists that the work of the risen Christ is not yet ended, this insight does not sufficiently motivate him to revise his notion of eternal eschatology along lines more receptive to mankind's graced part in realizing God's pledge of a definitive self-revelation at the completion of the cosmos.[32] Why is this the case? Once again it is the comprehensive nature of Barth's christology which hinders him from developing a thoroughly eschatological Spirit theology. Instead, Barth specifies the eschatological activity of the Spirit as the spatio-temporal transition of the Lord Jesus from resurrection to final coming. The christological categories with which Barth describes the Spirit's contribution to the parousia force one to ask just what God's distinct self-revelation as Spirit adds to the resurrection of Christ. Can Christians and men of good will increase Christ's glory? The Spirit is constantly given the didactic role of disclosing to all men what already is attained for them in the glorification of Christ; the future, as the work of the Spirit among human communities, cannot foster a totally new turn in history as such. In short, Christians confess, but do not contribute to the coming of Christ. This concentration of eschatology in the second article of the creed, and the subsequent neglect of the parousial mission of the Spirit are major flaws in Barth's understanding of Christian service and explain why he does not see theological implications in the hope of all men.[33] Nothing new can occur; all has happened in the history of Jesus Christ.

An ultimate reason for this neglect of the Spirit and of man in Barth's christologically-colored eschatology can be found in his doctrine of predestination, according to which man is already included from eternity in God's Word and is thus caught up in God's future before the beginning of time. This doctrine assures that the objective faith of all men is an intra-divine act achieved by Jesus Christ with the consent of the Holy Spirit; in the unfolding of salvation history this *de jure* human condition is to become a *de facto* acknowledgement of grace through Christian witness. The Spirit thus carries out in time what He already pledged to effect from eternity in affirming the eternal election of the one man Jesus on behalf of all mankind. Eberhard Jüngel is accurate in interpreting Barth to mean that the Christian's actual faith, his historical Yes to God's gracious love for him, is eternally grounded in the man Jesus; He is the first creature to be moved by the Spirit's power to accept God's future salvific plan so as to reveal divine mercy with the Spirit's assistance in the course of history.[34] The Spirit's work points back to His eternal origin. As profound and legitimate as such a description of the genesis of man's faith within the eternal pledge of the Holy Spirit might be, it rests too much on the "originative" concept of the Trinity and calls for a corrective. This model of the Trinity and of election causes man's role, as a free agent distinct from Jesus Christ and as a partner in the Father's encounters with him through the Holy Spirit, to lose its own salvific importance. Barth's eternal eschatology warps his entire pneumatology since it results in eclipsing the unfinished work of the Spirit and in disregarding the new possibilities of salvation which He opens up for man as the life-giving Spirit of the Father until the end of time.[35] At this point, the reflections which were offered in the previous chapter on the "eschatological" Trinity serve as the needed corrective to Barth's overly transcendental and thus unhistorical understanding of God's being and man's salvation. An end-time concept of the Trinity and of election would facilitate presenting the Holy Spirit as the first-fruits and as the guarantee of the Kingdom's presence in the historical pilgrimage of the Church and in the strivings of all men for peace and justice.

Barth's wholly christological eschatology seems to belie a dangerous confusion of the second and third articles of the creed. Ernst-Wilhelm Wendebourg discovers in this eschatological perspective serious consequences for Barth's ecclesiology. There appears to be a christological anticipation of the entire anthropologico-pneumatological problematic, in that Christ absorbs into Himself the historical process of sanctification which is properly the work of the Holy Spirit in the domain of the Christian community. If everything necessary for man's salvation is already preliminarily revealed in the Christ-event, what does the eschatological nature of the Church, which rests on the immanent presence of the Spirit in its midst, really append to christology? Barth's ecclesiology skirts the possibility that God the Spirit can effect a transformation in the course of history that would supplement the incipient salvation of mankind in the Father's resurrection of His Son.[36] Barth's theology of the Christian overlooks the possibility of a truly salvific encounter with God's Spirit; a soteriologico-pneumatological history which is being worked out with man's cooperation is lacking in the *Church Dogmatics*. The Christian is already so caught up in the eschatological history of Jesus Christ, that his own personal history becomes void of any soteriological and eschatological significance. The Church's mission simply involves furthering a process of enlightenment concerning what already is firmly fixed in God Himself.[37] Salvation history is thus eternal history; the promised eschatological future, for which man longs, becomes the ever-present now of transcendental glory which is fully determined before it can ever be augmented in history through the Spirit's new revelatory acts. These, it must be said in contrast to Barth, are sparked by men of hope or blocked by men of despair.

This reference to the existence of human holiness and sinfulness, as it fosters or frustrates the Spirit's activity in history, is not introduced as an afterthought. Barth's pneumatology seems to be so programmed that the evil or good actions of man can neither thwart nor advance its goal; the Spirit's main work is that of enlightening man's mind and not of justifying man's perversity. Gustaf Wingren accuses Barth of basing his dogmatics on an implicit modern philosophical view of man which identifies his main problem as knowledge about God and not redemption from his guilt. Thus Barth's purely noetic pneumatology is not aimed at the renovation of the Church and the cosmos but at the intellectual apprehension of a saving history which was worked out without their vigilant cooperation and continual repentance.[38] Barth gives the impression that the end of history will correspond to its eternal beginning and to its unique center. The whole span of salvation history from the resurrection to the final coming of Christ is thus merely a period of transition. Such a decidedly christological conception of man's history inevitably creates in Barth's theology the latent tendency to advocate a type of universal restoration of all creation to its original unity with God. The ontic role of Jesus Christ in man's history is so determinative in the *Church Dogmatics* that the noetic function of the Spirit who is to liberate man's freedom for Christ becomes almost superfluous. For the work of the Holy Spirit and the role of man's freedom is anticipated in Barth's christology, where all is already ontically assured in the eternal history of one man. Thus Barth's christocentric notion of predetermined history and his subsequent neglect of man's own precarious venture in time, which must be worked out in freedom and hope, opens his thought to the charge of apocatastasis.[39]

The source of this serious flaw in Barth's theology of history, which in turn causes substantial difficulties for his pneumatology and ecclesiology, is once again the distinctions which he makes between the objective and the subjective, the ontic and the noetic, the *prius* and the *posterius*, the *illic* and the *hic*, the actual and the virtual, the *de jure*, and the *de facto*. Such dichotomies lead Barth to attribute ontic relevance only to the Christ-event, whereas the Pentecost-event and the future of God's ecclesiological promises to man have only noetic meaning; the latter are valid insofar as they lead back to what already is and cause man to wait in hope for the future of the One who is now what He will be. The critics of Barth's objective-subjective schema protest against two important theological consequences which derive from this basic thought pattern of the *Church Dogmatics*.[40] One group centers on the ecclesiological problem by stating that the historical function of the Church, its proclamation and its sacramental character are seriously jeopardized by conceiving the ecclesial work of the Spirit as the creation of a noetic reflection of what is previously realized for man through Christ before it is ever applied to him and freely accepted by him. The second group of critics concentrates on the consequences for the whole of world history in relation to the being of God. The openness of mankind to the promise of the Father, which is to come in a totally new revelation of Himself, is omitted from the *Church Dogmatics* because of a constant emphasis on the ontological character of the Christ-event alone as the absolutely final self-manifestation of God. For both groups of critics the historical encounter of man and the Spirit produces nothing new in Barth's pneumatology except a *de facto* disclosure of what is antecedently disclosed *de jure* in Christ.

Despite Barth's insistence on the pneumatic nature of the Church, his treatment of the proclamation of the Word and the celebration of the sacraments deprives these events of their soteriological force as means of God's continual self-revealing presence; the sacraments of word and action are viewed as human responses to Christ's prior victory but not as divine initiatives aimed at fulfilling, at a particular point in history, the future promise which is indicated and given along with their sign-character. Barth refuses to comprehend them as instruments of a refreshingly new, salvific and eschatological act of God's Spirit.[41] The omnipresent Christ of the end-time, who is triumphantly at work since the resurrection, absorbs the role of the Spirit who is actively bringing about the Kingdom through the preaching and the sign-giving of the Church. Thus the crucial task of furthering Christ's glory by making it ontically present to many, which is traditionally attributed to the sanctifying mission of the Spirit in the Church, is fully anticipated by Barth's comprehensive understanding of the justifying work of Jesus Christ.[42] The Spirit can only affirm Christ's victory and make it known, but He cannot complete it and thereby allow the Christian to enjoy a foretaste of the Kingdom which is truly his own and not simply a reflection of Christ's.

The description of the ecclesial function of the Spirit, which Barth claims is his attempt finally to bring man into the *Church Dogmatics* as a real recipient of salvation, seems in the end to be only a transitory and superfluous office which does not cause man to come face to face with a final action of the Father's will on his behalf which is different from the Christ-event yet its real fulfillment. Barth permits the Spirit to do no more than direct man to the promise which Christ has previously received; the Spirit cannot actualize the not yet attained promise of the Father in the course of His ecclesial mission. Such a position has grave consequences for the very meaning of the Church: "One would destroy the ability of the gifts of the Holy Spirit to point beyond themselves, if one overlooks the fact that eschatological fulfillment actually comes about in the outpouring of the Holy Spirit."[43] This important aspect of sacramental theology is missing from Barth's pneumatology; the work of the Spirit in the kerygmatic and sacramental life of the Church is not regarded by Barth as an end in itself. The Spirit has no proper eschatological office except that of alluding backwards and forwards to the past and future eschatological events which are ontically grounded in the person of Christ alone. These the Christian community, which receives the sacraments, can only intellectually apprehend as its extrinsic identity.

Not only the explicitly religious nature of the Church is undermined by Barth's weakened pneumatology but its socio-political mission as well. Friedrich-Wilhelm Marquardt has provocatively argued that Barth's entire theology cannot be fully appreciated if one fails to grasp its socialistic intent.[44] Yet the serious problem with the *Church Dogmatics* is that the undeniable socio-political aspect of Barth's life and thought does not open the eschatological aspects of his pneumatology to sufficient concern for the hungers and longings of Christians and of all mankind for a more just social order. Why does Barth's theology almost counteract his biography? The germ of this difficulty can be found in Barth's very concept of the Holy Spirit's being. The reasoning here is not farfetched, since Barth holds that theology and politics are not mutually interchangeable but inextricably interrelated; one's theology of God has social implications, just as one's social activity has theological ramifications. Is Barth's theology of the Spirit capable of adequately grounding Christian social involvement and of ultimately explaining the quest of the secular realm for a just future? Instead of embodying God's final outpouring of love into history, the Spirit seems to carry out in time the function which Barth attributes to Him from eternity: that of completing the inner love of God. Once again it is evident that the Latin model of the Trinity and the Western institutionalization of pneumatology induces Barth to conceive the Spirit in terms of introverted rather than extroverted love.[45] Above and beyond the history of man, God is complete in Himself; creation is simply to reflect the history of God which transcendentally borders on it at each moment. Since God's economic activity totally mirrors His immanent divine life and since the divine life is completed by the Holy Spirit, there is little evidence in Barth's theology that the Spirit is God's openness to the world, who unites God and man in a spontaneous act of love and who makes man freely search and hope for divine approbation of his efforts towards the totally new.

The concept of the Spirit as God's opening of Himself to man's future happiness and as God's willingness to participate in such a goal would imply that God has freely chosen to enjoy complete oneness within Himself only by sharing His life with man. Thus in a real sense the triune God is waiting for and is fashioning this future through His Spirit, but on the condition that man fully cooperate with such a divine overture. In this way, the Father, Son and Spirit will reach a three-in-oneness only at the point in time when man attains his own social and political goals with the aid of the incessant eschatological power of the Spirit. In the process of liberation the Spirit accompanies, guides, corrects, makes way for and transforms man's own struggles towards unity, justice, peace and love. Barth seems needlessly to shy away from the insight that the Spirit is in labor with the whole cosmos until it reaches its superhistorical goal. Only then, in the transformed history of the entire creation, will God's Spirit bring about the inner harmony of the Father and the Son as well as the promised fulfillment of man's hopes. Until that point the Holy Spirit continually opens Father and Son up to the world, suffers with man and groans for God's own inner unity as well as for man's joy in the fulfillment of the Kingdom.[46] No doubt, Barth and many contemporary theologians would find these particular improvisational thoughts not only a serious threat to the self-sufficiency and perfection of God but also the very type of vague philosophical speculation, bordering on outright Hegelianism, which Barth's pneumatology meant to avoid at all costs. Yet, if divine compassion is to be more than a Christian tenet devoid of social relevance and if ecclesial and secular movements for a better world are to be more than transitory events with little meaning for God's future, such daring insights based on the Gospel have to be entertained. They rest on the humility and the freedom of the God who purposely chooses to extend love outside Himself and to suffer along with the world He has freely promised a share in His own glory.[47]

If it is true that both the role of the Spirit of God and that of the Church and of society are neglected in Barth's christologically biased pneumatology and eschatology, this oversight could have been prevented had Barth rested his Spirit theology on a thorough description of the third mode of God's existence as His self-surpassing love. The Spirit should have been described as divine love continually extended towards the world and actively engaged in creating new possibilities for man's future with God. In this way, the Spirit is not the last thing to be said about God, but the first; He is the outward-reaching freedom in love of the Father and the Son.[48] Barth rather starts with a consideration of the Spirit's inward-reaching role as the bond of love between Father and Son, and subsequently carries over this restrictive rather than expansive concept of the Spirit into his theology of history and of history's goal. Pneumatology and the concomitant explanation of man's vocation in the Church and in society are thus simply appended onto an antecedently rounded-out christology which in effect usurps the importance of the Spirit and of man. Barth should have recognized that his christology as well as his eschatology demanded a prior treatment of the Spirit as the divine presupposition and ground of possibility for the incarnation of the Word and for the eschatological being of the Church.[49] A discrepancy exists, therefore, between the subservient noetic role which the Spirit is to play with regard to Christ and the *eschaton*, and the biblically attested dynamism of the Spirit as the very precondition of the eschatological breakthrough into history which the Christ-event itself represents. This discrepancy accounts for the fact that the Spirit enjoys only a docile part in the ecclesiological and eschatological sections of the *Church Dogmatics*.

Instead of allowing the Spirit to set man free, even when He binds him to the person and work of Christ, Barth fuses man and the Spirit to Christ in such a way that the Spirit is not able to exert an independent ontic influence on man's future. In effect, the Spirit cannot complete the Christ-event through His mission in the Church and in the world. The sanctity and the sinfulness of Christians in the service of others for the Kingdom's sake, and the agelong search of mankind for a form of life based on respect for human rights, even though personal actions and social structures often stand in glaring dissonance with his best dreams, cannot effect the outcome of Christ's mission one way or the other. If Christ, the Church and the *eschaton* were subsumed under a biblically inspired pneumatology, Christ's victory would not be overshadowed, but given power to penetrate into dimensions of reality which are neither existentially influenced by it nor ontically prepared for it.[50] Barth does not opt for this possibility; all is a function of the triumph of grace in Christ. Yet the Church's hope for salvation—and also the many secular drives for a transformed cosmos—must not be christically restricted, but pneumatically freed. For, the Spirit liberates man for the new acts which the Father will perform on behalf of His creation. Spirit theology must be removed from purely noetic and transcendental categories, so that the Spirit's work with man towards the realization of the Father's Kingdom, which surely began in Christ and must be measured and informed by His glory, will find its proper place in a socially oriented and restlessly hopeful Christian theology.

3. The Advantages of a Revitalized Spirit Christology

Barth's total or comprehensive christology poses modern theology with a considerable dilemma. Given the fact that his Logos Christology not only towers above the work of the Holy Spirit by confining His mission to the noetic realm but also pales the meaning of ecclesial and secular history by contrasting its transitory nature to the once-for-all glory of the Messiah, the theologian must find a way to restore ontic significance to the Spirit and to man without denigrating the role of Christ. Is there any precedent in the history of christology which attributes a central place to the divine Spirit and to human mediation within a christological model which claims at the same time to protect the absolute uniqueness of Jesus Christ? Surprisingly Barth himself suggests a solution to this question when at two key points in the *Church Dogmatics* he introduces the insights of the earliest christology of the New Testament: the Pneuma-Sarx Christology of Jewish Christianity. When Barth turns to the incarnation of the Word, he explains the miracle of Christmas as one brought about by the Holy Spirit who alone, according to the Synoptic Gospels and to primitive Christian creeds, enables Jesus' conception to be a real union of the divine Word and human flesh. In other words, Barth's Logos Christology actually depends on the essential cooperation of the Holy Spirit. Furthermore, when Barth is faced with accounting for the distinctive constitution of Jesus' humanity, he claims that as the Word incarnate Jesus possesses the Holy Spirit lastingly and totally; whereas other human persons have continually to be gifted with the Spirit, Jesus has this privilege primarily, originally and definitively.[51] The intriguing possibility arises, therefore, that Barth's christology could be expanded and thus balanced by reintroducing the insights of christological models predating the Apologists' preference for the Logos model, which has dominated Western theology ever since.

A recent attempt to investigate the most primitive christologies has been made by Piet Schoonenberg. The genesis of his research is the patent yet astounding fact that, except for the prologue of John's Gospel and the beginning of his first Letter, the prevailing New Testament paradigm of Jesus' being is the Spirit-bearer; Jesus is the Christ, the one anointed fully with the Holy Spirit; for this reason He is Messiah and Lord, equal in glory with the Father. With time, however, this paradigm gave way to that of the incarnate Word, even to the extent that Jesus' unction with the Holy Spirit came to be viewed in the Middle Ages as a purely secondary factor in Jesus' divinity: "Scholasticism considered the hypostatic union as the *substantial* sanctification of Jesus. Besides this, Jesus' human reality had to receive an *accidental* holiness by the created gifts of grace, the 'habitual grace' as distinct from the 'grace of union' which is the hypostatic union itself. Now this accidental sanctification was considered as the fruit of Jesus' anointing by, or with, the Holy Spirit, and so this working of the Spirit is seen as accidental . . . The result of this whole process is that we are far removed from Holy Scripture and also from many Church Fathers, especially the Greeks."[52] In the light of these observations, it seems fair to say that Barth's references to the work of the Holy Spirit in the person of Jesus are of the accidental variety, since the primary ground of Jesus' divinity is not His anointing with the Spirit but His hypostatic union with the eternal Word. Must Spirit Christology be viewed simply as an appendage to Logos Christology, and not as an independent theological model which might better explain the uniqueness and universality of the Christ-event? If the Holy Spirit is seen to play only an accidental role in christology, will a Christian theologian not be prevented from lending the Spirit more than a secondary function in his treatment of the Church, the world and the *eschaton*?

Since this present improvisation accuses Barth of needlessly suppressing pneumatology for the sake of christology, it becomes clear that the root of this indictment is Barth's preference for an unmitigated Logos Christology. As is the case with most Western theology, the work of the Spirit is introduced in a decidedly accidental fashion into the christological sections of the *Church Dogmatics*, a decision which has rather dire consequences for an understanding of the Spirit's activity in all creation, and most especially in the human person, in the ecclesial community and in the socio-political order. Yet it is also clear that Barth's penchant to shun a christology "from below" is an understandable defense against Schleiermacher's teaching on Jesus as the man who brings to its highest level the innate God-consciousness which is found in all men. Barth thus rejects every anthropological starting point of christology since such a starting point invariably reduces Jesus to a noteworthy example of that closeness to God which all men potentially share.[53] Was Barth's basically healthy reaction to excesses in Neo-Protestantism and in Christian Existentialism to some degree an overreaction? Barth's own choice of an unmistakable christology "from above" which is reinforced by a pervasive Word theology risks the opposite danger of coming too close to a Gnostic concept of the eternal Word in the process of realizing itself throughout natural and human history. The choice of such a Logos Christology, although it is in consonance with Christian tradition, does not adequately do justice to the biblical notion that the Father broke His silence and poured out His Spirit in full measure on Jesus Christ.[54] Thus, it is tenable that the fragmentary Spirit Christology, which Barth himself at times weaves into the *Church Dogmatics* as an auxiliary way of comprehending the Christ-event, could have afforded him a more adequate approach to the mystery of Christ if he had developed it at greater length. As it is, his exaggerated Logos Christology seems blatantly to bypass the biblically attested truth that Christ must be understood in the context of God the Spirit's continual interactions with man, all of which are aimed at the attainment of man's salvation.

As soon as it is advocated that Christ be placed in a larger pneumatic framework, the objection naturally comes to mind that this methodology can only result in a new expression of Adoptionism. A Pneuma-Sarx Christology is perpetually in danger of minimizing the uniqueness of Jesus by categorizing Him as a special case of the Spirit-filled king, judge or prophet.

The heresy of Adoptionism was in fact the reason why the early Church departed from Jewish-Christian christologies and opted instead for Logos Christology which seemed at the time to be a necessary corrective to the ambiguities inherent in the earlier models.[55] This debate still goes on today and has lately increased due to revitalized interest in a more relevant christology, a theological priority which interestingly cuts across denominational lines. Hendrikus Berkhof was one of the first to voice the opinion that the danger of Adoptionism is overestimated and that the biblical data in favor of a Spirit Christology far outweigh the suspicion that this type of model, which had sufficed for the Synoptics, will automatically give rise to the thesis that Jesus was a mere man: "All this leads us to the conclusion that it is possible and even obvious to design christology from a pneumatological viewpoint, that is, to conceive the person and work of Jesus Christ as the result and the starting point, as the center of God's life-giving presence, of the work of the Spirit among men. Nevertheless, attempts to design such a pneumatic christology are very rare in the history of theology. I suppose this is mainly due to the fear of Adoptionism. It is not the dominating concept of the Spirit as such, however, which leads to Adoptionism, but the neglect of the strictly unique way in which the Spirit is united with Christ."[56] Since Barth feared that precisely the strictly unique nature of Christ would be compromised, especially if it were subsumed under the rather vague pneumatologies to which he so strongly objected, the most he could do was to enhance the anthropological dimension of his Logos Christology with biblical references to the power of the Spirit operative in Jesus' humanity.

Barth's hesitancy with regard to Spirit Christology is surprisingly confirmed by Wolfhart Pannenberg, whose own christology as well as basic theological method are decidedly anti-Barthian. Pannenberg points out that characteristics of illegitimate patristic Adoptionism mark the christologies of Kant, Schleiermacher, Ritschl and von Harnack, since these thinkers view the Spirit as an impersonal power of the transcendent God and depart from a trinitarian theology which inherently guarantees that the Spirit is substantially and not merely accidentally conjoined with the Father and the Son. As a result, Pannenberg suspects that the many contemporary endeavors at a Spirit Christology will likewise not preserve the pristine belief that Jesus is essentially united with God the Father through the Holy Spirit. It is difficult for modern man to adhere to the initial forms of validly conceived Adoptionism which understood the Spirit to be the consubstantial bond with the Father in which the humanity of Jesus fully partook. It would be better, therefore, to abandon any such revitalized Spirit Christology and to concentrate on an historically rooted theology of Jesus which is primarily based on the uniqueness of His resurrection and not of His incarnation.[57] Thus, it is widely admitted today that there is both a valid and an invalid form of Adoptionism. The valid type, as Piet Smulders explains, is that of the earliest Jewish Christology which has unfortunately been judged to be heretically Adoptionistic by later standards, but which entertains the question of Jesus' pre-existence through an affirmation of the singular indwelling of the eternal Spirit in Him.[58] Furthermore, Aloys Grillmeier attests that in the early Church Christ was seen as the union of Spirit (=Logos) and Sarx even by orthodox theologians such as Clement of Rome and Ignatius of Antioch. Only later, when the Stoa was unable to view the term Pneuma as excluding a material nature, did the concept Logos consistently replace it.[59] Invalid Adoptionism, however, totally skirts the need to link Jesus substantially with the Father since it is chiefly concerned with Jesus' temporal function as Spirit-led mediator between God and man and not with his divine being as such. Given such ambiguity, is Barth wise in adhering to a Logos Christology which inextricably unites Jesus' function and His being?

Other theologians follow Berkhof and Schoonenberg in maintaining that a revitalized Spirit Christology can avoid illegitimate Adoptionism by situating both the person and the work of Jesus not into an arbitrary philosophical theory, but into the theological and anthropological framework which the Bible itself provides: the eschatological power of the divine Pneuma. In this way both Old and New Testament pneumatology is seen to form the overarching system in whose encompassing unity the prophets, Christ and the Church are interrelated. Pneumatology is the means the Scriptures employ so that Israel, the Messiah and the Kingdom are incorporated into the total plan of God's gracious self-communicating love. Particularly notable is Walter Kasper's contribution to this understanding of the Holy Spirit as the divine mediator of grace between the Father and Jesus and between Jesus and the Church: "The Spirit is God as self-surpassing and self-excelling, overflowing and outgoing love, which is precisely self-contained in that it communicates itself and gives itself away. The Spirit is therefore the self-communication between God and man in Jesus Christ *(gratia unionis)* as well as between Jesus Christ and us *(gratia capitis)*."[60] Thus the decided advantage of a Pneuma-Sarx Christology is that its explicitation does not preclude, but in fact necessitates a discussion of God's activity in Israel, in the Church and in all human situations where the Spirit is beckoning creation to an increase of love because, as God's own love poured out to the world, the Spirit draws man into actual union with God. Nor does a Pneuma-Sarx Christology confuse the unmatched presence of the Spirit in Jesus with His pervasive indwelling in the rest of creation. For, the Spirit's immeasurable closeness to Jesus means that in this absolutely single case Jesus is led so fully into the being of God that His reciprocal dialogue with the Father constitutes Him as God's Son from the very moment of His existence. Such a primary and unparalleled relationship to the Father, however, does not deprive Jesus of an essential connection with all men who are also called to union with the Father through the outpoured grace of the Holy Spirit. Jesus' distinctive bond with the Father makes Him for that reason the Lord of all creation, the One through whom the Spirit is now given in a particularly intensive way. Thus Jesus surpasses the universal work of the Spirit while at the same time He furthers and condenses the Spirit's ongoing cosmic action.[61]

Barth's objection at this point would surely be that, by beginning with the humanity of Jesus of Nazareth as Spirit Christology necessarily must, it is not at all certain that such a christological model will conclude with any result other than the affirmation of Jesus' humanity. Although the goal of situating Jesus into the fabric of Israel's promise and into the context of world history is laudable, will Jesus' human nature be viewed as so absolutely remarkable in this model that, while it belongs to Him who is the fulfillment of creation's yearning, it is still the human nature of the transcendent Lord? Will a Pneuma-Sarx model make the divinity of Jesus as clear as does the Logos-Sarx paradigm? A response to this central question would begin by stating that, although Logos Christology begins "from above" with the eternal divine Word, and Spirit Christology starts "from below" with the humanity of the Spirit-filled Jesus, both models are capable of describing the mystery by which God Himself is present among men in a singular act of self-communication. As long as both Logos and Pneuma are understood to be identical with the self-revealing Father, the human nature of Jesus can be interpreted to be not only accidentally or functionally joined to God in a Father-Son relationship, but substantially or ontologically as well. In response to G. W. H. Lampe whose pneumatic christology would be content with abstaining from metaphysical questions altogether and who thus asserts that Jesus is divine not "substantively" but only "adverbially," that is, that He only acts in a Godlike manner,[62] Piet Schoonenberg insists on the inner unity of function and being: "Because the Spirit is equally divine as the Logos, the Spirit too is not only present in Jesus but also embraces, contains, and sustains his human reality, although we do not say that it is enhypostatic in the Spirit. In Spirit christology as well, the Spirit is connected with Jesus not only functionally but also ontologically, because function is the expression of being and being includes function. Nor can Jesus be divine only 'adverbially,' because 'the human Jesus acting divinely' also *is* divine by the Spirit's presence pervading him. Once again I come back to the conclusion formulated above: in both christologies Jesus can be seen as fully divine and fully human."[63]

Though the christological model which Barth himself employs in the *Church Dogmatics* is almost diametrically opposed to that espoused here, his theology is not totally closed to the centrality of the *"conceptus de Spiritu Sancto."* What would Barth's christology have gained, had he incorporated the biblical texts dealing with the Spirit's activity in Jesus' person and work more integrally into the structure of his thought? A number of distinct benefits come to mind which a Pneuma-Sarx design, either as a replacement for the Logos-Sarx model or as its complement, can procure for contemporary christology: such a model would be biblically grounded, centered on the paschal mystery, sensitive to Jesus' human consciousness, eschatologically oriented, in consonance with a theology of grace and open to inter-Christian, inter-faith and inter-national dialogue.[64] In short, this christological model would offset the serious difficulties which plague Barth's pneumatology. This present improvisation can conclude by doing no more than briefly sketching out the lines of a christology which is permeated by a pneumatic viewpoint. Before undertaking this sketch, a few general remarks must be made. The cultural and religious climate in which Barth fashioned his christology and pneumatology was considerably different from that prevailing at this writing. Though on the one hand the forces opposed to transcendent faith may have increased, so that the theologian is constantly constructing his thought with an eye to the practical atheism even within the Church, on the other the rise of biblical fundamentalism, the widespread existence of lively charismatic groups and the growing socio-political consciousness of many leading believers compel the theologian to develop a christology which is both apologetical in tone, pneumatic in character and socio-political in intent. Thus the advantages of a charismatic and liberational christology are not purely academic but predominantly pastoral. Given Barth's entire theological orientation, he would sympathize at least with the intention of the following "draft" of Spirit Christology.

A contemporary Spirit Christology which is to be both charismatic and liberational would begin with an investigation of mankind's global search for a just human community which is marked by freedom and united in harmony as well. But where is one to find any guarantee that man's intellectual and spiritual vision of the future will indeed be realized?[65] Is there any community which claims to possess a solid hope that mankind will be liberated from its own unjust creations and attain a goal which transcends its continually new-found limits? If no one can speak with certainty about such a dream and indicate that he is willing to sacrifice everything for its realization, then ceasing to question further may indeed by the only feasible option, unless one were to choose blind humanism, unblinking materialism or sheer fatalism.[66] The Christian community speaks out at this juncture that it is convinced of its own interaction with the powerful personal Spirit of a truly exceptional son of Israel who gave His life away for precisely such a kingdom of total justice which surpasses all man's hopes. This community can initially point to its own lively hope and dogged, even if often selfish, activity on behalf of all men as the proof of the legitimacy of its message. But the ultimate validity of its claim is that a totally Spirit-filled man, Jesus of Nazareth, was singularly united with God, the Father of all, in a bond of intimate sonship effected by the Spirit who propelled Him to heal the brokenhearted and to proclaim unprecedented hope for liberation to the most oppressed of peoples in the name of His Father. (*Lk*. 4:14-21).[67] Jesus not only professed this message, but lived it and died for it, all the while anointed by the Father's Spirit who continually deepened His conscious state of sonship and who made of His entire existence a messianic breakthrough of the Father's future into man's present. This same Father's Spirit vindicated Him by raising Him from the dead and passing on to Him not only the function of unmatched Spirit-bearer but also of messianic Spirit-sender (*Jn*. 1:33, 6:63). Jesus has become a life-giving Spirit for the community which bears His name and for all men, but His new office is rooted in His very union with His Father from the beginning of His temporal mission and since then for all time.[68] Yet Jesus did not simply become Spirit-anointed Messiah and Lord, since His resurrection reveals that He is one with the very being of the Father. In encountering Jesus and the Spirit one meets the Father.[69] This divine community of outstretched love offers hope of ultimate union to all men.

The tentative impromptu outline of a Spirit Christology, sketched above in the form of a short credal statement, is based on a biblical presentation of Jesus' existence which is obviously guided by the needs of contemporary believers and unbelievers. By starting with the living Christian community and moving from there to the paschal mystery and then to the ministry, baptism and incarnation of Jesus, the argumentation is sensitive to recent biblical and dogmatic scholars' attempts to account for the apparent growth in Jesus' consciousness of His messianic identity and mission which is present in the Bible itself.[70] The entire sketch is future-oriented, yet not incognizant of the solid foundation for what is to come that is found in the present and in the past both of the human and the divine community. Jesus' meaning is set in the current pneumatic framework of the Church, in the pneumatic context of the Scriptures and in the pneumatic setting of Israel's messianic expectations. Consideration of Jesus' ontic being follows an examination of His singular historical function; in this way, Jesus' union with all men is the gateway to the indispensable questions about the ultimate possibility of His unique cosmic office. Furthermore, Jesus' own experience of the Spirit *(gratia unionis)* is shown to have relevance for man's own encounter with grace *(gratia capitis)*. This is true primarily of the Christian community, but, since the Spirit of the Father does not cease His mission in history by bestowing on Jesus an unequaled intensification of His own universal work, grace is also available to the Jew, the Hindu and the atheist.[71] In fact, the Spirit is at work everywhere to allow the original creation of the Father and the recreation of the God-Man to achieve "transcreation" through the Spirit's presence in the socio-political efforts of all mankind in anticipation of the Kingdom. With the aid of the Spirit who raised Jesus from the dead, all men are invited to move beyond that normative event of joy to hopeful transformation of the world. The Spirit thus continues to act in the pattern of the Christ-event, though not explicitly in a christic form.[72]

Setting christology in a pneumatic framework is a clear and challenging mandate of present-day theology. Barth's own christological achievement, however, serves as a warning that it will be no easy task. In fact, his contribution to the theology of the second article is a continual reminder that an entire previous generation of Christian theologians and philosophers attempted an implicit pneumatic christology and, as Barth analyzed their efforts, failed to present the Gospel in its pure form to the modern world. Instead of a genuine Spirit Christology, if such were possible, what emerged was a vague spiritual universalism which undercut the Church's true relevance and led theology itself into disarray. With full awareness of the grave difficulties which Barth would most probably point out in the sketch outlined above, a growing number of theologians feel impelled to move in the direction of a Spirit-centered and socially oriented christology. This prognostic statement is made at the conclusion of Barth's entire pneumatology, however. What is the reason for putting such great stress on the need for a revitalized Spirit Christology here at the end of this study? No doubt, it is because Barth himself might be more amenable to this christic approach to a Spirit theology in a new key than he would be to the more cosmic approach advocated in the first improvisation on the role of the Holy Spirit in nature and in man. At least here the emphasis is where Barth was convinced that it should be, that is, on the second article of the creed as it enlightens the first and the third. It is obvious, nevertheless, that the previous thoughts on the transforming work of the Creator Spirit are employed in this present improvisation to furnish a backdrop for a pneumatic christology.[73] Both a theology of the *Spiritus Creator* and of the *Spiritus Redemptor* is called for along lines different from those drawn by Barth. This study concludes that the lessening of man's place in Barth's theology due to an insufficient pneumatic understanding of creation is more understandable, given the issues which he had to defend, than is the curtailment of both the Spirit and of man in an area where one would have least expected it, namely, in his christology.

EPILOGUE

A study of Karl Barth's pneumatology must unfortunately conclude with the same ambiguity and embarrassment which Barth himself expresses concerning the Spirit theology of his adversaries. Perhaps this is because, with regard to the Holy Spirit, all Christian theologians are almost necessarily novices. The study of the divine Pneuma, whose transparent person and work reaches into the recesses of God and of creation, is not easily definable and can quite readily be colored by the particular theological bent of the observer. Barth, however, is more than a mere novice in the quest for a theology of the Holy Spirit. In fact, his entire life's work simply cannot be categorized as christocentric; it is pneumatocentric as well. The activity of the Holy Spirit in God's and in man's being is treated in great detail throughout the *Church Dogmatics* and in many of Barth's shorter writings. Since Barth realizes the necessity of an elliptical model for theology, he is intent on guaranteeing that the Christ-focus be balanced by the Christian-focus and on demonstrating that the Holy Spirit forms the connection between God's turning to man and man's turning to God. It is Barth's pneumatology which prevents him from composing either a theology or an anthropology as such and which induces him to opt instead for a "theanthropology." Theology must be pneumatology if the equipoise between Christ and the Christian is to be kept intact. In this sense Barth can be interpreted not only as "secondarily" a pneumatologian but as "primarily" a pneumatologian as well, since he deeply desires to counteract the aberrations of his rivals' understanding of the third article by producing a great counterwork which would be a valid pneumatology but not one marked by a deficient christology. Once this has been said, the embarrassment spoken of above comes to the fore. Barth so surrounds his Spirit theology with a christological bulwark that in the end his elucidations of the Spirit and of the Christian both are overshadowed. For the sake of safeguarding the Spirit's revelatory work in the Christian with an impregnable christology, Barth in effect permits the protecting wall of the city to tower over its inhabitants.

If the results of Barth's pneumatological contribution are so ambiguous, why then this lengthy study of his Spirit theology? Would it not have been better to start afresh and to fashion a pneumatology of one's own? The very privilege of meditating on Barth's *Church Dogmatics* and of glimpsing its scope and depth, however, is such a reward in itself that it needs no defense. This is particularly true of Barth's pneumatology, which leads the reader to the core of his thought on every major dimension of Christian theology. One learns from Barth the inestimable value of a systematic presentation of the Spirit. It is thus undeniable that Barth is faithful to his original intention of constructing a theology of the third article which allows the divine Pneuma to be comprehended in more than a superficial way. In comparison with Barth's Spirit theology much that is being written today by spokesmen of the Charismatic Movement, for example, lacks the desired breadth and complexity which alone can do justice to the grandeur and power of the topic. Barth is in fact a great pneumatologian, even if the problems which beset his individual theses on the Spirit are grave. Not only is there a vast panorama opened up by his reflections on God's own Revealedness, but there is an astounding beauty manifest in his treatment of the humanity of the God who reveals Himself in Christian experience. Barth's pneumatology is an ingenious and incomparable achievement of 20th-century theology since it consists of more than academic theology; it is a profound spirituality in the genuine sense of this term: a linguistically and intellectually pleasing description of the Holy Spirit's activity in the Christian. In this spirituality, God encounters man and man encounters the God who communicates His very Self as the definitive sign of His unswerving graciousness and love. Barth's pneumatology contains more than a detailed account of the Spirit's work *ad extra* in the world; it is characterized by a pervasive attempt to penetrate *ad intra* into the being of God. Far more important than any critique of Barth's pneumatological accomplishment is the fact that, except for Paul Tillich and Karl Rahner, no other theologians have produced as thorough and lasting a masterpiece on the Holy Spirit in this century.

Precisely because Barth's theology of the Spirit is so impressive, its individual parts invite close scrutiny. What one discovers is that the architectonic structure of his pneumatology, while it is sturdy and attractive, is at the same time not as free-wheeling and imaginative as it perhaps could be if its plan were designed differently. This is true, for example, of Barth's treatment of the trinitarian aspects of the Spirit's being and mission. Few theologians have conducted as painstaking a review of traditional Christian teaching on the Trinity and refashioned it in as startling a thorough way. Yet, Barth's trinitarian reflections move only in one direction, that is, back in time to the eternal history of grace in the divine community. The Spirit is to effect in time an analogy between the inner being of God and God's economic activity. In such a retrospective framework the Spirit's achievements in the present and the future seem relativized by His everlasting function as the reciprocity or communityness between the Father and the Son. The Spirit continually makes known the timeless perfection of God by creating an image of this tranquility in the life of the believer. This approach lends Spirit theology a distinctly noetic, static and nostalgic character. The Spirit is so bound to the primeval election on behalf of man's salvation which was determined by the Father and the Son that He can do little more than assure the programmed correspondence between history and eternity. What is proposed in this study is that the Spirit must be attributed the forward-pointing, eschatological task of bringing the Father and the Son, along with all creation, to a not yet achieved unity. If the Father is the Creator, and the Son the Recreator, then the Spirit has to be conceived as the Transcreator of the cosmos, or else God's triune being will be viewed as such a closed case, that the Spirit offers the freedom of mankind no possibility of enhancing divine glory. As a result, the contemporary theologian cannot weave the doctrine of the Trinity into the fabric of God's ongoing and future cooperation with man towards the liberation of the world. Without espousing that theologians blindly repeat what Joachim of Fiore and Georg Hegel have done in excess, one has to ask whether a fresh consideration of the distinctive nature of *Spiritus Transcreator* has not to be undertaken today in a serious manner.

Just as the Father forms the universe before man's existence, and the Son reforms the human community through the mediation of a man of Israel at the center of history, so the Spirit transforms cosmic and human history by working ahead of man and enticing him to the completion of creation. If such new formulations are not worked out, perhaps along the lines of the traditional *Veni Creator Spiritus*, the Spirit's truly exciting task of making the world pliable, energetic and hopeful for the Father's promise of the Kingdom can be interpreted as a meaningless divine venture; then not only the Spirit's relevance but also man's destiny with God is lost sight of. If the Spirit is viewed as the spearhead of a movement from the Father through the Son, and then through the Son forwards to the Father, the anthropological and eschatological dimensions of Christian revelation will not be overclouded by the doctrine of the Trinity, but highlighted and intensified through theology, preaching and pastoral practice. Such a theology of the Spirit as Transcreator and Transformer does not detract from the work of the Father and the Son; rather the Spirit can be seen to carry on and to bring to completion the "Father-Son-Spirit" movement to man through the "Spirit-Son-Father" movement with man towards the *eschaton*. This schema is not to be interpreted as happening over the heads of human communities which are in search of a totally new future, but in their midst. Thus, a proper theology of the Transformer Spirit presupposes a theology of nature, so that God's being fashions, refashions and transfashions man with the graced yet free cooperation of man himself. This is the deepest enigma of revelation: the triune God graciously chooses to open His own being outward to the world so that man is able to contribute to the moment when both God and all human beings will find the harmony which God's generosity purposely keeps from Himself so that it can be shared by man. It is precisely the "resurrection of the dead" and the "life everlasting," with which the creed ends, that should inspire a theology of the distinctive transforming work of the Spirit in the world.

Yet a dynamic vision of the eschatological Trinity is impossible if, as is the case with Barth, everything in theology is interpreted "pan-christologically." In effect such a position is anti-trinitarian, even though Barth would insist that the Trinity was formulated with the Christ-event at the center and represents a defense of the uniqueness of the second article. It could just as well be argued, however, that it was the unexpected experience of the Spirit's outpouring on them which compelled early Christian writers to view Jesus Christ through a pneumatic lens. Thus, actually living the third article of the creed originally rendered the confession that "Jesus Christ is Lord" possible and intelligible, because the power of the Spirit who filled Jesus had met and enlivened them personally. To suggest that the Spirit be reintroduced as the central category of Christian dogmatics is not to urge that Christ become unimportant, but that His prior pre-eminence in Western theology be mitigated by a truly trinitarian and eschatological perspective. Barth situates creation within the circumference of Christ, whereas a more valid biblical outlook would necessitate placing both creation and Christ in the sphere of the Spirit. The most convincing argument for this position is the very theology of the Synoptics, of John and of Paul, for whom Jesus patently belongs in the matrix of the spiritual power of Yahweh who fills His humanity with messianic dignity and causes his being to be transformed. This absolutely singular occurrence enables one to grasp in retrospect that in the Spirit-filled Jesus the Father conducted a dialogue with His own Son in the flesh. Thus, in addition to the need to develop an eschatological rather than on originative doctrine of the Trinity, Barth's too narrow understanding of the Spirit calls for a new investigation of early Spirit Christology. This is urgent so that Pentecost does not simply perpetuate Easter but opens salvation history into a new era which is patterned on the Christ-event but aimed at broadening both Christ's glory and that of the Father through the Spirit's rejuvenation of all nations.

In the light of these remarks it seems tenable to propose the thesis that the *Church Dogmatics* (III) contains the most innovative Spirit theology within the Barthian corpus. This is because two important themes are developed here which are usually neglected when Barth considers matters which more easily lend themselves to a christological truncation. These two central ideas are the notion of *Spiritus Creator* and the possibility of a Spirit Christology. There is no need to explain further the vast importance of these pneumatic insights for Barth's theology. It may seem strange indeed, but the *Church Dogmatics* (III) finally brings Barth to a genuine theology of the Father. This is so significant since only in the perspective of the first credal article does Barth actually put Christ and the Spirit on equal ground, as it were. It is also true, of course, that Barth presents the Spirit's work both in every man and in the person of Jesus as fulfilling a rather accidental role; the reality of the covenant of grace on the one hand and that of the incarnation of the Word on the other relegate the Spirit's function to that of assuring that man is ready to hear the Word spiritually and that Jesus' humanity is prepared to receive the Word personally. The Spirit is thus given even here an ancillary office. But this should not detract from the fact that here the Spirit is at least incorporated into Barth's theological vision in more than a purely noetic fashion. The Spirit enjoys an ontic role in man's very being to the extent that He constitutes the human person as body and soul and makes him ontically disposed to accept the covenant. The Spirit also guarantees Jesus' integral humanity so that the Word of God can dwell uniquely in Him. Though Barth's pneumatology occupies a pre-eminent position over his anthropology in the *Church Dogmatics* (III), it is refreshingly evident that the Spirit shares great responsibility in this entire area. In the light of creation's vastness and of the Father's goodness, the Spirit is for a moment seen to play an indispensable part in the very occurrence of the incarnation and not to be totally subservient to the already accomplished Christ-event.

This is not true, however, of Barth's ecclesiology. Although the Spirit is theoretically given much space in the treatment of the Christian community in the *Church Dogmatics*, Christ so controls the being of the Christian that the Spirit's mediating function becomes rather lifeless. There is no prophetic thrust to the ecclesial dimensions of Barth's pneumatology. No doubt a major contradiction is involved here, since it is precisely in the doctrine of reconciliation that the Spirit is to win the center of attention. What Barth seems actually to mean is that the noetic function of the Spirit will be even more intensified, but not that the death-destroying, life-giving power of the Spirit Himself will be underscored. It is in Barth's theology of the Church, in fact, that all the difficulties in his pneumatology are accentuated. Most prominent among these is the lack of mediation which is attributed to the members of the Church, let alone to all mankind, in the accomplishment of the Spirit's mission of bringing about the consummation of the world. Once Barth turns from what he considers the cosmological excesses of the 1919 *Letter to the Romans*, he does not permit his lived concern for social issues sufficiently to influence, if not the text, the tone of the *Church Dogmatics*. Consequently, man's graced part in the ultimate salvation or condemnation of the world is not seen as a logical outcome of Barth's pronounced stress on man's pride, lies and sloth. Rather, all is interpreted in the context of the eternal decree of election in which the Son of God took condemnation and salvation upon Himself. The Spirit had affirmed this decision and is now executing its wide pronouncement, not its very realization, however. The work of the Church is essentially that of witnessing to the reconciliation won by Christ and not that of furthering the but incipient victory of Christ by cooperating in the transfashioning action of the Spirit who first anointed Jesus and who enabled Him to become the inaugurator of liberation for the oppressed. The dangerous tendency in Barth's ecclesiology is that, where the Spirit should be most prominent, Christ's death and resurrection distort the picture, and an ecclesial community is described which is not the painful concern of the triune God who through preaching and sacrament grants the Church a share in the very arrival of the Kingdom; the Church is huddled around Christ the Victor, but not sent out on the liberating mission of the Kingdom's harbinger, the Lord and Giver of Life.

How can the claim that Barth is a great pneumatologian be maintained when so many serious flaws are discovered in this central dimension of his theology? What Barth understands he must do to underline the sovereignty, holiness and promise of the Spirit he does exceptionally well. The problem is that Barth does not dialogue with others concerning the Holy Spirit. His unfortunate propensity is to view the other as the adversary and not as the possible channel through whom God's grace is subtly leading him to the balance and breadth needed in Spirit theology. Some obvious dialogue partners, such as Brunner, Gogarten and Tillich, were needlessly spurned. The same is true of contact with Roman Catholic and Orthodox thinkers. This last group in particular has emerged from the research done for this study as a most helpful dialogue partner in the area of pneumatology. If it can be said that Protestantism tends to stress the cross, or the second article of the creed, and Catholicism emphasizes nature, or the first article, Orthodoxy stresses exultation, or the work of the Spirit described in the third article. There is a most astounding emphasis among Eastern theologians on the centrality of pneumatology. This is evident not only in their developed understanding of the Holy Spirit as the outpoured love of the Father through His Son on behalf of creation which forms the germ of their doctrine of the Trinity, but also in their comprehension of the parousial nature of the Church and in their almost natural affinity for the insights of Spirit Christology. In fact, the pneumatocentrism of the East, which reacts incessantly to the West's christocentrism, offers such richness to ecumenical dialogue on the person and work of the Holy Spirit that it provides a major corrective not only to Barth's pneumatology but to that of the whole Western Church. Nor is Orthodoxy's insistence on the *ex patre* to be overlooked. A future pneumatology will have to plumb these insights and discover once again that it is not just a matter of piety when the Holy Spirit is described as the joy of the Father in His Son's resurrection which is communicated to the universe and which permeates it with an unction that gladdens the face of the earth.

The mention of dialogue brings this study back to the point at which it began and to the germ of Barth's own noetic pneumatology, namely, his reaction to Neo-Protestantism, Christian Existentialism and Roman Catholicism with their ubiquitous stress on anthropology. Since their pneumatology seemed only to serve as a thin veneer on an otherwise poorly disguised natural theology, Barth sets out to assure that the divine Spirit in his own system really is the Holy Spirit, that is, the Spirit of the eternal Word, the Spirit of another man, the outreaching power of Jesus' resurrection. In other words, Barth counters his opponents' search for a theology of *Spiritus Creator* with a redoubled stress on *Spiritus Redemptor*. The judgment of many competent theologians, both Protestant and Catholic, is that Barth is equally guilty of erring in the opposite direction. For, instead of incorporating the insights of his rivals into a theology centering on the Redeemer Spirit, Barth globally repudiates their more mediated stances. The result is that his pneumatology, noteworthy in other respects, lacks precisely the anthropological and ecclesiological dimensions which he profitably could have culled from their positions. Their concern for man's being allows the Holy Spirit to work within the confines of human freedom and reason, and their regard for the Church's mediating role permits the Holy Spirit to meet the Christian in and through the words and actions that comprise ecclesial sign-giving. In this way man's autonomy would not be stifled by the Holy Spirit, and the being both of man and of the Holy Spirit not obscured by Christ. Thus there are valid, even if overstated, points of view represented by those towards whom Barth expresses an inquisitive though suspicious attitude. This study suggests that the reason for the haunting attraction which other pneumatological formulations continue to exert on him throughout his life is that they direct Spirit theology into domains which Barth could not fully appreciate. Instead of patient and probing dialogue, Barth chooses to go his own way and not to meet with others in some sort of cautious compromise. The lacunae in his own pneumatology are the consequence of such unwillingness to reach a guarded agreement with Spirit theologies of a different kind.

It may well be, of course, that Barth was wiser than all his past and present critics. His theological and sociological common sense in adhering and giving new meaning to the perennial truths of the Scriptures and to the tenets of the Reformation in their pure form afforded his generation a fixed point by which to measure its position in an atmosphere of jolting change. Certainly the recent rise of the Charismatic Movement in all Christian denominations is proof enough that return to the original sources of Christian life can rejuvenate the Church and foster new communities which in the power of the Holy Spirit listen to the Word of God and gather to pray and to discern what it is that they are called to heal in their world. It may well be the case that Barth's charism was not that of compromise but of fiery yet serene restatement of the traditions in the West that have nurtured faith for centuries. Certainly the critique offered in this study, which would essentially point Barth's pneumatology forward and insist on granting a mediating role in Spirit theology to contemporary man's growing concern for the future of the world, may indeed make God's divine Pneuma seem to be a bit poor. Barth's enticing quality is that he allows the Spirit's sovereignty to attract the mind and move the will in a way that a cosmic or existential, world-history or liberational approach to pneumatology may not. Thus, the positive aspects of his Spirit-centered theology of the Christian cannot be passed over lightly. Barth presents the Holy Spirit as the Lord of Christian existence and as the triune God's own self-impartation who graciously reveals His being not only to but also within man; Barth's pneumatic ethics powerfully incites the Christian to accept his calling by erecting signs of God's eternal grace in a world which neither knows nor wants to know of its redemption in Jesus Christ; there is little vagueness here, since the Spirit is clearly the extension of Christ's triumph over all obstacles; the Spirit executes the eternal divine Yes amid man's age-old No. Particularly striking is Barth's account of God's own inner tension which is resolved by the same Holy Spirit who instills in man the courage to hold out in his own frustrations and to live restlessly at rest. If these deeply joyful aspects of the pneumatology within the *Church Dogmatics* are not appreciated, Barth's Christian wisdom, attested to by a life of constant service of the Church and the world, can be glossed over by too exacting a critique of his entire system.

Granted the majesty and profundity of Barth's pneumatology, it must nevertheless be added that his achievement is not so much an original exposition of the third article of the creed as a detailed description of the Christian's subjective appropriation of the second article. In other words, Barth does not begin with the Father's life-giving Spirit who spoke through the prophets and who, having filled the person and ministry and effected the glorification of Jesus, is now present in His Church, allowing its graced holiness and unity, universality and apostolicity to contribute at least partially to the communion of all men, to the forgiveness of sin, to the resurrection of the body and to life everlasting. Barth keenly sensed that his opponents were attempting an innovative pneumatic starting point which commenced at the end of the creed and then moved "upwards" as it were, to the second and first articles. It is clear that Barth sets out from the second article, moves on to the third and then to the first. To proceed from the experience of sanctification and then to consider reconciliation and finally creation remained for Barth a distinct theological possibility, but one which only the most gifted scholar could undertake without the effort degenerating into a form of anthropology. Certainly the main lines of the two improvisations sketched in the last part of this study would be judged intellectually hazardous by Barth. By advocating a theology of *Spiritus Creator* active everywhere in the universe and by affixing to it a theology of *Spiritus Redemptor* at work in Christ and in His community, one would seem to fragment the Spirit and deprive Him of His essential relationship to the eternal Word. Furthermore, to suggest that man be awarded an ontic part in the salvific mission of the Holy Spirit, even beyond those who explicitly confess Jesus Christ as Lord, would be deemed an excessively dangerous concession to an innocuous philosophy of spirit which leaves the very identity of this so-called "Holy" Spirit in question. In a real sense, therefore, the issues raised here place this study in the camp of Barth's rivals: Is this really a theology of the Holy Spirit?

Barth's "second article" pneumatology seems to leave the Father and the Spirit somewhat inhibited from action, and man decidedly sheltered from responsibility, by the Son. Is there some compromise possible between Barth and his pneumatological opponents? If so, where does the middle lie between a theology of Creator Spirit and a theology of Redeemer Spirit? Have Tillich and Rahner indicated the path with their particular blend of philosophy and theology? Or are Moltmann and Pannenberg right in directing the Church away from past positions towards forward-looking pneumatologies? Will Küng's and Kasper's studies of the Idealists, and the more anthropologically oriented pneumatologies which result, strike the right balance? Have Schoonenberg and Lampe been correct in developing tentative Spirit Christologies as the solution? Or is Gutierrez's and Sobrino's call for a prophetic liberational pneumatology the way to link creation and recreation? In short, Barth's pneumatology raises anew the perennial questions concerning the Holy Spirit without answering them in a sufficiently nuanced way. But Spirit theology will never be quite the same because of Barth. His pounding reaction to—and ironic incorporation of—Scholastic, Neo-Protestant and Existential methodologies, which induced him to refashion a traditional, even if christologically biased, theology of the Spirit for this century is an unique achievement. His particular attempt at a correlation of biblical and Reformational pneumatology slights man, the Spirit and the Father for the sake of the Son. But in other respects it serves as a touchstone for the future. His intention to make the Spirit God's Spirit once again has succeeded. In consonance with Barth's own self-doubt, therefore, one is compelled to ask a final question. Who will be the "geistlich und geistig kundiger Thebaner" capable of writing a pneumatology which is not an anthropology, and which is not—as in Barth's case it patently is—anthropologically wanting as well?

NOTES TO CHAPTER I

1. Karl Barth, *Dogmatics in Outline* (New York: Harper and Row, 1959) pp. 137-138. One earlier reference occurs in 1937; cf. *KD* I/2, 403-404; *CD*, 367-368.
2. Karl Barth, *The Heidelberg Catechism for Today* (Richmond: John Knox, 1964), pp. 84-85.
3. Karl Barth, *Protestant Theology in the Nineteenth Century: Its Background and History* (London: SCM Press, 1972), p. 460. Hereafter, *Protestant Theology*.
4. Karl Barth, *Protestant Theology*, p. 514.
5. *KD* III/3, 370-71; *CD*, 324. In most cases, reference to the original German version *(KD)* and the English translation *(CD)* of *Die Kirchliche Dogmatik* is given.
6. Karl Barth, "Evangelical Theology in the 19th Century," in *The Humanity of God* (Richmond: John Knox, 1968), pp. 24-25.
7. Karl Barth, *Evangelical Theology: An Introduction* (New York: Holt, Rinehart and Winston, 1963) p. 55.
8. Karl Barth, *Schleiermacher-Auswahl*, p. 311.
9. *Ibid.*
10. *KD* IV/2, 61; *CD*, 57.
11. *KD* IV/1, 372-73; *CD*, 337-338.
12. *KD* IV/2, 902; *CD*, 795.
13. *KD* IV/2, 403-404; *CD*, 361.
14. *KD* II/2, 174; *CD*, 160.
15. *KD* I/2, 275; *CD*, 252.
16. *KD* IV/3², 572-73; *CD*, 498. The influence of Barth's pneumatic interpretation of Schleiermacher is evident; cf. Felix Flückiger, *Philosophie and Theologie bei Schleiermacher* (Zurich: Evangelischer Verlag, 1947), p. 217; Henri Bouillard, *Karl Barth* I: Genèse et Évolution de la Théologie Dialectique (Paris: Aubier, 1957), pp. 154-55; Friedrich Hertel, *Das theologische Denken Schleiermachers: Untersucht an der ersten Auflage seiner Reden "Über die Religion"* (Zurich: Zwingli Verlag, 1965), p. 18.
17. Karl Barth, *Protestant Theology*, p. 463.
18. *KD* IV/1, 136; *CD*, 124.
19. *KD* IV/4, 21; *CD*, 19.
20. Karl Barth, *Rudolf Bultmann: Ein Versuch Ihn zu Verstehen* (Zurich: Evangelischer Verlag, 1952), p. 47.
21. *KD* I/2, 228; *CD*, 209.
22. Karl Barth, *Rudolf Bultmann: Ein Versuch Ihn zu Verstehen*, p. 50; also pp. 48 and 52.

23. *KD* IV/2, vi; *CD*, ix.
24. *KD* I/2, 273; *CD*, 251.
25. Karl Barth and Heinrich Barth, *Zur Lehre vom Heiligen Geist* (Munich: Chr. Kaiser Verlag, 1930), p. 95.
26. Karl Barth and Hans Urs von Balthasar, *Einheit und Erneuerung der Kirche* (Freiburg: Paulusverlag, 1968), p. 12.
27. *Ibid*.
28. *KD* III/4, 185; *CD*, 166.
29. *KD* III/4, 692; *CD*, 602.
30. *KD* IV/2, 13-18; *CD*, 13-18.
31. *KD* I/2, 160; *CD*, 146.
32. *KD* IV/2, 47-48; *CD*, 45.
33. *KD* IV/2, 570-71; *CD*, 504-505.
34. Hans Küng, *Justification: The Doctrine of Karl Barth and a Catholic Reflection* (London: Thomas Nelson and Sons, 1964), pp. 93-94.
35. Karl Barth, *Protestant Theology*, p. 514 (F. A. Tholuck); p. 585 (I. A. Dorner); and pp. 594-95 (Julius Müller).
36. Karl Barth, "Brunners Schleiermacherbuch" *Zwischen den Zeiten* II (1924) 63-74.
37. Karl Barth, *Protestant Theology*, p. 458.
38. Karl Barth, *Protestant Theology*, p. 459.
39. *Ibid*.
40. Karl Barth, "Schleiermacher," *Zwischen den Zeiten* V (1927) and *Protestant Theology*, pp. 430-32 and 471-73. For a corroboration of Barth's opinion, cf. Felix Flückiger, *Philosophie und theologie bei Schleiermacher*, pp. 174-185; Paul Seifert, *Die Theologie des jungen Schleiermachers* (Gütersloh: Verlagshaus Gerd Mohn, 1960), p. 111.
41. Karl Barth, *Protestant Theology*, pp. 447-48 and 467.
42. Richard R. Niebuhr, *Schleiermacher on Christ and Religion: A New Introduction* (New York: Charles Scribner's Sons, 1964), pp. 11-12.
43. Karl Barth, *The Heidelberg Catechism for Today*, p. 84; *Protestant Theology*, pp. 426-28.
44. Hans Urs von Balthasar, *The Theology of Karl Barth* (New York: Holt, Rinehart and Winston, 1971), pp. 177-78. Von Balthasar supports the theory that from Schleiermacher's "God-consciousness" Barth derives his understanding of the Holy Spirit as the intermediary between Christ and the Christian; Barth is to stress, however, the "objectively efficacious" source of Christian life in the historical Jesus.
45. Karl Barth, *Protestant Theology*, p. 460.
46. Karl Barth, *Protestant Theology*, p. 431; cf. Gerhard Spiegler, *The Eternal Covenant: Schleiermacher's Experiment in Cultural Theology* (New York: Harper and Row, 1967), p. 178.
47. Karl Barth, *Protestant Theology*, pp. 462-64.
48. Karl Barth, *Protestant Theology*, pp. 471-72; cf. E. Troeltsch, *Gesammelte Schriften* II (Tübingen: J. C. B. Mohr, 1919), pp. 657-58; Friedrich von Hügel, *Essays and Addresses* (London: J. M. Dent and Sons, 1921),

p. 166; Paul Tillich, *Systematic Theology* III (Chicago: University of Chicago Press, 1963), pp. 326-331. All these authors situate theology between two focal points, an historical and a personal; they thus confirm the elliptical pattern which Barth distills from Schleiermacher.

49. *KD* IV/3¹, 513; *CD*, 445.

50. *KD* IV/1, 858; *CD*, 767-68.

51. Karl Barth, "The Humanity of God" in *The Humanity of God*, p. 44. In this lecture of 1956 Barth indicates that von Balthasar, "the shrewd friend from another shore," represents for him the Catholic position on his theological achievement.

52. Karl Barth, *Schleiermacher-Auswahl*, pp. 307-310.

53. Karl Barth, *Schleiermacher-Auswahl*, p. 312.

54. Karl Barth, *Die Theologie und die Kirche*, *Gesammelte Vorträge* II (Munich: Chr. Kaiser Verlag, 1928) pp. 165-66.

55. Hans Urs von Balthasar, *The Theology of Karl Barth*, p. 170; Hans Küng, *Menschwerdung Gottes: Eine Einführung in Hegels Theologisches Denken als Prolegomena zu einer Zukünftigen Christologie* (Freiburg: Herder Verlag, 1970), p. 656.

56. Hans Urs von Balthasar, *The Theology of Karl Barth*, p. 171.

57. Karl Barth, "Hegel," in *Protestant Theology*, pp. 384-421. Barth's essay on Hegel is surprisingly positive and has awakened new interest in the theology of the Idealists. This is especially noticeable in the works of Jürgen Moltmann among Protestants and Hans Küng among Catholics.

58. Karl Barth, "Schleiermacher," *Zwischen den Zeiten* V (1927) and *Protestant Theology*, pp. 463-67.

59. Wilfried Brandt, *Der Heilige Geist und die Kirche bei Schleiermacher* (Zurich: Zwingli Verlag, 1968), p. 17; Holger Samson, *Die Kirche als Grundbegriff der theologischen Ethik Schleiermachers* (Zurich: Evangelischer Verlag, 1958), pp. 55-59; Robert Stalder, *Grundlinien der Theologie Schleiermachers* I: *Zur Fundamentaltheologie* (Wiesbaden: Franz Steiner Verlag, 1969), pp. xxvii-xxviii. These authors generally agree that there is a more solidly based christology behind Schleiermacher's pneumatology than Barth is willing to admit.

60. Hans Urs von Balthasar, *The Theology of Karl Barth*, pp. 172-73.

61. Hans Urs von Balthasar, *The Theology of Karl Barth*, p. 174.

62. *KD* IV/1, 316; *CD*, 287.

63. *KD* IV/1, 802-805; *CD*, 718-721.

64. *KD* I/2, 222 and 257; *CD*, 203 and 240. Hans Urs von Balthasar makes use of these texts to point out that Barth's theology of Christian rather than philosophical identity centers on the key mediating role of the Holy Spirit, the very point of identity between God and man. (*The Theology of Karl Barth*, p. 179). In agreement with this interpretation are: Richard R. Niebuhr, *Schleiermacher on Christ and Religion*, p. 147 and Wolfhart Pannenberg, *Theology and the Philosophy of Science* (Philadelphia: The Westminster Press, 1976), pp. 297-298. Henri Bouillard, *Karl Barth* III: *Parole de Dieu et existence humaine* (Paris: Aubier, 1957), pp. 298-99 argues that Barth is not an Hegelian.

65. Barth employs this "analogy" between the three forms of the one revealed Word (=*Dei loquentis persona*) and the Trinity itself in *CD* I/1, 136-37.

66. Cf. Gordon H. Clark, *Karl Barth's Theological Method* (Philadelphia: Presbyterian and Reformed Publishing Company, 1963), pp. 176-177.

NOTES TO CHAPTER II

1. Karl Barth, "Dank und Reverénz," *Evangelische Theologie* 14 (1963) 339.

2. Hans Urs von Balthasar, *The Theology of Karl Barth*, pp. 79-80.

3. Henri Bouillard, *Karl Barth* I, pp. 20-21.

4. Colin Brown, *Karl Barth and the Christian Message* (Chicago: Inter-University Press, 1967), pp. 21-22.

5. Eberhard Busch, *Karl Barth: His Life from Letters and Autobiographical Texts* (Philadelphia: Fortress Press, 1976), p. 490.

6. Colm O'Grady, *The Church in the Theology of Karl Barth* (London: Geoffrey Chapman, 1970), p. 8.

7. B. A. Willems, *Karl Barth: An Ecumenical Approach to His Theology* (New York: Paulist Press, 1965), pp. 21-22.

8. Henri Bouillard, *Karl Barth* I, p. 145.

9. Hans Urs von Balthasar, *The Theology of Karl Barth*, pp. 48-52.

10. Karl Barth, *Der Römerbrief*, unaltered reprint of the 1st ed. of 1919 (Zurich: EVZ-Verlag, 1963), p. 197.

11. *Ibid.*, p. 227 and also p. xii.

12. Henri Bouillard, *Karl Barth* I, pp. 87-88.

13. Emil Brunner, "The Epistle to the Romans by Karl Barth: An Up-to-Date Unmodern Paraphrase," in *The Beginnings of Dialectic Theology* I, ed. James M. Robinson (Richmond: John Knox Press, 1968), pp. 69-70.

14. Karl Barth, *Der Römerbrief* (1919), p. 80.

15. Eberhard Busch, *Karl Barth*, pp. 118-119.

16. Karl Barth, *The Epistle to the Romans*, rev. ed. of 1922 (London: Oxford University Press, 1933), pp. 284-285.

17. *Ibid.*, p. 283.

18. See the last section in Chapter I of this study.

19. Karl Barth, *The Epistle to the Romans* (1922), p. 315.

20. *Ibid.*, p. 314.

21. Herbert Hartwell, *The Theology of Karl Barth: An Introduction* (Philadelphia: Westminster Press, 1964), p. 11.

22. Karl Barth, *The Epistle to the Romans* (1922), p. 30.

23. Hans Urs von Balthasar, *The Theology of Karl Barth*, p. 56. On pp. 53-58 von Balthasar offers what he admits is a harsh presentation of Barth's early theology, since he characterizes it as "super-Christian and therefore un-Christian" (pp. 57-58).

24. Henri Bouillard, *Karl Barth* I, pp. 29-30. Cf. also E. L. Allen, *The Sovereignty of God and the Word of God: A Guide to the Thought of Karl Barth* (London: Hodder and Stroughton, 1951), pp. 16-17.

25. Jürgen Moltmann, *Theology of Hope: On the Ground and Implications of a Christian Eschatology* (New York: Harper and Row, 1967), pp. 39-40.

26. Henri Bouillard, *Karl Barth* I, p. 121.

27. *Ibid.*, p. 130.

28. Karl Barth, "Abschied," *Zwischen den Zeiten* XI (1933) 538.

29. Karl Barth, "Vom Heiligen Geist: Eine Pfingstbetrachtung," *Zwischen den Zeiten* IV (1926) 277.

30. Henri Bouillard, *Karl Barth* I, pp. 125-126.

31. *Briefwechsel Karl Barth-Edward Thurneysen*, 1921-1930 (Zurich: TVZ Verlag, 1974), p. 442.

32. *Ibid.*, p. 448.

33. Eberhard Busch, *Karl Barth*, p. 173. Busch quotes from Barth's self-portrait of 1964.

34. Karl Barth, *Die Christliche Dogmatik im Entwurf: Die Lehre vom Worte Gottes, Prolegomena zur Christlichen Dogmatik* (Munich: Chr. Kaiser Verlag, 1927), p. 205.

35. *Ibid.*, p. 199.

36. *Ibid.*, pp. 206-207.

37. *Ibid.*, p. 206.

38. Hans Urs von Balthasar, *The Theology of Karl Barth*, p. 74.

39. Karl Barth, *Die Christliche Dogmatik*, pp. 203-204.

40. *Ibid.*, pp. 295 and 325.

41. Henri Bouillard, *Karl Barth* I, pp. 129-130.

42. *KD* I/1, vii; *CD*, ix.

43. Karl Barth and Heinrich Barth, *Zur Lehre vom Heiligen Geist* (Munich: Chr. Kaiser Verlag, 1930), pp. 39-40 and 95. Cf. Eberhard Busch, *Karl Barth*, p. 188.

44. *Zur Lehre vom Heiligen Geist*, p. 101.

45. *KD* I/1, 131; *CD*, 147.

46. Karl Barth, *Anselm: Fides Quaerens Intellectum*, trans. of 2nd German ed. (Cleveland: Meridian Books, 1962), p. 11.

47. *Ibid.*, pp. 170-171.

48. B. A. Willems, *Karl Barth: An Ecumenical Approach to His Theology*, pp. 33-34.

49. Karl Barth, *Anselm*, pp. 17-18.

50. *Ibid.*, p. 46.

51. *Ibid.*, p. 47.

52. *Ibid.*, p. 48.

53. *Ibid.*, p. 50.

54. *Ibid.*, p. 53.

55. *Ibid.*, p. 55.

56. Sebastian Matczak, *Karl Barth on God: The Knowledge of the Divine Existence* (New York: Alba House, 1962), pp. 25-27; 116-119.

57. Eberhard Busch, *Karl Barth*, p. 216. Cf. also *KD* I/1, 257ff.; *CD*, 243ff.

58. Henri Bouillard, *The Knowledge of God* (Paris: Aubier, 1967), pp. 94-95. Though in general agreement with Barth's evaluation of the theological intent of Anselm, Bouillard claims that Anselm's arguments take on a philosophical character with logical validity even in the eyes of the unbeliever: "This leads us to relativize the Barthian critique of all philosophical proofs."

59. Wilfried Härle, *Sein und Gnade: Die Ontologie in Karl Barths Kirchlicher Dogmatik* (Berlin: Walter de Gruyter, 1975), pp. 191 and 195.

60. See Chapters IV, VI and VII of this study.

61. Already in 1937 (*KD* I/2, 403-414; *CD*, 367-368) Barth prefigures the theme of 1947 and afterwards. He asserts that von Harnack's stress on "man himself believing in the divine" is a valid insight; "it has a legitimate place within the doctrine of the Holy Spirit."

NOTES TO CHAPTER III

1. *KD* I/1, 155; *CD*, 170.
2. *KD* I/1, 155-56; *CD*, 171.
3. *KD* I/1, 189; *CD*, 207-208.
4. *KD* I/1, 19-20; *CD*, 21-22.
5. *KD* I/1, 189-190; *CD*, 208.
6. Barth distinguishes his controversial use of *Seinsweisen* or "modes of being" from the tenets of heretical Modalism, and argues that his option expresses more clearly what the term "person" always intended to connote (*KD* I/1, 378 and 380; *CD*, 412 and 414). Cf. Karl Rahner's preference for his own term *Subsistenzweisen* or "modes of subsisting" in *The Trinity* (New York: Seabury Press, 1974), pp. 109-115, and Hendrikus Berkhof's proposal of the term *modi revelationis* or "modes of revelation" in *The Doctrine of the Holy Spirit* (Atlanta: John Knox Press, 1976), pp. 111-115.
7. *KD* I/1, 190; *CD*, 208-209.
8. *KD* I/1, 494; *CD*, 539.
9. *KD* I/1, 331-32; *CD*, 361.
10. For Barth's presentation of the very special unity which Christian monotheism asserts of the God of revelation who is totally independent of a reciprocal relation with the world and yet not singular or lonely, cf. *KD* I/1, 374; *CD*, 407.
11. *KD* I/1, 332; *CD*, 361.
12. *KD* I/1, 350; *CD*, 380.
13. *KD* I/1, 347-48; *CD*, 378.
14. *KD* I/1, 352; *CD*, 382-83.
15. *KD* I/1, 314; *CD*, 342.
16. *KD* I/1, 351; *CD*, 382.
17. *Ibid.*
18. Since Barth insists that all analogies between the Trinity and the world are set up by revelation and are not independently present, he is critical even of his own use of such triads as Pure Giver—Receiver and

Giver—Pure Receiver, Beginning—Middle—End, Speaker—Word—Meaning, lest he cross into the zone of the *vestigia trinitatis*. Cf. *KD* I/1, 383-84 and 393; *CD*, 417-18 and 428.

19. *KD* I/1, 354; *CD*, 385.
20. *KD* I/1, 194; *CD*, 212.
21. *KD* I/1, 319; *CD*, 348.
22. *KD* I/1, 320; *CD*, 349.
23. *KD* I/1, 392; *CD*, 427.
24. *KD* I/1, 394-95; *CD*, 430.
25. *KD* I/1, 402; *CD*, 438.
26. *KD* I/1, 370; *CD*, 403.
27. *KD* I/1, 402-403; *CD*, 439.
28. *KD* I/1, 387-88; *CD*, 422.
29. *KD* I/1, 403-404; *CD*, 440.
30. *KD* I/1, 472; *CD*, 515.
31. *KD* I/1, 473; *CD*, 516.
32. *KD* I/1, 489; *CD*, 533-34.
33. *KD* I/1, 492; *CD*, 537.
34. *KD* I/1, 504; *CD*, 549-550.
35. *KD* I/1, 491; *CD*, 535-36.
36. *KD* I/1, 491-92; *CD*, 536.
37. *KD* I/1, 505; *CD*, 551.
38. *KD* I/1, 494; *CD*, 538.
39. Throughout the *Church Dogmatics* Barth consistently applies to various aspects of dogma his conviction that God's own inner life with the Son and the Spirit is reflected in His acts *ad extra*. Cf. *CD* III/2, 324 where Barth grounds man's very existence as likeness of God and as hopeful creature in the intradivine life of the Trinity.
40. *KD* I/1, 512; *CD*, 559.

NOTES TO CHAPTER IV

1. *KD* I/2, 230; *CD*, 211.
2. *KD* I/1, 475-76; *CD*, 518-19.
3. *KD* I/2, 217-18; *CD*, 199.
4. *KD* I/1, 510; *CD*, 556.
5. *KD* I/2, 217; *CD*, 198.
6. *KD* I/2, 268-69; *CD*, 246.
7. *KD* I/2, 302; *CD*, 277.
8. *KD* II/1, 181; *CD*, 161-62.
9. *KD* I/1, 480; *CD*, 523-24. Though in this passage Barth stresses the soteriological and only indicates the anthropological work of the Spirit, he does more adequately distinguish and conjoin the two functions in his treatment of creation in *CD* III/2. Cf. Chapter V of this study.
10. *KD* I/2, 228-29; *CD*, 209.
11. *KD* II/1, 167; *CD*, 150.
12. *KD* II/1, 8-9; *CD*, 10.

13. *KD* II/1, 177-78; *CD*, 158-59. Barth generally confines himself to the terms "objective and subjective" throughout the middle volumes of the *Church Dogmatics*. The justification of the use of "ontic" and "noetic" here is that Barth had already introduced them in *CD* I/1, 350: "God's revelation has its reality and truth wholly and in every respect—i.e. ontically and noetically—within itself"; furthermore, these terms play a key part in *CD* IV/3[1], e.g. p. 213: "The distinction between ontic and noetic, or objective and subjective elements in the intercourse between God and man inaugurated and ordered in Jesus Christ."

14. *KD* I/1, 486-87; *CD*, 530-31.

15. *KD* I/2, 272-73; *CD*, 249-50.

16. *KD* I/1, 484-85; *CD*, 528.

17. *KD* I/1, 509; *CD*, 555. Since every man is free because of the eternal free decision of God on his behalf in Jesus Christ, the man who is to believe is already objectively free to do so: the Holy Spirit activates this freedom to a new state. The Spirit's role is more corroborative than creative in Barth's system. Once this has been said, it is clear why Barth insists that it is man himself who believes and not the Holy Spirit in him; cf. *KD* I/2, 402-403; *CD*, 366-67.

18. *KD* I/2, 242; *CD*, 221-22.

19. *KD* I/2, 247-48; *CD*, 226-27.

20. *KD* I/2, 258; *CD*, 236.

21. *KD* I/2, 251; *CD*, 230. Here Barth describes the "pre-given-ness" of the sacraments as their special feature as compared to preaching. A few pages later Barth, after calling the sacraments "indispensable means of grace," observes: "and no complaints about 'Roman sacramentalism' will prevent us from declaring that on its objective side the Church is sacramental; that is to say, it has to be understood on the analogy of Baptism and the Lord's Supper." *CD* I/2, 232.

22. *KD* I/2, 252; *CD*, 231.

23. *KD* I/2, 270-71; *CD*, 248.

24. *KD* I/2, 377-79; *CD*, 344-45.

25. *KD* I/2, 394-395; *CD*, 359.

26. *KD* I/2, 383, *CD*, 349.

27. *KD* I/2, 394; *CD*, 358-59.

28. *KD* I/2, 579; *CD*, 522.

29. *KD* I/2, 560; *CD*, 505. Cf. Klaas Runia, *Karl Barth's Doctrine of Holy Scripture* (Grand Rapids: William B. Eerdmans, 1962), pp. 137-168.

30. *KD* I/2, 597; *CD*, 537.

31. *KD* I/2, 845-847; *CD*, 756-57.

32. *KD* II/2, 202; *CD*, 184. Even with the first reference to the Holy Spirit in *CD* I/1, 170-171, Barth includes election as one of the functions of the Word's spiritual power: "The concepts election, revelation, setting apart, calling, rebirth . . . all signify a promise, a judgment, a claim regarding man, by which God binds him to Himself."

33. *KD* II/2, 109; *CD*, 101-102.

34. *KD* II/2, 183; *CD*, 159.

35. *KD* II/2, 113; *CD*, 105-106.

36. *KD* II/2, 346; *CD*, 315.
37. *KD* II/2, 338; *CD*, 308.
38. *KD* II/2, 338-39; *CD*, 308.
39. *KD* I/2, 275; *CD*, 252.
40. *KD* I/2, 260; *CD*, 238.
41. In *CD* II/2 Barth introduces the calling of man as his response to the divine election; in *CD* IV/3[1] he expands and conretizes this central concept in treating "The Holy Spirit and the Sending of the Christian Community." For an appreciation of how significant a contribution Barth has made to pneumatology by appending the category of calling or mission to the more usual treatment of the Spirit's work as sanctification, cf. Hendrikus Berkhof, *The Doctrine of the Holy Spirit*, pp. 33 and 78.
42. *KD* II/2, 383-84, *CD*, 348.

NOTES TO CHAPTER V

1. *KD* III/1, 219; *CD*, 195.
2. *KD* I/2, 408; *CD*, 371.
3. *KD* II/2, 780; *CD*, 699.
4. *KD* I/2, 408; *CD*, 371.
5. *KD* I/2, 441-442 and 453; *CD*, 400 and 411.
6. *KD* III/2, 369; *CD*, 306.
7. *KD* III/4, 103-104; *CD*, 94.
8. *KD* II/2, 854; *CD* 763. The context of this passage reveals that Barth not only links prayer with freedom, but also with truth. Since it appears in the section dealing with man's ability to understand the doctrine of justification through divine election, Barth views prayer as the way to a genuine knowledge about the reality of justification and not simply about the Church teaching on such. Broadening and deepening one's theological understanding of doctrine is not sufficient; justification is proven true only when it becomes a matter of prayer. This the Holy Spirit assures by making man free to pray and thus to discover the truth of salvation.
9. *KD* III/4, 110-11; *CD*, 101.
10. *KD* III/3, 500; *CD*, 430.
11. *KD* I/2, 416; *CD*, 378.
12. *KD* I/2, 418; *CD*, 380.
13. *KD* I/2, 491; *CD*, 444.
14. *KD* II/2, 816; *CD*, 730.
15. *KD* III/4, 205; *CD*, 184.
16. *KD* I/2, 404-05; *CD*, 368. For a detailed treatment of the Spirit's role in Barth's ethics of Christian freedom, cf. Robert E. Willis, *The Ethics of Karl Barth* (Leiden: E. J. Brill, 1971), pp. 240-272.
17. *KD* III/2, 402; *CD*, 334.
18. *KD* III/3, 292-93; *CD*, 258. Just as Barth argues that it is really man who believes, though the Spirit is Lord of Christian faith, he likewise argues that the omnipotence of the Word along with the omnipresence of the Spirit "does not prejudice the autonomy, the freedom, the responsibility, the in-

dividual being and life and activity of the creature, or the genuineness of its own activity, but confirms and indeed establishes them" (*KD* III/3, 163-64; *CD*, 144). Barth is thus aware of the critique that his theocentric theology robs man of a participatory role in divine providence, and does not respect the creature's authentic freedom to rebel against God or to cooperate with Him.

19. *KD* III/2, 565; *CD*, 470.

20. *KD* III/2, 560-61; *CD*, 467.

21. *KD* III/2, 562, *CD*, 468.

22. *KD* I/1, 494-95; *CD*, 539. While Barth takes a bold step in the direction of a Pneuma-Sarx-Christology in the *Church Dogmatics* (III/2), this earlier passage acts as a reminder that he deems such a christology valid only if it preserves the absolute uniqueness of Jesus; He is not a "living soul" as Adam was, but a "living spirit." Thus Barth is consistent when he points out that Jesus is not the Messiah and the Son of God due to His privileged anointing by the Holy Spirit: "On the contrary, it is because this man is the Messiah and the Son of God that He stands to the Holy Spirit in this special relationship" (*CD* III/2, 333 and 341). It is the classical Logos Christology which affords Barth the sure foundation on which to base a view of Jesus which in fact antedates the development of Logos theology. Cf. Chapter VIII of this study.

23. *KD* I/2, 263; *CD*, 241.

24. *KD* III/1, 63; *CD*, 59.

25. *KD* III/1, 282-83; *CD*, 249.

26. *KD* III/2, 431; *CD*, 358-59.

27. *KD* III/2, 436; *CD*, 363.

28. *KD* III/2, 432 and 439; *CD*, 360 and 366.

29. *KD* I/1, 475; *CD*, 518.

30. *KD* III/2, 435-36; *CD*, 362-63. The importance of this "may" and this "transcendent enabling" cannot be overemphasized. Here Barth comes as close as possible to suggesting a precondition of faith which is in the possession of the nascent believer due to his human condition. Barth is adamant that it is all gift. Man does not have this potential; it is given to him continually by the life-giving Spirit. However, this openness on Barth's part to the anthropological tenets of his rivals marks a definite, though guarded, development of his theology. Cf. Chapter VII of this study.

31. *KD* III/2, 474-75; *CD*, 396.

32. *KD* III/2, 475; *CD*, 396.

33. *KD* III/2, 437; *CD*, 364.

34. *KD* III/2, 433; *CD*, 361.

35. *KD* III/2, 447; *CD*, 373.

36. *KD* III/2, 426; *CD*, 355.

37. *KD* III/2, 429; *CD*, 357.

38. *KD* III/2, 431; *CD*, 358.

39. *KD* III/1, 229-30; *CD*, 204. Passages such as this support the conviction that the *Church Dogmatics* (III) contains a considerable broadening of Barth's pneumatology. Though here as elsewhere he remains christocentric in outlook, more sensitivity to the Spirit's role as *Spiritus Creator* is

evident. As a result, man is presented as a being in whom the Spirit of the Creator is active prior to a conscious knowledge of Jesus Christ, although the Spirit Creator is necessarily identical to the Spirit Redeemer.

40. *KD* III/2, 260-61; *CD*, 218.
41. *KD* III/2, 264; *CD*, 221.
42. *KD* III/2, 262; *CD*, 220.
43. *KD* III/3, 356; *CD*, 312.
44. *KD* III/2, 23; *CD*, 21.
45. *KD* III/1, 7-8; *CD*, 8-9.
46. *KD* III/2, 535; *CD*, 446.
47. *KD* III/2, 8; *CD*, 9.
48. *KD* III/2, 92; *CD*, 79.
49. *KD* III/1, 19; *CD*, 19.
50. *KD* III/1, 60; *CD*, 56.
51. *KD* III/3, 132-33; *CD*, 117-18.
52. *KD* III/3, 106-07; *CD*, 94. In addition to presenting the Holy Spirit as the guarantor of man's similarity to the eternal Godhead, Barth considers the Spirit's role in creating a likeness between man's earthly existence and that of Jesus Christ. In the faith, obedience and prayer of the Christian, the Spirit insures that Jesus' birth and death, solidarity with and influence on mankind is repeated and returned to the Father. Cf. *KD* III/3, 503; *CD*, 432.
53. *KD* III/1, 14; *CD*, 15.
54. *KD* III/3, 161; *CD*, 142.

NOTES TO CHAPTER VI

1. *KD* IV/2, vi, *CD*, ix.
2. *KD* IV/2, 379; *CD*, 339.
3. *KD* IV/2, 373, *CD*, 334.
4. *KD* IV/4, 20-23; *CD*, 19-21. To avoid excessive stress either on *extra nos* (christomonism) or *in nobis* (anthropomonism), Barth claims that the *extra nos* included a *pro nobis*. Thus, the "new being of every man" happened in the being of Jesus Christ: "If He acts *extra nos pro nobis*, and to that extent *in nobis*, this necessarily implies that in spite of the unfaithfulness of every man, He creates in the history of every man the beginning of his new history, the history of a man who has become faithful to God." The Holy Spirit allows man freely to respond to his divine change which is secured in Jesus' "fruitful history which newly shapes every human life."
5. *KD* IV/4, 29-30; *CD*, 27.
6. *KD* IV/3², 868; *CD*, 759.
7. *KD* IV/3², 870; *CD*, 760.
8. *KD* IV/3², 861; *CD*, 752.
9. *KD* IV/3¹, 414; *CD*, 358.
10. *KD* IV/1, 87; *CD*, 83.
11. *KD* IV/1, 416; *CD*, 376.
12. *KD* IV/1, 844; *CD*, 755.
13. *KD* IV/1, 846; *CD*, 757.

14. *KD* IV/4, 5; *CD*, 5. Barth understands Christian transformation not as the "infusion of supernatural powers" or as "the fulfillment of natural and moral impulses," but as a living connection to the history of Jesus Christ. The Christian "is a man to whom Jesus Christ has given not just a potential, but an actual share in that history of His" (*CD* IV/4, 14). Man's very essence is exalted along with that of Jesus Christ: "It is the exaltation of our essence with all its possibilities and limits into the completely different sphere of that totality, freedom, correspondence and service" (*CD* IV/2, 30). Again, the Holy Spirit makes man willing and ready to accept the share in Jesus' history and exaltation which he already has.

15. *KD* IV/1, 729-30; *CD*, 652-53.
16. *KD* IV/4, 37; *CD*, 34.
17. *KD* IV/4, 112; *CD*, 102.
18. *KD* IV/1, 858; *CD*, 767-68.
19. *KD* IV/1, 858-59; *CD*, 768.
20. *KD* IV/2, 570-571; *CD*, 504-505.
21. *KD* IV/3[2], 863-64; *CD*, 754-55.
22. *KD* IV/3[1], 340-41; *CD*, 295.
23. *KD* IV/3[1], 406; *CD*, 351-52. Why this penultimate form of the parousia? Why not its immediate consummation? Barth's answer is that God intends man "not merely to see, but actually to share in the harvest which follows from the sowing of reconciliation" (*CD* IV/3[1], 331). Cf. John Thompson, *Christ in Perspective: Christological Perspectives in the Theology of Karl Barth* (Grand Rapids: Wm. B. Eerdmans, 1978), p. 130.
24. *KD* IV/3[1], 340; *CD*, 295.
25. *KD* IV/2, 360-61; *CD*, 322-23.
26. *KD* IV/2, 403-04; *CD*, 360-61.
27. *KD* IV/2, 375; *CD*, 336.
28. *KD* IV/2, 372; *CD*, 333.
29. *KD* IV/2, 384; *CD*, 343.
30. *KD* IV/2, 378; *CD*, 338-39.
31. *KD* IV/3[1], 208-209; *CD*, 182.
32. Spirit Christology comes to the fore whenever Barth attempts to explain how the humanity of Jesus is free to correspond to the freedom of the Word. Thus, even in Jesus' case, the Holy Spirit is the power of the Word to be united with human nature. Unadulterated Word Christology would deny that the Word only exists with the Spirit both in the trinitarian life, in the person of Jesus Christ, in the life of the Christian, and potentially in every man. Cf. *CD* I/2, 199 and *CD* III/2, 334, passages already discussed in Chapters IV and V of this study.
33. *KD* IV/2, 103; *CD*, 93-94.
34. *KD* IV/2, 362-63; *CD*, 324-25.
35. *KD* IV/2, 186; *CD*, 167.
36. *KD* IV/1, 169; *CD*, 153 and *KD* IV/2, 59-60; *CD*, 55-56.
37. *KD* IV/1, 52; *CD*, 49.
38. *KD* IV/1, 835; *CD*, 747.
39. *KD* IV/2, 305; *CD*, 275.

40. *KD* IV/4, 127-28; *CD*, 116.
41. For a corroboration of the interpretation offered here, cf. Eberhard Jüngel, "Karl Barth's Lehre von der Taufe: Ein Hinweis auf ihre Probleme" *Theologische Studien* 98 (1968) 18, where Jüngel makes an informative comparison between two passages in which Barth speaks of the "new being of every man" (*KD* IV/2, 305; *CD*, 275 and *KD* IV/4, 23; *CD*, 21).
42. *KD* IV/1, 835-36; *CD*, 748.
43. *KD* IV/2, 410; *CD*, 366-67. Cf. Wilfried Härle, *Sein und Gnade: Die Ontologie in Karl Barths Kirchlicher Dogmatik*, pp. 300-313.
44. *KD* IV/3¹, 44; *CD*, 41.
45. *KD* IV/1, 392-93; *CD*, 354-55.
46. *KD* IV/3¹, 344; *CD*, 299.
47. *KD* IV/3¹, 243; *CD*, 213.
48. *KD* IV/3¹, 245; *CD*, 215.

NOTES TO CHAPTER VII

1. Hans Urs von Balthasar, *Karl Barth: Darstellung und Deutung seiner Theologie* (Cologne: Verlag Jacob Hegner, 1951), p. 218. The English edition unfortunately does not contain this section. The translation is the author's.
2. David L. Mueller, *Karl Barth* (Waco: Word Books, 1972), pp. 76-79.
3. Karl Rahner, *Theological Investigations* VIII (New York: Herder and Herder, 1972), p. 40.
4. Eberhard Busch, *Karl Barth*, p. 487. Busch quotes from a letter of Barth to Wolfhart Pannenberg on Dec. 7, 1964.
5. Wolfhart Pannenberg, *Gottesgedanke und menschliche Freiheit* (Göttingen: Vandenhoeck and Ruprecht, 1972), p. 32.
6. Hans Albert, *Traktat über Kritische Vernunft* (Tübingen: Paul Siebeck, 1968), pp. 108-115.
7. Hans Urs von Balthasar, *The Theology of Karl Barth*, pp. 217-247.
8. Eberhard Jüngel, *Gottes Sein ist im Werden*, pp. 15-16.
9. Jürgen Moltmann, *The Crucified God: The Cross of Christ as the Foundation and Criticism of Christian Theology* (London: SCM Press, 1974), p. 240.
10. Wolfhart Pannenberg, *Jesus, God and Man* (Philadelphia, Westminster Press, 1968), p. 171; Paul Tillich, *Systematic Theology* III, pp. 111-138.
11. John Thompson, *Christ in Perspective: Christological Perspectives in the Theology of Karl Barth*, p. 139.
12. Eberhard Busch, *Karl Barth*, p. 494.
13. Hans Küng, *On Being a Christian* (New York: Wallaby Books, 1978), p. 472.
14. Henri Bouillard, *Karl Barth* III: *Parole de Dieu et Existence Humaine*, p. 291.
15. Heinrich Zahrnt, *Die Sache mit Gott* (Munich: Piper Verlag, 1967), pp. 141-142.

16. André Dumas, *Une théologie de la realité*: *Dietrich Bonhoeffer* (Geneva: Labor et Fides, 1968), p. 16.

17. Jürgen Moltmann, *The Crucified God*, p. 255.

18. Wolfhart Pannenberg, *The Apostles' Creed in the Light of Today's Questions* (Philadelphia: Westminster Press, 1975), pp. 133 and 155.

19. Wolfhart Pannenberg, *Gottesgedanke und menschliche Freiheit*, p. 23.

20. Jürgen Moltmann, *Theology of Hope*, p. 58.

21. Walter Kasper, *Glaube und Geschichte* (Mainz: Matthias-Grünewald Verlag, 1970), p. 86, and *Jesus the Christ* (New York: Paulist Press, 1977) p. 184.

22. Hans Urs von Balthasar, *The Theology of Karl Barth*, p. 57.

23. Karl Rahner, *Theological Investigations* I (Baltimore: Helicon Press, 1961), pp. 146-148; Hans Urs von Balthasar, *Skizzen zur Theologie* III, *Spiritus Creator* (Einsiedeln: Johannes Verlag, 1967), pp. 97-100; Walter Kasper, *Jesus the Christ*, pp. 257-259.

24. Theodore de Régnon, *Études de théologie positive sur la Sainte Trinité* I (Paris, 1892), pp. 335-340, 428-435; Michael Schmaus, *Die psychologische Trinitätslehre des heiligen Augustinus* (Münster: Aschendorffsche Verlagsbuchhandlung, 1927), p. 19.

25. Karl Rahner, *Theological Investigations* IV (Baltimore: Helicon Press, 1966), p. 85.

26. Karl Rahner, *Theological Investigations* I, p. 146.

27. *Ibid.*, p. 148.

28. Wolfhart Pannenberg, *Jesus, God and Man*, pp. 173-174, where Pannenberg points out that Barth, while dependent on the soteriological argument of the Cappadocians, does not arrive at the divinity of the Spirit through experience of salvation alone, but through the realization of one's own incapability of believing. Only God can bring one to faith; this God is the Holy Spirit.

29. H. Dörries, *De Spiritu Sancto*: *Der Beitrag des Basilius zum Abschluß des trinitarischen Dogmas* (Göttingen: Vandenhoeck and Ruprecht, 1956), pp. 59-69; 132-146. The Greek Fathers understood the Holy Spirit to manifest Himself through human potentialities so that man's search for God is fulfilled when he meets the Spirit who graciously comes to him.

30. Hans Küng, *On Being a Christian*, pp. 446-447 and 475-476. Küng supports Barth's christological starting point since Küng claims that one only knows the Father in Jesus Christ and that all theology bears a "christological imprint". The Trinity really is aimed at explaining the Christ-event, how God acted economically in Jesus Christ and in the Spirit. Yet Küng seems to give the Spirit-experience more weight than Barth does, e.g., p. 477.

31. This question is the entire point of Simon van der Linde's critique of Barth in *De leer van den heiligen Geest bij Calvijn*: *Bijdrage tot de kennis der reformatorische Theologie* (Wageningen: Veenman, 1943).

32. In support of the essential role of pneumatology in the formation of the trinitarian dogma, cf. Joseph Ratzinger, "Bermerkungen zur Frage der Charismen in der Kirche," in *Die Zeit Jesu*, *Festschrift für Heinrich Schlier*, ed. G. Bornkaam and K. Rahner (Freiburg: Herder Verlag, 1970), p. 261;

K. Rahner and W. Thüsing, *Christologie—Systematisch und Exegetisch: Arbeitsgrundlagen für eine interdisziplinäre Vorlesung* (Freiburg: Herder Verlag, 1972), p. 270.

33. Eberhard Jüngel, *Gottes Sein ist im Werden*, pp. 51-53. Barth is defended here as having maintained through his teaching on the Trinity the existence of God as a concrete happening. Jüngel would thus disagree with the critique of Barth presented in this study.

34. Walter Kasper, *Jesus the Christ*, p. 250; G. Wagner, "Der Heilige Geist als offenbarmachende und vollendende Kraft," in *Erfahrung und Theologie des Geistes*, ed. C. Heitmann and H. Mühlen (Hamburg, 1974), pp. 216-220.

35. Walter Kasper, "The Spirit Acting in the World to Demolish Frontiers and Create the Future," *Lumen Vitae* 34 (1979) 86-99.

36. Joseph Ratzinger, *Introduction to Christianity* (New York: Seabury Press, 1969), pp. 255-256.

37. Hans Urs von Balthasar, "Der Unbekannte Jenseits des Wortes," in *Spiritus Creator*, p. 97.

38. Jürgen Moltmann, *The Church in the Power of the Spirit: A Contribution to Messianic Ecclesiology* (New York: Harper & Row, 1977), pp. 56-65.

39. Eberhard Busch, *Karl Barth*, p. 487. Busch quotes from a letter of Barth to Moltmann on Nov. 17, 1964. When Moltmann makes "the whole of theology end up in eschatology," Barth claims, "God seems to be a bit poor."

40. Ewert Cousins, "Teilhard and the Theology of the Spirit," *Cross Currents* XIX (1969) 165-166; Pierre Teilhard de Chardin, *The Phenomenon of Man* (New York: Harper and Row, 1965), pp. 264-265.

41. Alan Paton, "The Nature and Ground of Christian Hope Today," in *Knocking on the Door* (New York: Scribner's, 1975), pp. 290 and 292.

42. Jürgen Moltmann, *The Church in the Power of the Spirit*, pp. 50-56.

43. Heribert Mühlen, "Die epochale Notwendigkeit eines pneumatologischen Ansatzes der Gotteslehre," *Wort und Wahrheit* 28 (1973) 275-287.

44. George S. Hendry, *The Holy Spirit in Christian Theology* (London: SCM Press, 1965), p. 109.

45. Arnold B. Come, *Human Spirit and Holy Spirit* (Philadelphia: Westminster Press, 1959), pp. 85-86.

46. Wilfried Härle, *Sein und Gnade: Die Ontologie in Karl Barths Kirchlicher Dogmatik*, pp. 121 and 313.

47. Albert Ebneter, *Der Mensch in der Theologie Karl Barths* (Zurich, 1952), p. 40.

48. Wilfried Härle, *Sein und Gnade*, pp. 98 and 167.

49. Walter Kasper, *Geheimnis Mensch* (Mainz: Matthias Grünewald Verlag, 1975), pp. 20-21. Cf. also: Karl H. Schelkle, "Die Schöpfung in Christus," in *Die Zeit Jesu: Festschrift für Heinrich Schlier*, p. 217.

50. Karl Rahner, *Theological Investigations* I, p. 83.

51. G. C. Berkouwer, *The Triumph of Grace in the Theology of Karl Barth* (Grand Rapids: Wm. B. Eerdmans, 1956), p. 190.

52. Eberhard Jüngel, "Die Möglichkeit theologischer Anthropologie auf dem Grunde der Analogie' " *Evangelische Theologie* 22 (1962) 548.

53. Hans Urs von Balthasar, *The Theology of Karl Barth*, pp. 149-150. Cf. also: Ulrich Hedinger, *Der Freiheitsbegriff in der Kirchlichen Dogmatik Karl Barths* (Zurich: Zwingli Verlag, 1962), pp. 103-104.

54. Gottlieb Söhngen, "Wesen und Akt in der scholastischen Lehre von der *participatio* und *analogia entis*" *Studium Generale* 8 (1955) 650. Cf. also: Martin Storch, *Exegesen und Meditationen zu K. Barths Kirchlicher Dogmatik* (Munich: Chr. Kaiser Verlag, 1964), p. 151.

55. Edgar H. Friedmann, *Christologie und Anthropologie: Methode und Bedeutung der Lehre vom Menschen in der Theologie Karl Barths* (Münsterschwarzach: Vier-Türme Verlag, 1972), p. 393.

56. Hendrikus Berkhof, *The Doctrine of the Holy Spirit*, pp. 19-20.

57. Walter Kasper, "Aufgaben der Christologie Heute," in Arno Schilson and Walter Kasper, *Christologie im Präsens: Kritische Sichtung neuer Entwürfe* (Freiburg: Herder Verlag, 1974), pp. 147-148.

58. George S. Hendry, *The Holy Spirit in Christian Theology*, pp. 112-114.

59. John C. Haughey, *The Conspiracy of God: The Holy Spirit in Us* (New York: Doubleday, 1976), p. 56-77.

60. Karl Rahner, *Theological Investigations* VI (New York: Seabury Press, 1974), pp. 72-73; Hans Urs von Balthasar, *The Theology of Karl Barth*, pp. 269-270; Walter Kasper, *Einführung in den Glauben* (Mainz: Matthias-Grünewald Verlag, 1972), p. 30; Avery R. Dulles, *Revelation Theology* (New York: Herder and Herder, 1969), pp. 97-98 and 130-134.

61. Paul Tillich, *Systematic Theology* I, pp. 59-68; G. W. H. Lampe, *God as Spirit* (Oxford: Clarendon Press, 1977), pp. 176-205.

62. Colm O'Grady, *The Church in Catholic Theology: Dialogue with Karl Barth* (London: Geoffrey Chapman, 1969), p. 339.

63. Karl Rahner, *Theological Investigations* IV, pp. 216-218. Cf. also: Hans Küng, *Justification: The Doctrine of Karl Barth and a Catholic Reflection*, pp. 144-147.

64. Thomas Merton, *The Seven Storey Mountain* (New York: Mentor Books, 1948), pp. 175-176.

65. F. A. Cockin, *God in Action* (Harmondsworth: Penguin Books, 1961), pp. 25-26; Jürgen Moltmann, *The Church in the Power of the Spirit*, pp. 64-65.

66. Hendrikus Berkhof, *The Doctrine of the Holy Spirit*, pp. 115-116.

67. Langdon Gilkey, *Catholicism Confronts Modernity: A Protestant View* (New York: Seabury Press, 1975), pp. 196-197. Cf. also: Harold H. Ditmanson, "The Significance of the Doctrine of the Holy Spirit for Contemporary Theology," in *The Holy Spirit in the Life of the Church*, ed. Paul D. Opsahl (Minneapolis: Augsburg Publishing House, 1978), p. 216.

68. Otto Weber, *Karl Barths Kirchlicher Dogmatik: Ein Einführender Bericht zu den Bänden I/1 bis IV/3²* (Neukirchen: Verlag des Erziehungsvereins, 1963), p. 110.

69. Ernst-Wilhelm Wendebourg, *Die Christusgemeinde und ihr Herr: Eine Studie zur Ekklesiologie Karl Barths* (Berlin: Lutherisches Verlagshaus, 1967), p. 158.

70. Karl Rahner, *Theological Investigations* VIII, p. 34; David L. Mueller, *Karl Barth*, p. 150.

71. Heinrich Fries, *Bultmann, Barth und die katholische Theologie* (Stuttgart: Schwaben Verlag, 1955), p. 120.

72. Wolfhart Pannenberg, *Grundfragen systematischer Theologie: Gesammelte Aufsätze* (Göttingen: Vandenhoeck and Ruprecht, 1967), p. 228.

73. Joseph Ratzinger, *Introduction to Christianity*, p. 96.

74. Walter Kasper, *Jesus the Christ*, p. 251.

75. Martin Storch, *Exegesen und Meditationen zu K. Barths Kirchlicher Dogmatik*, p. 123; Eberhard Jüngel, *Gottes Sein ist im Werden*, pp. 118-120.

76. Hans Urs von Balthasar, *Spiritus Creator*, pp. 98-99.

77. Jürgen Moltmann, *The Church in the Power of the Spirit*, pp. 60-64.

78. Avery R. Dulles, *Models of the Church* (New York: Doubleday, 1974) pp. 79-80.

79. G. W. H. Lampe, *God as Spirit*, pp. 34-35.

80. Wolfhart Pannenberg, *Jesus, God and Man*, pp. 169-171.

81. Walter Kasper, *Jesus the Christ*, p. 266.

82. Friedrich Schmid, *Verkündigung und Dogmatik in der Theologie Karl Barths: Hermeneutik und Ontologie in einer Theologie des Wortes Gottes* (Munich: Chr. Kaiser Verlag, 1964), p. 183.

83. Wilfried Härle, *Sein und Gnade*, pp. 327-328.

84. Paul Tillich, *Perspectives on Nineteenth and Twentieth Century Theology* (London: SCM Press, 1967), p. 20.

NOTES TO CHAPTER VIII

1. G. W. Bromiley, *Karl Barth* in *Creative Minds in Contemporary Theology*, ed. P. E. Hughes (Grand Rapids: Wm. Eerdmans, 1966), pp. 27-59; Colin Brown, *Karl Barth and the Christian Message*, pp. 149-153.

2. Hans Küng, *On Being a Christian*, pp. 468-472; Hans Urs von Balthasar, *Spiritus Creator*, p. 98.

3. Jürgen Moltmann, *Theology of Hope*, pp. 279-281.

4. Paul Althaus, *Die Christliche Wahrheit: Lehrbuch der Dogmatik* (Gütersloh: Gerd Mohn, 1966), pp. 56-57; Hans Urs von Balthasar, *The Theology of Karl Barth*, pp. 198-200.

5. Walter Kasper, *Glaube und Geschichte*, pp. 85-86.

6. Max Schoch, *Karl Barth: Theologie in Aktion* (Stuttgart: Verlag Huber, 1967), p. 225.

7. Ernst-Wilhelm Wendebourg, *Die Christusgemeinde und ihr Herr*, pp. 57-58.

8. Heribert Mühlen, "Die Christusereignis als Tat des Heiligen Geistes," *Mysterium Salutis* III/2 (1969) 524-530; Walter Kasper, *Einführung in den Glauben*, p. 121.

9. Jürgen Moltmann, *The Crucified God*, pp. 255-256; Walter Kasper, *Jesus the Christ*, p. 249.

10. George T. Montague, *The Holy Spirit: Growth of a Biblical Tradition* (New York: Paulist Press, 1976), pp. 3-17.

11. C. K. Barrett, *The Holy Spirit in the Gospel Tradition* (London: SPCK Press, 1947), pp. 113-121.

12. Ernst-Wilhelm Wendebourg, *Die Christusgemeinde und ihr Herr*, pp. 175-177.

13. Karl Rahner, *Theological Investigations* I, p. 110.

14. David L. Mueller, *Karl Barth*, p. 152.

15. James Dunn, "Spirit and the Kingdom," *The Expository Times* 82 (1970) 38.

16. Carroll Stuhlmueller, "The Gospel according to Luke," *Jerome Biblical Commentary* (Englewood Cliffs, N. J.: Prentice-Hall, 1968), II 117.

17. S. Boulgakof, *Le Paraclet* (Paris: Éditions Montaigne, 1946), pp. 236-256.

18. Nikos A. Nissiotis, *Die Theologie der Ostkirche im ökumenischen Dialog: Kirche und Welt in orthodoxer Sicht* (Stuttgart: Evangelisches Verlagswerk, 1968), pp. 73-74.

19. Paul Evdokimov, *L'Orthodoxie* (Paris: Delachaux et Niestlé, 1949), pp. 147-148.

20. V. Lossky, *The Mystical Theology of the Eastern Church* (London: James Clarke and Company, 1957), p. 159.

21. Walter Kasper, "Einmaligkeit und Universalität Jesu Christi," *Theologie der Gegenwart* 17 (1974) 8-9.

22. Alexander Schmemann, "The Orthodox Tradition," in *The Convergence of Traditions: Orthodox, Catholic, Protestant*, ed. Elmer O'Brien, S. J. (New York: Herder and Herder, 1967), pp. 27-28.

23. Avery R. Dulles, "The Theology of Hans Küng: A Comment," *Union Seminary Quarterly Review* XXVII (1972) 141-142.

24. Henri Bouillard, *Karl Barth* III, p. 292. Bouillard remarks that the action of the Father and the Spirit is not sufficiently detached from that of Christ in Barth's thought: "Theology may be christology, but only if christology encompasses a *the*ology."

25. Norman Pittinger, *The Holy Spirit* (Philadelphia: United Church Press, 1974), p. 72.

26. G. W. H. Lampe, "The Holy Spirit and the Person of Christ," in *Christ, Faith and History*, ed. S. W. Sykes and J. P. Clayton (Cambridge: University Press, 1972), pp. 129-130.

27. Hans Urs von Balthasar, *Spiritus Creator*, p. 100.

28. Wolfhart Pannenberg, *The Apostles' Creed in the Light of Today's Questions*, pp. 141-143.

29. Hans Urs von Balthasar, *Spiritus Creator*, p. 153.

30. Wolfhart Pannenberg, *Jesus, God and Man*, pp. 369-372.

31. Jürgen Moltmann, *Theology of Hope*, pp. 86-87. Moltmann is aware that in *CD* IV/3¹, 326ff. Barth does admit that "Christ's intrinsically perfect work is still moving towards its consummation" (p. 327). The question is whether Barth is consistent in following through with this insight.

32. *Ibid.*, pp. 57-58.

33. G. W. H. Lampe, *God as Spirit*, pp. 187-188.

34. Eberhard Jüngel, *Gottes Sein ist im Werden*, pp. 96-97.

35. Jon Sobrino, *Christology at the Crossroads: A Latin American Approach* (Maryknoll, N.Y.: Orbis Books, 1978), p. 226.

36. Ernst-Wilhelm Wendebourg, *Die Christusgemeinde und ihr Herr*, p. 208.

37. G. Sauter, *Die Theologie des Reiches Gottes beim älteren und jüngeren Blumhardt, Studien zur Dogmengeschichte und systematischen Theologie* 14 (1962) 159. Sauter shows the similarity between Barth's ecclesiology and that of the younger Blumhardt.

38. Gustaf Wingren, *Theology in Conflict: Nygren, Barth, Bultmann* (Philadelphia: Muhlenberg Press, 1958), pp. 71-74 and 109-120.

39. Hans Urs von Balthasar, *The Theology of Karl Barth*, p. 163.

40. The works of David L. Mueller and Ernst-Wilhelm Wendebourg are particularly helpful in clarifying the problem which the objective-subjective schema causes for Barth's ecclesiology; Jürgen Moltmann, Wolfhart Pannenberg and the advocates of Liberation Theology are able to draw out the significance of the Church's mission in the world which derives from a future-oriented theology of Christ.

41. Ernst-Wilhelm Wendebourg, *Die Christusgemeinde und ihr Herr*, pp. 84-85.

42. Jürgen Moltmann, *The Church in the Power of the Spirit*, p. 201.

43. Ernst-Wilhelm Wendebourg, *Die Christusgemeinde und ihr Herr*, p. 175.

44. Friedrich-Wilhelm Marquardt, *Theologie und Sozialismus: Das Beispiel Karl Barths* (Munich: Chr. Kaiser Verlag, 1972), pp. 16-24, 33ff. and 312; George Hunsinger, *Karl Barth and Radical Politics* (Philadelphia: Westminster Press, 1976), pp. 224-227.

45. Walter Kasper, "Aufgaben der Christologie heute," pp. 149-151.

46. Jürgen Moltmann, *The Crucified God*, pp. 248-249.

47. John Macquarrie, *The Humility of God* (Philadelphia: Westminster Press, 1978), pp. 4-5 and 81-82.

48. Warren A. Quanbeck, "Developmental Perspective and the Doctrine of the Spirit," in *The Holy Spirit in the Life of the Church*, pp. 165-171.

49. Walter Kasper, *Jesus the Christ*, pp. 254-258.

50. Gustavo Gutierrez, *A Theology of Liberation: History, Politics and Salvation* (Maryknoll, N.Y.: Orbis Books, 1973), pp. 198, 259 and 265.

51. For an exposition of Barth's openness to Spirit Christology, cf. Chapters V and VI of this study.

52. Piet Schoonenberg, "Spirit Christology and Logos Christology," *Bijdragen* 38 (1977) 355.

53. Walter Kasper, "Einmaligkeit und Universalität Jesu Christi," pp. 5-6. Kasper would agree with Barth that christology in an evolutionary, existential or world-history perspective can lose its uniqueness. Kasper opts instead for the pneumatological framework of the Scriptures.

54. C. K. Barrett, *The Holy Spirit and the Gospel Tradition*, pp. 39-40.

55. Jean Daniélou, *The Theology of Jewish Christianity* (Chicago: Regnery Press, 1964), pp. 57-64 and H.-J. Schoeps, *Jewish Christianity: Factional Disputes in the Early Church* (Philadelphia: Fortress Press, 1969), pp. 68-73.

56. Hendrikus Berkhof, *The Doctrine of the Holy Spirit*, pp. 21-22.

57. Wolfhart Pannenberg, *Jesus, God and Man*, pp. 120-121; in agreement with Pannenberg is Bertold Klappert, *Die Auferstehung des Gekreuzigten: Der Aufsatz der Christologie Karl Barths in Zusammenhang der Christologie der Gegenwart* (Neukirchen: Neukirchener Verlag, 1971), pp. 28-29 and 144.

58. Piet Smulders, "Dogmengeschichtliche und lehramtliche Entfaltung der Christologie," *Mysterium Salutis* III/1 (1970) 391-399.

59. Aloys Grillmeier, *Christ in Christian Tradition: From the Apostolic Age to Chalcedon* (London: A. R. Mowbray and Co., 1965), pp. 68 and 105.

60. Walter Kasper, "Aufgaben der Christologie heute," p. 149 and *Jesus the Christ*, p. 253. Cf. also: George Johnston, *The Spirit-Paraclete in the Gospel of John* (Cambridge: The University Press, 1970), p. 151.

61. James Dunn, *Jesus and the Spirit: A Study of the Religious and Charismatic Experience of Jesus and the First Christians as Reflected in the New Testament* (Philadelphia: Westminster Press, 1975), pp. 46-49. Dunn argues that Jesus' ongoing messiahship is only understandable in terms of the Holy Spirit, since the Messiah is the one equipped and anointed with the end-time Spirit of Yahweh.

62. G. W. H. Lampe, "The Holy Spirit and the Person of Christ," p. 124. Also in disagreement with Lampe on this point is Olaf Hansen, "Spirit Christology: A Way Out of our Dilemma?" in *The Holy Spirit in the Life of the Church*, pp. 194-196.

63. Piet Schoonenberg, "Spirit Christology and Logos Christology," p. 365. Cf. also: Norman Hook, "A Spirit Christology," *Theology* 75 (1972) 229.

64. Cf. Philip J. Rosato, "Spirit Christology: Ambiguity and Promise," *Theological Studies* 38 (1977) 447-449.

65. Avery R. Dulles, *The Survival of Dogma: Faith, Authority and Dogma in a Changing World* (New York: Doubleday and Co., 1971), pp. 69-77.

66. Patrick Masterson, *Atheism and Alienation: A Study of the Philosophical Sources of Contemporary Atheism* (South Bend: University of Notre Dame Press, 1971), pp. 154-173.

67. The prophetic anointment of Jesus as liberator of the poor and oppressed forms the center of Liberation Theology's christology. Cf. Leonardo Boff, "Salvation in Jesus Christ and the Process of Liberation," *Concilium* 96 (1974) and Jon Sobrino, *Christology at the Crossroads*, pp. 33-37.

68. Oscar Cullmann, *The Christology of the New Testament* (Philadelphia: Westminster Press, 1963), pp. 221-227. Cullmann argues that, since the Spirit's presence in and possession of Jesus first became fully known in His glorification, only then was it evident that the power of the Spirit was operative in Jesus even before His vindication as Lord.

69. Karl Rahner, *The Trinity* (New York: Seabury Press, 1974) pp. 41-42 and 119-120.

70. Raymond E. Brown, *Jesus God and Man: Modern Biblical Reflections* (New York: Macmillan Publishing Co., 1967), pp. 94-99 and 103-105 where the author sees Jesus' true humanity as proof of the depth of God's

love for man in allowing His Son to experience ignorance and to grow in awareness of His deep-seated sense of mission and of His unique identity. Cf. also: James Dunn, *Jesus and the Spirit*, pp. 53-62.

71. This position is based on Karl Rahner's "Anonymous Christianity," *Theological Investigations* VI (Baltimore: Helicon Press, 1969), 390-398; for a more strictly confined notion of what is Christian, cf. Hans Küng, *On Being a Christian*, pp. 97-98 and 122-126.

72. This interpretation of the Spirit's post-resurrection work as God's new actuality beyond Christ, yet in the pattern of Christ, is supported by Piet Schoonenberg, *The Christ: A Study of the God-Man Relationship in the Whole of Creation and in Jesus Christ* (New York: Herder and Herder, 1971), pp. 186-187. G. W. H. Lampe also affirms such a view in "The Spirit and the Person of Christ," p. 128. For a decidedly christocentric understanding of the Holy Spirit, cf. Olaf Hansen, "Spirit Christology: A Way Out of Our Dilemma?", pp. 198-201.

73. Juan Alfaro, "Incarnation and Revelation" *Theology Digest* XVII (1969) 131: "Human Nature can be appropriated personally by God in the incarnation because human nature, by its very spirituality, is radically capable of the personal self-communication of the Absolute Spirit and capable of reflecting in its acts the personal presence of God Himself." Cf. also: Dietrich Wiederkehr, "Entwurf einer systematischen Christologie," *Mysterium Salutis* III/1 (1970) 500-506.

INDEX OF NAMES

INDEX OF SUBJECTS

The majority of items in this index deal either solely with Karl Barth's theological standpoints or with objective references to them on the part of others. In contrast, such entries as "Protestant Theology" and "Theological Models Treated" include some trains of thought with which Barth disagrees, whereas "Various Distortions of Revelation" and "World-views Dangerous to Theology" catalogue those systems which he almost invariably treats in a negative manner and which are thus to be demarcated from his own. Moreover, so as to afford a clear distinction between Barthian views on pneumatology and the favorable or unfavorable commentary of other theologians on the same or related topics, the index provides the categories "Barthian Traits", "Critique of Barth's Pneumatology" and "Positive Aspects of Barth's Pneumatology". As regards the entry "Church Dogmatics", the page numbers recorded outside parentheses refer to sections of the present work where an individual sub-volume is rather extensively discussed; one can thus easily locate the notes which correspond to these references; furthermore, in parentheses are given pages of the notes containing additional references to the *Church Dogmatics* which crisscross the orderly progression of the various chapters of this study. Acquainting oneself from the start with the above-mentioned classifications will facilitate a profitable use of the following table.

215

DATE DUE

HIGHSMITH   #LO-45220